J. Christoph Amberger's
Hot Trading Secrets

J. Christoph Amberger's Hot Trading Secrets

*How to Get In and Out of the Market
with Huge Gains in Any Climate*

J. Christoph Amberger

WILEY

John Wiley & Sons, Inc.

Published by John Wiley & Sons, Inc., Hoboken, New Jersey.
Published simultaneously in Canada.

Limit of Liability/Disclaimer of Warranty: While the publisher and author have used their best efforts in preparing this book, they make no representations or warranties with respect to the accuracy or completeness of the contents of this book and specifically disclaim any implied warranties of merchantability or fitness for a particular purpose. No warranty may be created or extended by sales representatives or written sales materials. The advice and strategies contained herein may not be suitable for your situation. You should consult with a professional where appropriate. Neither the publisher nor author shall be liable for any loss of profit or any other commercial damages, including but not limited to special, incidental, consequential, or other damages.

For general information on our other products and services or for technical support, please contact our Customer Care Department within the United States at 800-762-2974, outside the United States at 317-572-3993 or fax 317-572-4002.

Wiley also publishes its books in a variety of electronic formats. Some content that appears in print may not be available in electronic books. For more information about Wiley products, visit our web site at www.wiley.com.

Library of Congress Cataloging-in-Publication Data:

Amberger, J. Christoph.
    J. Christoph Amberger's hot trading secrets : how to get in and out of the market with huge gains in any climate / J. Christoph Amberger.
        p. cm.
    Includes bibliographical references and index.
    ISBN-13: 978-0-471-73872-5 (cloth)
    ISBN-10: 0-471-73872-7 (cloth)
    1. Investments. 2. Investment analysis. 3. Stocks. I. Title.
    HG4521.A456 2005
    332.6—dc22
2005018249

Printed in the United States of America.

10 9 8 7 6 5 4 3 2 1

To
Joanna, Maximilian, Sebastian, and Sophia

CONTENTS

PART III
THE TRADING SECRETS

FOREWORD

I have an intellectual weakness for contrarian investing. Buy quality when it is unpopular and prices are cheap. Sell it when the crowds have finally caught on and prices are zooming.

This is the sort of moneymaking philosophy that appeals to a certain snobbish tendency in me: that most investors, the lumpeninvestoriat (as Bill Bonner calls them in his *Daily Reckoning*) are financial lemmings who don't have the sense to recognize value when they see it. Instead, they buy on hype and frenzy and contribute to bubbles that inflate and burst, as bubbles must do, and are justly punished for their folly.

Or, to paraphrase Mick Jagger: You can't always get what you want as an investor, but if you live long enough you will get what you deserve.

As I say, that's the way I *like to think* about the financial markets and when I talk about investing and investors, that's the sort of perch I'm happy to acquire.

But when I look at what I have *actually done* as a businessman and investor, I have to admit that most of my wealth has been accumulated by doing almost exactly the opposite. Of the considerable money I have made in my lifetime, the great majority of it has come from investing in trends—not foolishly running behind the herd (I'd like to think), but shrewdly going with the flow.

I once heard it said that there is a rule of probability that states that there is a seven-to-one chance that any trend that exists today will continue to be in place tomorrow. That dovetails with my experience as a builder of businesses. Yes, trends change. But most of the time they go in exactly the same direction that they were going in yesterday.

Betting against the trend can provide rich emotional rewards, but it's generally bad for the pocketbook. If kids today like low-cut pants so that their boxer shorts can show, chances are they will like them tomorrow. Sometime in the future higher-cut jeans and cotton briefs will be back in vogue, but I'm not going to invest in a business that is starting to manufacture them now.

If you look at the history of the stock market over the past 25 years (since I've been more or less involved with it) you will notice that there have been about a half dozen major trends. The pattern of investing during those trends is pretty well documented: as one trend gradually or somewhat suddenly comes to a halt another trend almost immediately takes up movement. Those who get in the new trend at the beginning do very well, but those that get in toward the end often get killed.

The secret to becoming wealthy as a trend investor is timing. And for every trend there are at least a half dozen investment theories that aim to profit from it. As a consultant to the financial publishing industry, I've been studying those theories for almost three decades, and if there is one thing I've learned about them, it is this: there are all sorts of investment strategies that work, but very few—if any—that work consistently.

Which brings me to Christoph Amberger and his exciting new book *Hot Trading Secrets*.

There is an inside secret in the investment advisory business that goes something like this: if the investor likes the shade of your glasses he won't care so much that the numbers he's looking at don't add up to that much. Put differently: if your reader likes your political and economic worldview, he will stay with you when your track record for recommending winning stocks is in the toilet.

As someone who has watched the investment advice business for many years, I believe that perspective is largely true. And there's a good reason for it. Most investors—most people—are not all that concerned about what return on investment they get. They feel that they should be. And it can indeed affect their purchasing power. But when you consider all the uncertainties that are incorporated in the world of investing and after you've had the experience of seeing your winning streak turn bad on you several times, you gradually start to pay attention to other things.

Those other things are often more philosophical in nature: Why, for example, is there such a variance between the average income of a new family in the United States and the average cost of a start-up home? If the world were a reasonable place, you'd think that there would be a clear and calculable connection.

Or, given the fact that most new wealth in America is created by small companies, shouldn't investors who put their money in small-cap stocks do better than the rest of the investing public?

Or, considering the fact that God created the world and it's meant to have some sublime order (though we may not know what that order is), shouldn't good investors—that is, investors who put their faith in solid, value-producing companies—be rewarded in the end when the universe rights itself?

Such speculations are endlessly entertaining for those investors who have (subconsciously or wittingly) given up the goal of attaining wealth through stocks (or even, in many cases, the much less ambitious objective of beating market indexes.) But Mr. Amberger is not content to merely entertain. A compelling theoretician and amusing lampooner, he has spent 15 years as the publisher of the Taipan division of Agora Publishing's financial newsletter empire excoriating fools, lambasting intelligent dimwits, and poking fun at pundits whose theories are always richer than those who follow their recommendations.

That said, he has never given up the goal of finding investment theories that actually work. In fact, he's been so dedicated to what seems to most industry insiders to be an impossible task that he has practically invented a process of hiring, training, and then testing young people with a talent for this game and has, in the process, developed an enviable record of gurus and investment newsletters with impressive performances.

A few years ago I had a conversation with Christoph about his success. I told him I was impressed with the individual results of individual writers who had matured their game under his direction, but I still wasn't convinced that any one of them can sustain their records indefinitely.

"And that's why I start them young," he explained. "Because I want them young enough to change as the market changes—to correct and refine and, if necessary, entirely reinvent their systems in order to get those good returns."

I wondered aloud whether that would be possible.

"Look at it this way," he said. "During every market trend, isn't there always one predominant investment theory that is working?"

"Yes," I said. "But that's exactly my point. As the market changes, so do the investment systems. What worked ten years ago doesn't work today, and what's working today won't be working ten years from now."

"In fact, you are making my point," he said. "My program is meant to take advantage of that one irrefutable fact about the stock market: that it is endlessly changing. In an endlessly changing environment, only a fool or zealot would stick to a single, unchanging system for dealing with it.

"My system is dynamic. It's a dynamic market theory."

"You should write a book on that idea," I told him.

And so he did. And that's why I'm excited to introduce you to *Hot Trading Secrets*. In this book, Christoph not only lays out the analytical approaches of his ambitious young team of editors and analysts, but also provides you with his big-picture view of how he sees the next five years unfold in the global markets. It's no pretty picture. Worse even, Christoph has an uncanny track record of being right in his analyses and forecasts.

But despite the looming crisis in the financial markets, this book has a very optimistic message: By explaining how his analysts harness each move in the markets for fun and profits, he provides you with the tools needed to meet this crisis head-on—enabling you to come out not only wiser, but potentially vastly richer.

—Michael Masterson
December, 2005

PREFACE

We at 247profits, the Taipan Group, and its affiliate publications and web sites consider ourselves researchers, compilers, and publishers of independently assessed information and opinion. We do not nor will we ever accept compensation, fees, or payment for promoting or publicizing a company, stock, or any other entity as part of our editorial content. All opinions we publish are the result of independent analysis on the part of our editors.

The Taipan Group and 247profits are services for readers with a strong sense of individual responsibility and the ability to perform their own risk assessment before acting upon the information provided.

Every effort is made to ensure the utmost accuracy of all information, opinion, research, and commentary contained in our publications, web sites, monthly bulletins, and special reports. But while this information is obtained from sources believed to be credible and reliable, such credibility and reliability cannot be guaranteed. Forecasts and projections of events are based on the subjective evaluations, analysis, and personal opinions of our editors. The maxim of *caveat emptor* applies—let the buyer beware!

The Taipan Group and 247profits do not provide personal investment, financial, or legal advice to individuals; act as personal financial, legal, or institutional investment advisers; or individually advocate the purchase or sale of any security or investment or the use of any particular financial or legal strategy.

Before pursuing any legal or financial strategies discussed in this book, our monthly publications, or on our web sites, you should consult with your legal or financial adviser or CPA. Investments discussed in any form should be made only after reviewing the prospectus or financial statements of the respective company.

Some of the information our editors and associates gather could be considered "insider information." When we get it, we publish it—because regulations prohibit us, or anyone else, from trading on insider information not available to the public.

Members of the organization, its officers, directors, employees, and associated individuals may have positions in investments referred to herein and may add to or dispose of the same at any time. But while we encourage our editors and analysts to put their own money where their mouths are, the editors, staff, and associates of 247profits and the Taipan Group, as well as its directors, employees, and associated individuals, are prohibited from trading on this information until after such information is published—that is, at least three days after the publications have been mailed to our subscribers or posted to our web sites.

Our network seeks to take advantage of the disparity of knowledge and the inequality of its distribution to maximize investment profits for our network associates and subscribers. And even though in the past certain investment recommendations from the Taipan Group, 247profits and their affiliates have produced huge gains, past performance is no guarantee of future gains.

ACKNOWLEDGMENTS

No work successfully undertaken and completed by man is ever the result of one person's efforts. Writers especially rely on other people's intellects to come up with something worth saying—copying, adapting, adopting, and developing (sometimes even pilfering!) thoughts and ideas from thousands of sources until they're convinced it's all their own.

This book in particular owes its publication to the direct and indirect influence of many friends and colleagues: the editors and staff of the Taipan Group: Sandy Franks, Christian DeHaemer, Siu-Yee Ng, Erin Beale, Ian Cooper, Bryan Bottarelli, Alex Chinn, Martin Denholm, Brad Colburn, Briton Ryle, Abe Said, Adam Lass, Sarah Nunnally, Ann Sosnowski, Mike Wiles, Zhan Caplan, Amy London, Mia White, Jerome McLennon, Sherri Green, Sheryl Ivey, Alexa Landrus, Ned Humphrey, Howie Ng, Erick Hienz, and Alex Ferguson.

I am greatly indebted to my boss, William R. Bonner, for entrusting me with the responsibility of developing the Taipan Group into one of the most successful international trading publication groups in the world, and paying my salary during that time; Michael Masterson and Mark Ford for showing me how to create and run a business based on good products; and my mentor and Taipan's founding editor emeritus Robert W. Czeschin for guiding me in the early years of my career.

Special thanks go to John "W." Forde, Don Mahoney, Bob Bly, Brian Hicks, and James Passin for originally putting into words many of the ideas we came up with and have expressed in the pages that follow.

This book would not have been written without the valiant efforts of Wayne Ellis and Michael Ward, and the critical eye and indispensable hands-on help of Michael Thomsett.

Thanks also to my aikido senseis Brian Sutherland and Jeff Mims, without whom I never would have grasped the complex concepts of flow, and to my fencing coach Bin Lu, for teaching me more about timing and positioning than a library of trading literature can offer. And my special gratitude to Dan and Phyllis Strayer for always asking the right questions.

INTRODUCTION

A VISIT
FROM THE FBI

Social mood trends represent changes in human attitudes. Changes in social mood trends precede compatible changes in history and culture, indicating that the former causes the latter. Thus, there is powerful evidence that the pattern of mood change produced by social interaction of men is the underlying engine of trends of social progress and regress.

—Robert R. Prechter, Jr., *The Wave Principle of Human Social Behavior and the New Science of Socionomics* (2002)

In retrospect, it seemed like it was a particularly gray and depressing day. Outside, there was just enough of a drizzle coming down to make the late fall chill unpleasant. You heard car tires hiss on the asphalt and yet—when traffic had stopped and you happened to listen closely—windshield wipers were squeaking on glass that was neither quite dry nor quite wet enough for them to do anything but leave broad, sticky smears of whitish residue.

Inside our headquarters at 808 St. Paul Street in downtown Baltimore, the mood was tense. My colleague Adam Lass, our in-house attorney Matt Turner, and I were seated uncomfortably in our glass-enclosed conference room. At the head of the table, a stern-looking visitor, a Washington, D.C.-area FBI field agent, was readying a ballpoint pen. In front of her were a stack of papers, printouts of our daily e-mail letter, the *247profits e-Dispatch*, and various printouts of our web pages.

"We all know why we're here," the agent began the conference. She handed photocopies to all of us.

I didn't have to look at the papers. I knew exactly what was on them.

Dated September 10, 2001, they contained an urgent warning that we had broadcast to the 400,000 readers of the Taipan Group's e-letter, the *247profits e-Dispatch*. This is what we wrote:

> We were seeing a rally in the NASDAQ today. Don't, however, confuse that with a RALLY. Rather, it is a completely predictable move from the bottom of the 10-day trend. Expect this short-lived upward move to peter out between 1,725 and 1,750 when it hits the top of the short-term trend.
>
> Then put your head between your legs and kiss your gains goodbye: WaveStrength™ indicates this will be followed by a geometrically accelerating arc down toward my target of 1,619, now less than 75 points away.
>
> But beware! 1,619 is no longer the worst thing you have to worry about. I am now working on my next long-term WaveStrength™ prediction, and my preliminary studies are indicating a move so gruesome, ambulances will be cueing up below Wall Street brokerage windows.

How could we possibly have known? Did we have tip-offs from people who were in the know about the attacks to come the very next day? If yes, who were they? Why exactly did we choose these words to convey our message?

I must say that I've had more than a few sleepless nights since we sent that message. Even for us at the Taipan Group, it is no everyday occurrence that our financial predictions unfold in as horrific and literal a fashion as the terrorist attacks of September 11, 2001. After all, we had no prior warning outside our own resources. No mysterious phone calls. No e-mails from anonymous servers in Yemen or Russia. There was no stranger in a parking lot dropping an envelope before disappearing in a dark SUV with tinted windows.

All we had were data. Reams of data. Charts as long as scrolls of wallpaper that took up the entire length of our polished mahogany conference table. And we had Adam, who translated the muddle of pencil lines, curves, and annotations into probabilities according to the principles he established for his WaveStrength analytical system, the macro perspective tool of our Dynamic Market Theory.

Two long hours later, the agent left—and I like to think her good-bye was a bit more cordial than her hello. Did she understand all the mathematical intricacies of Adam's theories and methods? Frankly, I doubt it: I myself occasionally have problems following when Adam is on a roll. But she seemed satisfied that this particular bunch of geeks she had just spent the better part of the morning with had no involvement with terrorism whatsoever, just an uncanny knack for making the right call at the right time.

Which still doesn't explain just why Adam's prediction was so eerily correct, or why we managed to turn one of the most horrifying crimes perpetrated on American soil (and one of the most drastic market drops) into hands-on investment opportunities for our subscribers.

MONEY, MARKETS, AND MAYHEM

In this book, I try to explain how our investing and trading philosophy works, how over the years we have established one of the best batting averages in the financial publishing industry, and what methods and tricks our analysts use to create superior profits not only in days of global crisis, but day in and day out—methods that will help you profit handsomely in the markets in the coming years, independent of where the various domestic and international indexes are headed.

At the Taipan Group, we have been doing just that since 1988. We took our name from the swashbuckling entrepreneurs who amassed great fortunes from the China trade during the nineteenth century. The Chinese called these ambitious, moneymaking men "taipans" or big bosses.

The name suits us because we, too, are after great fortunes. Our flagship publication *Taipan*, a small-circulation bulletin that is available by private subscription only, has always understood itself to be a window on the future, a preview of what is to come, an accurate source for advance information on the big ideas that will change the way we work, live, and play in the years ahead.

We call our trading philosophy Dynamic Market Theory. Like the theory of evolution, it is a convenient and descriptive rather than a specific handle that we use to reduce the complexities of market phenomena and the human behavior that cause them and translate them into dynamic new trading opportunities. Much like the theory of evolution, Dynamic Market Theory is based on an explanation for a set of facts that has been repeatedly tested and that can be used to make predictions about those phenomena.[1]

As such, the individual facets of Dynamic Market Theory that we let you in on in this book are part and parcel of a constant process of evolution and adaptation themselves; data patterns that translate into excellent buying and trading opportunities rarely remain undetected by a wider circle for long. This system is subject to change. With growing volume caused by a further permeation of an "exclusive" set of indicators, the dynamics of the pattern itself can and do evolve dramatically. A new pattern emerges, with different segments that, at least for a time, can be analyzed and translated to create the basis of yet another (modified) trading strategy.

This flux creates a conundrum for the writer: Books are rather static objects that can only provide a snapshot of the current conditions. A year from now, market psychology and the further permeation of information—such as a wider public use and application of the unique constellations of catalysts our editors use to determine entry and exit opportunities of particular trades—may have created new challenges to be addressed and harnessed by further adaptation to the new parameters.

Despite having been in the business of publishing trading and investing information since the late 1980s, this is the first book the Taipan Group has ever produced. It's not like we didn't have enough to say. There is a very good reason for this: being part of a dynamic market environment and being steeped in the daily, even hourly, flux of information. Accordingly, we specialize in instant communication of these opportunities to the readers of our free e-letters and to the subscribers of our electronic trading information services.

This book is an attempt at putting on paper the principal ideas and thoughts that have gone into creating these services and to enable you to apply them for your own benefit. We make no claim that ours is the only or perfect way of profiting in the markets in the crucial years that lie ahead. But forgive my self-centeredness when I say it is one of the most successful and yes, most fun ways I've seen so far.

PART I

DYNAMIC MARKET THEORY

CHAPTER 1

MARKETS RISE, MARKETS FALL— IT MATTERS NOT

(As Long As *You* Are Making a Profit)

A ruler placed on a globe will give one answer; the same ruler applied to every indentation as one traverses the coast will give a vastly different one.

—Robert R. Prechter, Jr., *The Wave Principle of Human Social Behavior and the New Science of Socionomics* **(2002)**

"Bulls make money, bears make money, pigs get slaughtered."

The idea at the core of this old chestnut of a trading rule is simple: If you pick an investment strategy and stick with it long enough, you're bound to make money at least half the time. Only the greedy pig—the one who chases profits without any strategy—loses money all the time. Likewise, the nervous chicken—one who flees the market even with a well-formed strategy as soon as it ticks downward— cannot expect to profit. The concept, at least, that you can profit at least half the time, is fine . . . assuming that you are satisfied with just beating 50–50.

Unfortunately, that concept has one major weakness. It would have you accept that you lose money half the time. That's something I find both distasteful and unnecessary. Besides, what's wrong with a bit of greed? Hunger, when properly controlled and channeled, is a fine motivator. So after the bull, the bear, the pig, and the chicken, I would like to introduce a fifth investment creature to our little menagerie: the wolf, *Canis lupus*, a predator equally competent at catching mice or elk, an animal that will dine with equal fervor on bears, bulls, pigs, and chickens.

To become this kind of market wolf, the first thing you need to do is *stop caring—at least morally—whether it's a bull or a bear market*. To the predator and trader alike, it's a near-meaningless distinction: Every market has wheels within wheels, upstrokes and downstrokes that offer profit opportunities to the quick and the strong of heart—and to the strong of stomach. This is the principal insight of our Dynamic Market Theory.

After all, who needs a bull market anyway when there's plenty of opportunity to make money all over the world?

GOLDEN JONQUILS

Just a few days prior to the terrorist attacks of September 11, the Dow Jones Industrial Average dropped 200-plus stomach-churning points in only three hours. The Nasdaq, long off its 2000 bubble-market highs, was heading into numbers woefully reminiscent of the early settlement dates of the American continent. Sitting at my desk and following the market carnage on my computer monitor, I leaned back and thought of golden jonquils.

In the Ozarks, hopeful homesteaders used to plant golden jonquil bulbs by their front doors. A century or more after they were planted, some of these flowers still keep appearing each spring. Often, they rise around bare foundation stones deep in a deserted stretch of sky-high oak woods—symbols of peace and hoped-for prosperity that "bloom sunshine yellow against a sea of green."

In *Country Living Is Risky Business*, author, fencing master, and gentleman farmer Nick Evangelista muses about the shattered dreams and ambitions that are evidenced by these empty, deserted farmsteads deep in the Ozark Mountains:

> Where did these people go? Where did their dreams disappear to? What sent them spiraling down to disaster and abandonment? When does a shout of assurance become a hollow cry of enough is enough?[1]

I looked at the Nasdaq back then and I felt an inkling of that pain. Even today, as most U.S. equity indexes are trading well above their post–September 11, 2001, lows, or are even approaching their bubble boom highs, the memory of financial hardships is still evident.

More than four years have passed since the sociopathic attacks on New York City and Washington, D.C., but the economic fallout is still as real as falling concrete, less damaging to human life but just as lethal to perceptions of value.

But mark my words: Even back in 2001, you didn't have to lose money. You didn't even have to give up on high returns. All you needed to know is what to buy, what to sell, and when to take profits.

In September of 2001, the market was providing amazing ultra-short-term profit opportunities. (No one can tell me that you can't make money on 3 percent drops and 2 percent recoveries, even if the indexes end down overall.) With the emphasis shifted to ultra-short-term, this market was a day trader's nirvana. One buying opportunity chased the next. It was as if a scatterbrained store clerk had inadvertently put up the discount sale signs for the dollar store instead of those meant for Bloomingdale's.

But unless you were ready and able to rapidly jump on buying—and profit-taking—opportunities, you might have been better served by watching from the sidelines.

So why do some win where most others lose?

Because those who lose in the market have no idea how the investment world really works. They're still trapped in the nice, cozy idea that markets are about logic, rationality, and analysis.

But think about what the market is telling us right now. The investment world doesn't follow formulas. And it is not for amateurs. In fact, if investing were easy, it wouldn't be fun. There would be no challenge. No excitement.

And no big profits.

The fact is that real investment—the kind that yields profits worth mentioning—can be as unpredictable as a day on the battlefield. The way General George Patton saw it, "War is won by blood and guts alone."

I think Patton would have made a shrewd investor, because playing to win is all about guts. Competitiveness. The timing and nerve to go for the jugular. It's also about hunger . . . the hunger to be rich and beat all the other bastards out there—because if you don't, they'll beat you first!

Let me be blunt: Those who are made nervous by crisis and upheaval shouldn't be in the market. Successful investing isn't always pretty. If you win and you make money, it's because the other guy lost. And if he wins, you lose. The rules change fast. But the plunder—the spoils of the investing war—can be huge.

Many American investors have turned their backs on the equity markets, liquidating their portfolios and reinvesting in real estate. (Germany, which had seen the number of households owning stock more than double from 8 percent to almost 19 percent between 1995 and 2001, saw almost all those new investors being shaken out of the market by the end of 2001.) The great majority of U.S. investors still remembers all of the money they've lost, wondering how long it's going to take to make it all back. That's a tall order. Consider that a 25 percent loser requires a 33 percent gainer just to get back to even. And a 50 percent loss demands you double your remaining money to break even. But you can make gains like this with relative ease by putting your money into the right kind of stocks *at the right time.*

It takes a sturdy disposition not to panic in the face of such prospects. And you may think—rightfully so—that these are the days for dynamic optimism in the face of adversity and a sense of gloom in the market.

THE TRUTH . . . VERSUS SMILING LIP SERVICE

To succeed in the fast-moving market, you need to have truth on your side. This is not a mere platitude. My associates and I call ourselves Taipan for a good reason. We don't believe in telling investors what they want to hear, or playing into the way they think things should be. We tell it like it is. That may get a few people hot under those crisp white collars. But let's be serious: a lot of investors lose out because they can't see past the way they want things to be. They need to find—and use—the truth.

Things are rarely what you're told. We're not ashamed to admit that we've always ranked high in insubordination. That's the way things have to be. Realistically, though, you know that all the pessimism and prissy judgments in the world won't help you invest wisely and well.

We've always encouraged our editors and analysts to develop their own ideas rather than slavishly adhere to the curriculum that forms today's bedrock of mainstream analysis. We admit that our approach makes no claim on being complete or generally accepted. Author James Surowiecki wrote:

> Human beings don't have complete information. They have private, limited information. It may be valuable information and it may be accurate (or it may be useless and false), but it is always partial. Human beings aren't perfectly rational, either.[2]

Markets aren't rational, because people aren't rational. Accordingly, much of the information the markets generate is at its core the result of compound irrationalities. An extreme example, the "Tulipomania" that gripped Holland in the seventeenth century, makes this point. Tulip bulbs, the story goes, became the mania among not just speculators, but average men and women as well:

> The rage for possessing them soon caught the middle classes of society, and merchants and shopkeepers, even of moderate means, began to vie with each other in the rarity of these flowers and the preposterous prices they paid for them.[3]

Indeed, by 1635 people paid as much as 100,000 florins for a tulip bulb. (To put this in perspective, the value of a suit of clothes was about 80 florins.) When the market for tulip bulbs crashed, no one would buy at any price. In hindsight, the irrationality of Tulipomania was apparent—especially to those who had lost money in that market by sheer greed, and to those who had not participated in the bubble out of a sense of morally righteous indignation or inactivity. Both groups were losers: those who had held on to their bulbs as prices crashed, and those who had stood aside as prices were rising. Even so, many investors today make decisions on the same irrational level, and that itself defines the market for what it is, and for how it operates.

The key to overcoming this "market insanity" is to take a step back with rationality and reassess all information you can possibly lay your hands on. Find fresh angles to old solutions. Reevaluate signals and ratios as to their usefulness as indicators. Identify market myths and avoid falling into those thinking patterns. And finally, cautiously begin to test your own market perceptions by paper trading.

MEN (AND WOMEN) OF ACTION

While the Taipan Group was deeply affected by the human tragedies in Manhattan and Washington back in 2001, we remained pragmatic. In his *Nicomachean Ethics*, the Greek philosopher Aristotle defines the moral man as the man of action. (And while Aristotle himself might be inclined to argue, we extend that definition to women as well.)

Taking action in the case of the 2001 attacks meant doing what was best for our way of life. Paralysis, grief, and mourning were appropriate and understandable responses. So was compassion. But these sentiments typically enforce passivity where the markets are concerned. Not so here at Taipan. The Taipan Group's editors decided to make "Open for Business" the motto of the hour. But let's get this straight: This was not about making a buck off other people's misery. It was about getting back to the basics of a free market society. Within a day after the collapse of the World Trade Center towers, we had organized our "Open for Business" fund drive for the American Red Cross. Within a month, Taipan members all over the world had contributed $40,000 to this effort.

This "Open for Business" philosophy also translates into investment action. In the days that followed the horrid massacre of September 11, 2001, I asked my editors to come up with some plays that you can use to show the world an indomitable free market spirit, something the terrorists don't understand.

It worked. We closed the year 2001 with an average gain of over 26 percent—and a large percentage of these gains was taken straight from our recommendations to investors: to use the epic Dynamic Market opportunity created by September 11.

NEW PARADIGMS

Successful investing invariably depends on adjusting your short-term strategy and taking advantage of the fastest means of delivery to find critical information in as timely a manner as possible.

In the immediate aftermath of the 2001 attacks, we identified what we considered to be valid buying ranges for a bunch of great investments. Be-

> **Valuable Resource**
>
> Sign up for Taipan's daily free e-mail service, the *Dynamic Market Alert*. This provides you valuable leads, not just once a month, but each and every day.

cause, terror or not, we're not opposed to buying cheap. Our mission is to enable you to prosper now and in your future.

You see, despite the incredible short-term market fluctuations we have experienced in the past few years, the people making a living commenting on what's going on haven't changed one bit. And while the bulls are still holding back, licking the wounds they sustained back in 2000 and 2001, the bears appear to be on a roll.

Half of the bulletins and editorials I read these days bemoan America's rising levels of personal debt. Others never tire of invoking the Bush administration's "twin deficits." Editors, commentators, and pundits build intricate causal strings based on these economic indexes, foreboding strings that inevitably involve bank runs, the collapse of the dollar, and crashing mutual fund and real estate industries—all, of course, to occur within the next few weeks.

I have to confess, sometimes they're very convincing. In fact, I'd be a believer by now if it were not for one simple fact: I've read the same dire predictions from the same editors since at least 1989, then again in 1992, 1995, 1997, and 2000. And I'm still waiting for the other shoe to drop. I am sure I will be waiting for a while.

Why? Personal and public debt levels really have little to do with how the markets work. If the personal savings of an individual in any given industrial nation were an indicator of that market's profit potential, we'd all be lining up outside the Frankfurt, Zurich, and Tokyo stock exchanges.

Oddly enough, these markets move with the same seeming randomness as the U.S. markets, no matter how solid the personal savings rates or local currencies of the respective countries may seem. In fact, many global markets still take their clues from what's happening on the American exchanges, notwithstanding the twin deficits!

BOOM, DOOM, AND GLOOM

The professional doomsday prophets are getting one thing right.

In a market whose mood swings make postpartum depression seem like an evening of Scrabble with your accountant—when even the Dow can gain and lose more than 200 points within a six-hour spell—investors must come to terms with one simple fact: if you want to come out ahead in this market, you need to be mobile, motivated, and disciplined. Maintain a healthy emotional detachment from the stocks you buy and be ready and willing to get rid of them at the drop of a hat.

After all, every 200-point rise and fall spells a double 200-point profit opportunity for those who know where to look—and who have the guts to take profits whenever they can make them.

The message of this book is quite simple:

> *There is always an opportunity to make exceptional stock market profits independent of where the domestic indexes are headed—as long as you know how to read the signs.*

The key to locating these opportunities is to keep your eye on the money. The opportunity to create wealth does not evaporate. It migrates—from the Nasdaq's Internet bubble into real estate, foreign bonds, or emerging markets and back into U.S. stocks.

You have to be selective in your choices and stay out of the way of the lemmings. Most important of all, you have to find a way to hitch your portfolio to some of the most powerful profit engines around.

Over the past two decades, I've sent out millions of annual investment forecast reports that contain a lot of the advice you'll be reading about in this book. And based on those forecasts, I've watched some subscribers to our various Dynamic Market Theory trading services pile up triple-digit profits, and even quadruple-digit profits in some instances—often in a *very short time.*

The pages that follow give you a blueprint for making money in the market today. I show you step-by-step how to read signals and interpret events—and how to transform these events into consistent investment returns. Much of what you're about to read here may sound familiar to you, simplistic even. But this is exactly what makes our approach so powerful: Dynamic Market Theory is a rags-to-riches investment philosophy that opens up doors of opportunity to investors of all experience and skill levels. Among our existing members and subscribers, professional traders rub shoulders with novice investors, seasoned money managers, amateur day traders, and I'm sure even a few punters who, according to mainstream investment opinion, have absolutely no business being in the stock market.

Each chapter of this book can be read in less than 15 minutes. You might find some of the catalysts and concepts we will be introducing easy, perhaps too easy. That's because they are built around information you yourself can extract from common information sources on the Internet. But to absorb the principles and put them to work will probably require a few weeks of study, thought, and practice. Of course, you can go faster if you wish, or take the program at a more leisurely pace. The only deadlines are the ones you set for yourself.

By the time you have finished this book, you'll know how to make yourself very, very rich. What's more, you'll have discovered a secret for making money that you can apply to any market: up, down, or sideways. In fact, you'll see it can be as easy as reading a road map. All you need to know is how to anticipate the unexpected turns. I'll give you all the tools you need, everything that you must know to make money in the market: how to look at fundamentals, company symbols, insider background, price-earnings (P/E) reports and statistics, trends, principles, and insights.

It's all here. And it's all yours.

That's one of my motives for putting together this book—to get you to understand the half dozen or so trading techniques and styles we use, collectively, to make fabulous profits for our readers. Your motive is to make more money investing.

CAST YOUR NET WIDE (AND PROFIT FROM BOTH UPWARD AND DOWNWARD MOVEMENTS)

It has been said that "all economic movements, by their very nature, are motivated by crowd psychology."[4]

A couple of months ago at the fencing club, my eyes fell on a book held by one of the fathers watching the exploits of their offspring. The book was Bill Bonner's "bible of the bears," *Financial Reckoning Day* (Wiley, 2003). What are the chances, I thought, a tingle of "soft depression" blending in with the sense of déjà vu. Have bearish market views really become so mainstream that you now encounter them at your local gym, just like you encountered overexcited bullishness among busboys and sales clerks during the Internet stock mania? Or is it just that fencing attracts people who like the challenge of being a step ahead of their opponent?

Over the years, I have found that fencing has a lot in common with trading. Both depend on timing and positioning, on reading the action accurately, on picking up on clues that seem meaningless to the untrained eye but contain the blueprint of the movement to come. Both require discipline and strategic thinking—but first and foremost the ability to adapt to and then exploit new conditions as they arise.

The favorite saying of my Chinese-born fencing coach Bin Lu is: "You can take a chance, or you can make a chance. If you can make the chances, you will be a great fencer." This holds true for the equity markets as well.

Foresight and planning certainly are laudable qualities in and of themselves. But they can become quite dangerous if based mainly on assumptions on how markets and opponents *should* react.

Typically, the execution of elaborate plans based on wrong assumptions is terminated quickly and resoundingly by an unforeseen (and seemingly irrational) counteraction. That's why fencers who expect too much of their opponent typically end up leaving competitive fencing before they've truly started.

Many years ago, I briefly served as the editorial director for the *Colby Report*, the private, small-circulation newsletter of Bill Colby, who served as director of the Central Intelligence Agency (CIA) under Presidents Richard Nixon and Gerald Ford. Up until his mysterious drowning death in the spring of 1996, Mr. Colby was a very proper and distinguished gentleman. And yet, he did not leave much of a lasting impression on me. I guess that was part of his strategy. Unfortunately, I found his letter equally unremarkable: I never really had the feeling that the content of his briefings exceeded the amount of intelligence you could gather from a middle school geography atlas.

But maybe that was part of the strategy as well. It always made me itch for more. I was looking for a catalyst, something that turned the academic insights and seductive opinions into something actionable: What does this information mean to me? What practical conclusions can I draw—and implement—from the historical facts, assumptions, and opinions expressed?

It is this same feeling that I have when reading *Financial Reckoning Day*: Is "buy gold" really the only answer to burgeoning American household debt, a declining U.S. dollar, or the rise and fall of equity valuations? If gold is really your best strategic defense against excessive market fluctuations and the decline of Western civilization, how come it is still priced at levels reflecting just one-third of its bubble valuations in the 1970s and 1980s? And how come you still can lose 20 bucks within a week or two on an ounce of gold, much like you can on the most flimsy technology stock?

(I'm not even going to touch on the fact that in the case of rare coins, you typically buy at retail and sell at wholesale. Add in sales tax, and you're down 20 percent in real terms before you cut the first check to pay for your safe-deposit box.)

Now don't get me wrong here: We at the Taipan Group actually like gold. We think it is part of a prudent diversification of assets to keep maybe 5 percent of your portfolio in bullion. We also have liked—and profited from—positions in select mining stocks, especially when entered and exited at the proper time. We love exchange-traded gold and precious metals indexes that enable you to profit from upward and downward movements of the gold price.

But gold is just an asset, one out of many that can be harnessed to build wealth in the Dynamic Market environment. And the more asset groups you include in your view of the markets, the better your chances to have one (or several) working for you at any given time.

This is the principal insight of Dynamic Market Theory:

Cast your nets wide enough, and you will be able to profit handsomely from the major and minor fluctuations—upward and downward—of equity markets, international indexes, currencies, hard assets, real estate, and technologies.

Supplement short- and medium-term profits with long-term protective strategies, such as calls or puts on individual indexes. And most importantly, don't get overly enamored with any particular investing philosophy. As long as you pay as much attention to financial planning as you would to the maintenance of your car, chances are you'll come out ahead of the game—because the only credible advice a bear could give you is: stay out of the markets.

And where would be the fun in that?

CHAPTER 2

WHAT EXACTLY IS VALUE?

History is a rhetorical weapon in influencing modern policy out-comes. In particular, the invocation of bubbles is one such use of history.

—Peter M. Garber, *Famous First Bubbles: The Fundamentals of Early Manias* (2001)

One chilly Saturday morning in April 2005, I was roused from my beauty sleep a half hour earlier than I had planned. Now, I can sleep through the demanding yowls of our cats and the whimpering of the dog. I don't even mind the sharp elbows and knees that my early-rising children like to apply to the paternal sides and back. What woke me up was a *New York Times* columnist on National Public Radio commenting on the most recent 200-point drop in the Dow Jones Industrial Average. Get used to it, his rather smug message was. Stocks are simply overvalued. Tech stocks in particular were trading at a price-to-earnings (P/E) ratio of over 40—and the historical average was 20. And stocks just shouldn't trade at a higher P/E ratio than that.

Annoyed, I turned off the radio. But our friend from the *New York Times* was just repeating what a generation of pundits and economics professors has said before him. Judging by their commentary, the stock market's final purpose is to move toward and establish a stable (if static) and ideally air-conditioned level from which it will progress

at an orderly, measured, and above all reasonable pace that is determined by the real value of its underlying equity.[1]

But if real value is what investing is all about, it begs the question:
what then is value?

Over the years in financial publishing, I've found a surprising variety in the personal definitions of value, which may be indicative of
"the slipperiness of that classic economic concept."[2] Indeed, there are
plenty of value indicators that financial analysts apply. First, there are a
company's business fundamentals: the cash value of a company's assets,
as well as its break-up value and cash flow value. There is the cost of
production versus the cost of the product. Then there is the market's
current appetite for a specific sector, technology, or industry that must
go into the definition of value.

These days, when asked what is value, I'm tempted to reply: when
the bearish view of the world starts cutting into your profits. This is
true in the negative sense of the word. Just as we can measure happi-
ness, love, wealth, or other positive things by the degree to which we
have lost them, value works in the same fashion. For all intents and
purposes, value in the stock market is the device by which we judge
our relative successes and failures, moods and attitudes, and the effectiveness of our own judgment and timing.

Classic value gauges, such as the historic P/E ratios of a sector,
certainly have their place in analyzing the relative qualities of a
company, especially when you're about to buy or sell a business. But
like all evaluative shortcuts, they contain enough arbitrary elements
to make me question their unqualified applicability.[3] In his book
The (Mis)Behavior of Markets, Benoit Mandelbrot muses on the
wildly fluctuating P/E ratios of Cisco Systems between 1999 and
early 2003:

> If [the market's appetite for technology companies . . . is as much
> a part of the measure of intrinsic value as balance sheet or cash
> flow] . . . then surely the "real" value of Cisco changes every
> month, every week, every day—even tick-by-tick on the stock
> exchange. And if that value changes constantly, then of what prac-
> tical use is it to any investor or financial analyst weighing whether
> to buy or sell? What use is a valuation model with new parameters
> for every calculation?[4]

In our view, stocks are about more than intrinsic value. They're about human behavior, human progress, and human ideals. In his groundbreaking book *The Wave Principle of Human Social Behavior,* Robert R. Prechter, Jr. wrote:

> The stock market is far more significant to the human condition than it appears to casual observers and even to those who make a living by it. The level of aggregate stock prices is a direct and immediate measure of the popular valuation of man's total productive capability.[5]

If aggregate stock prices, conveniently packaged within market indexes, are compound reflections of the moods and attitudes toward mankind's immediate future, what does that tell us about the concept of value?

Let's take another step back: Value—what a thing is worth, and why—is the heart of Dynamic Market Theory. Once you understand the way value really works in the stock market, you can avoid the misconceptions that cost investors trillions in the crash of 2000, and begin to see your portfolio's worth climb steadily upward.

To begin with, the *traditional* measures of value for investors all have to do with the actual or potential earnings of a company: What is it producing? What are its costs of production? What is its position in the marketplace? What is its competition? What is its future potential for earnings? How much merchandise can it possibly sell, and at what profit margin? Is its market growing or shrinking?

REMEMBER, ONLY THE NARCISSIST CAN FIND TRUE LOVE

How can we judge the true value of something, whether emotional or logical? How can we know what is true? We must have some means for making consistent and *informed* value judgments. Typical value investors, for example, look at the ability of a company to produce and sell products of value to consumers at a profit. They assume that a company with a good, healthy, and competitive business is a valuable company to own. Or at least they base their decision about whether the stock is a good buy at the current market price on the value of the business as measured by its earnings or potential earnings, because as investors, they have just one thing on their minds: arbitraging the difference between the current asset price and a future asset price into a profit, plain and simple.

Oddly enough, few investors these days seem to care about traditional value anymore. They sure didn't back in 1999, either, when all they wanted was an Internet-related business plan scribbled on a cocktail napkin. And unless they're seeing sales and earnings increase in U.S. companies where we can't find them, they still don't care now. This culture that preferred to shun profits was expressed by Amazon.com chairman Jeff Bezos in 2002, when he told a reporter that he did not believe in setting profit goals, explaining "It would be impossible for us to do so."[6]

That is one CEO's opinion. But how are investors to react to such a statement? Then again, maybe you don't have to care about value to make money. Maybe Bezos was onto something.

In fact, based on our research into Dynamic Market Theory, *the traditional views on value are all wrong.*

Most market theories deal with the intrinsic value of stocks or other commodities—in other words, the notion that the value comes from within the thing, and that it has value in and of itself, regardless of any associations with other things. But we believe that, for investors, *the only value of any importance is the value that someone else places on a stock, commodity, or investment* at any given point in time.

For instance, in early 2005, gold had a value around $435 an ounce. But is that value intrinsic in a bar of gold metal? What good is it? What can you do with it, other than use it as an expensive paperweight? And what makes an ounce of gold on February 8, 2005, $21 less valuable than on December 28, 2004, when it set a $16\frac{1}{2}$-year high at $456? This is what we mean by observing that value is defined by what someone else is willing to pay, or by what someone else wants to receive at any particular moment.

Ground beef sells for about 20 cents an ounce, a tiny fraction of 1 percent of the price of gold. Yet the hamburger meat has greater practical value than gold: if you are hungry, you can cook it and eat it.

The value of a gold bar is based on the value other investors place on it at a given point in time. When others want your gold, they are willing to pay more for it, and the price of gold goes up. But one ounce of gold at $435 has no more practical value than the same ounce you bought two years earlier at $280, or the ounce that your father bought at $800 back in 1980. Sure, its price can go up considerably—but not because its practical value increased but because more people believe that they can arbitrage the differential between gold's current price and a future price level into profits. And there are plenty of value factors that you can use to convince yourself that gold's future upside is virtually limitless. It just depends on how you look at it. For example, you can meld gold with your philosophy on how currencies ought to work. Referring to the fact that back in 1980 one ounce of gold cost around $800, Laurence Kotlikoff and Scott Burns argue:

> Divide the amount of U.S. currency in circulation in 1980 by U.S. gold reserves, and you find that a gold-backed dollar would require gold to be priced at $800 an ounce. Do the same math today, and U.S. gold reserves would have to be worth $4,600 an ounce for us to have a gold-backed currency. That's nearly twelve times the current market price of gold.[7]

Make sense? Sure. If the current dollar is overvalued by a factor of 12, and gold has been moving in sync with the other anti-dollar, the euro, you might even use your calculation to define value for the dollar-euro exchange rate. As I am writing this in July 2005, that's at $1.18 per euro. Furnishing our arithmetical house of cards, we could arrive at the razor-sharp conclusion that a euro really should be worth $15.60. Bad news for central banks around the world! Japan, with its $800 billion in dollar reserves, already sees the relative value of its holdings melt like frozen tofu on a hot summer day, by $8 billion every time the dollar sheds a cent.

When it comes to the markets, we have come to consider that a dogmatic view really is not all it's cracked up to be. I wager that during the five-year upsurge of the last big bull market from 1995 to 2000, more money was lost by those embracing fundamentally bearish attitudes—with ill-timed fundamentalist short sales, misplaced investments in precious metals and mining stocks, and plain missed opportunities—than was lost by all those chipper, bright-eyed irrational but exuberant market devotees combined. Once a bubble pops, you may have the satisfaction of being able to say "I told you so"—and maybe even write a book about it. But chances are that you, too, may have gum all over your face at that point.

Let me give you an example:

In early 2003, a radio talk show host asked me if I could comment on what he called the U.S. real estate bubble. My reply was cautious, Clintonian even: "Depends on what your definition of 'bubble' is."

Look around yourself, read the daily papers, surf the Web, and all you'll find is prudent warnings on this, that, and the other thing. Show me a market or asset that gains 10 percent in a year, and I'll show you a choir of pundits singing "bubble" at the top of their voices to the tune of Richard Wagner's "Ride of the Valkyrie": everything, from China to tech stocks to the equity in your suburban four-bedroom colonial, everything that rises these days apparently qualifies as a bubble or at least a bubble in the making.

If you follow our dyspeptic friends from the perma-bear encampment, only rising gold prices and the sky-high exchange rate of the euro against the dollar appear to be nonbubbles. In this mindset, the all-time highs of the gold and gold coin markets that were set in the 1970s and late 1980s represent these assets' fair valuation—even though price charts documenting their price development over three decades or more bear a closer resemblance to that of the Nikkei 225 from 1985 onward. (See Figure 2.1.) But more on that later.

We at the Taipan Group have never cared much about market bubbles, because in the nearly two decades we have been monitoring and uncovering profit opportunities in the world's equity, bond, and real-estate markets, we have made one quintessential discovery: you can make a lot of money on *irrational exuberance*, and you can make lots of money in markets that move sideways or even down.

Two of my colleagues examined the hubris and market frenzy surrounding the scandalous market debacle of Global Crossing (GX:Nasdaq). They arrived at the same seemingly obvious conclusion every other commentator has in the past half-decade:

"If you bought Global Crossing in 1998," a cynic might have retorted, "you would have lost 98% of your money."[8]

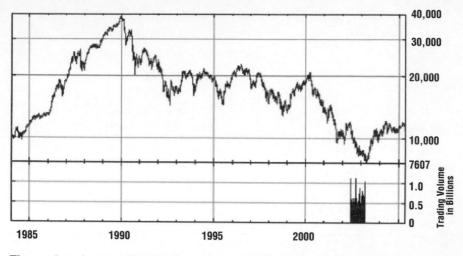

Figure 2.1 Japan Nikkei 225 Index as of April 27, 2005

This is one way of looking at things. Surely, many investors did lose money, and plenty of it. But even Global Crossing is not a clear-cut example of a bubble stock, given that its demise was the result of blatant large-scale fraud rather than the collapse of the Internet bubble. (Just think about it: Enron collapsed for the same reason, and not because there was anything wrong with the energy market.)

A graph from my colleagues' book appears in Figure 2.2, with my annotations. Here it is in a nutshell: Yes, if you bought GX in August of 1998 or at either of its $60-plus highs, put them into Al Gore's proverbial lockbox, and sat on your hands as you watched your position lose almost all of its value in the maelstrom of bad press before selling in the aftermath of September 11, you could have lost 98 percent of your investment.

But had you applied a simple risk-management strategy—such as the 20 percent or 30 percent trailing stop we at Taipan recommend that you observe on your more volatile positions—you would have had not one but two opportunities to walk away with triple-digit profits intact.[9] It took well into 2001 for the stock to reach its 1998 breakeven point. Those who still held on when it was delisted were either in a Rip Van Winkle-like trance or were day traders or hedge fund jockeys looking to squeeze double-digit profits from even the most minute price fluctuations.

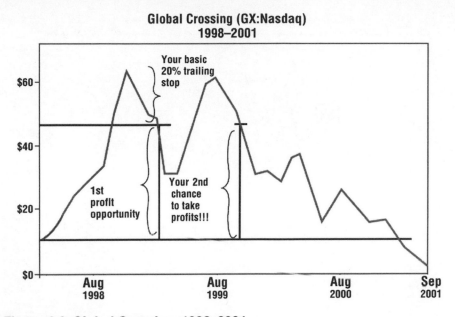

Figure 2.2 Global Crossing, 1998–2001

Source: William R. Bonner and Addison Wiggin, *Financial Reckoning Day: Surviving the Soft Depression of the 21st Century*, Hoboken, NJ: Wiley, 2003. Annotations by author.

Or how about this other poster boy for big, bad bubble stocks, Intel (INTL:Nasdaq)?

Here, too, in Figure 2.3, we're supposed to see a bubble followed by a cataclysmic collapse in the stock price. A valid if academic argument can (and should) be made that investors who bought INTL at its peak of $45 lost $35 a share when the stock plummeted into the single digits in the aftermath of September 11, 2001.

Even so, the *Financial Reckoning Day* view holds up only in the case of those who bought at the absolute top and bailed out at the ultimate bottom. A basic stop-loss provision would have locked in a majority of the gains and limited the losses of even the tardiest Internet Johnnies-come-lately to $9 and change per share. With a few well-placed puts as strategic insurance, this loss could have been turned into a profit, while the dynamic ups and downs of the stock price provided ample opportunity to make short and long gains on each movement.

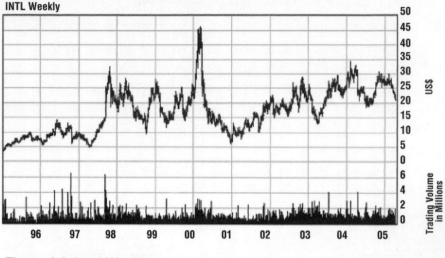

Figure 2.3 Intel Weekly

Heck, even those investors who bought at the top and then dollar-cost averaged over the next couple of years could have doubled and tripled their money on the portion invested after September 11.

Most of this, as you will rightfully interject at this point, is a result of perfect 20/20 hindsight. But so, my friend, are bubbles, if you consider it carefully. If anything, Intel's chart bears a striking resemblance to that of the CU 3000 index of rare US gold coins. (See Figure 2.4.)

If Intel stock were a quintessential bubble asset based merely on its price curve, we'd have to argue that at one point gold coins were, too. This only goes to prove one thing: there is no such thing as a safe investment. Every asset class carries risk and opportunity, downside as well as upside potential, both of which can be leveraged to your benefit by adopting the sweeping perspective of Dynamic Market Theory.

Valuable Resource

Check the Chicago Board Options Exchange (CBOE) web site at www.cboe .com not only for free 20-minute delayed quotes on stocks and all listed options, but also for important information concerning using puts for insurance. This is a conservative strategy when applied correctly.

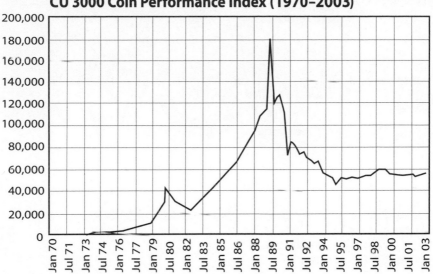

Figure 2.4 CU 3000 Coin Performance Index

In the Conclusion to his book *Famous First Bubbles*, Peter M. Garber wrote:

> Before we relegate a speculative event to the fundamentally inexplicable or bubble category driven by crowd psychology . . . we should exhaust the reasonable economic explanations. . . . Bubble explanations are often clutched as a first and not a last resort. Indeed, "bubble" characterizations should be a last resort because they are non-explanations of events, merely a name that we attach to a financial phenomenon that we have not investigated sufficiently in understanding.[10]

Following the notion of value we proposed earlier, we accept as our working hypothesis that there is no such thing as a bubble. If the price of a commodity like real estate, tulip bulbs, or Internet stocks rises to hyper-value based on demand, then that is not a false reading. It is the commodity's true value at that moment in time—not, however, for its intrinsic or absolute value at that time, *but for its perceived value as a tool to be leveraged into future profits*.

You see, at its core, a bubble is an argument about value—mostly made in retrospect, after a particular investment fad has gone bust. (Investment fads that don't go bust, conversely, are called strokes of genius, even if the underlying speculative analysis and risks are the same for both.)

For example, at the market peak in early 2000, it was said that the stock market had a valuation of $17 trillion. That amount had dipped to $8.5 trillion by October 2000. By the first quarter of 2005, the valuation of the stock market was about $10 trillion.

But—and here's what most investors don't seem to realize—all these figures are assignments of value based only on what a small percentage of shares trades for. Only a tiny fraction of a given company's shares are in play at a given time. Take Microsoft, for example. There are almost 11 billion shares of Microsoft outstanding, but on any one day only 25 to 30 million might change hands.

If you dumped all 11 billion shares on the market at one time, the price would plummet because of the monstrous excess in supply—no matter what was going on at the company, with the software, or in the stock market. So the valuation commonly given to any or all stocks is more or less arbitrary, not real, even if it is based on the latest sale of a few shares of the stock.

Those who hold a bearish view of the market like to say that around $8.5 trillion of equity valuation was destroyed in the bear market from early 2000 to October of that year. But since valuations are assigned arbitrarily anyway, they can't be destroyed. They change up; they change down. But they never go away. Conversely, that $8.5 trillion wasn't created, but was generated by the reallocation of savings and spending money put into stocks, which pushed share prices up overall, causing the higher valuation.

THE GLITTER OF GOLD

In early 2005, for example, gold was increasing in value. It sold for $435 an ounce, and an article in *Barron's* predicted that gold would hit $800 an ounce, based, I guess, on its 1980 valuation. Another expert source even predicted $1,000 gold. And one of my favorite gold bugs was quoted as saying that he "sees no reason why gold shouldn't be priced at $1,200 an ounce." Kotlikoff and Burns, as mentioned earlier, even make what could be considered a valid case for a $4,600-an-ounce price.

Why? Economic uncertainty and market volatility make investors less confident in currency, stocks, and other financial instruments. These investors are worried about the value of their holdings. So they start to shift assets away from paper instruments and toward hard assets—investments they can see, feel, and hold, like gold coins, bullion, or gems. Demand for gold—the "currency without a government" (Kotlikoff and Burns)—increases, and prices rise.

Plus, there is a political streak to the speculation as well, which has crystallized both the euro and gold as anti-dollars—presumably because economic conditions in the United States are deemed unsustainable. Given the economic and democratic carnage we expect the economies of Europe, and especially Germany and France, to undergo in the next couple of years—more about this in Chapters 5 and 6 of this book—this is by far the thinnest and flimsiest rationalization of blatant speculation we have seen in recent history.

And here's another interesting fact: In 1982, at the beginning of the most recent bull market, there were only about 1,500 companies listed on the New York Stock Exchange, with roughly 40 billion shares. The market valuation was around $1.3 trillion.

But by the year 2000 and the end of the bull market, there were more than 3,000 companies listed on the New York Stock Exchange with over 349 billion shares available. Granted, some of these were start-ups, but it's obvious that a lot of the wealth that was "created" actually came from existing private companies going public, taking advantage of a rising market, and putting shares of their company up for sale to the general public.

These companies were already in existence, with dynamic value. It's just that their value was now counted as part of the stock market. It shifted from the private owners to the shareholders who purchased the stock on the open market. In these cases, wealth wasn't created; it merely changed hands, from a few private owners to millions of stock investors. Realistically, since stock market valuations came down, the amount of money invested in stocks also came down. Much of that money was simply reallocated to other assets, like real estate, bonds, gold, energy, and other commodities.

Stocks are valuable to investors because their prices change, both up and down. If they didn't change, why would investors want them? It would be easier to hold cash. Cash is more liquid, and there are no transaction fees.

THE NATURE OF THE MARKET

Most investors think in linear terms about markets. A bull market is good, a bear market is bad, and a flat market is frustrating. A more rewarding way of looking at a bull market is to interpret it as an autocatalytic process. In chemical terms, a catalyst is an ingredient added to a chemical reaction for the purpose of speeding up that reaction. In his book *Collapse: How Societies Choose to Fail or Succeed*, Jared Diamond wrote:

> Some chemical reactions produce a product that also acts as a catalyst, so that the speed of the reaction starts from nothing and then runs away as some product is formed, catalyzing, and driving the reaction faster and producing more product which drives the reaction still faster.[11]

This kind of reaction is called autocatalytic.

Diamond takes this concept and applies it to the expansion of human populations, especially in view of emigration patterns:

> In an autocatalytic expansion of a human population, some initial advantages that a people gains (such as technological advantages) bring them profits or discoveries, which in turn stimulate more people to seek profits and discoveries, which result in even more profits and discoveries stimulating even more people to set out, until that people has filled up all the areas available to them with those advantages, at which point the autocatalytic expansion ceases to catalyze itself and runs out of steam.[12]

Translating this idea from the emigration of Norsemen to Greenland and Iceland or the human settlement of Polynesia to the equity markets, we gain a far better understanding of how a market bubble works than taking refuge in the proverbial "madness of crowds": The bubble is a natural phenomenon that occurs when a large number of human beings attempt to better their current living conditions.

In his recent book *The Wisdom of Crowds*, James Surowiecki takes the side of this maligned multitude:

> The wisdom of crowds has a far more important and beneficial impact on our everyday lives than we recognize, and its implications for the future are immense.[13]

Because the nature of such a process is not at all irrational or amoral, as the earliest treatises on Tulipomania, the still widely revered characterizations of the Victorian Charles Mackay, or even the poignant lines of Federal Reserve Chairman Alan Greenspan may suggest. Seeking gains and profits, whether by emigration, by discovery, or by investing in a bull market, is not at all irrational. To the contrary, it would be irrational not to. Because gains generated—and taken—during bubble events are just as real as those generated in a bear market.

In both cases, the operative term is "gains taken." For gains to materialize, however, you must find and invest in an asset that is growing in value, and sell before it declines in value. Too many investors overlook the cyclical tendency of prices, mainly because they are not looking at a bull market as an autocatalytic process that will slow down and cease once all catalysts have been used up. We are wise to remind ourselves that prices rise and fall; they do not continue rising indefinitely. The trick is first to find out what exactly the catalyst is that speeds the reaction in an upward direction, and then to identify the point in that process where the reaction is about to "run out of steam." This applies to markets *and* to individual equities and assets.

CONTROLLING RISK ITSELF

In the chapters that follow, my associates at the Taipan Group and I introduce you to their tried and proven methods of reading the markets for clues to these movements, to indicators and unique constellations of catalysts they apply to analysis. This proven technique is effective in localizing the proper timing of entry and exit strategies.

You can do it yourself, applying the catalysts that point you to a promising entry point, and you can put yourself in control, maximizing profits while limiting losses. It's easy. In fact, as I am writing this, what I am hearing in the background is oddly on point. I have not been able to locate the exact source of the melodious electronic jingles emanating from the depths of one of my children's rooms. I suspect the culprit is my middle son's Tamagotchi, an electronic pet parents worldwide have wished extinct for years.

For those of you able to eat your dinner in peace and escape the SpongeBob Squarepants movie and other trappings of a modern childhood, the Tamagotchi is a smallish, egg-shaped device on a key chain that consists of a small screen and various buttons. The screen is populated by crudely cutesy Japanese cartoon animals, whose maintenance requires periodic feeding and cleaning up digital digestive by-products. My son has developed a talent for nurturing these things past their natural life spans, surprising for a boy who can't find his bed for the piles of laundry covering the floor of his room.

Given the fact that an eight-year-old kid, living in apparent chaos, can be conditioned to respond to electronic alerts of a vaguely anthropomorphic collation of pixels, it always takes me by surprise to read or hear about people who apparently make do without stop-losses on their investment portfolios. If an "angry" Tamagotchi can be incentive enough to maintain it, how can watching the value of your investments decline past your preset pain threshold not be incentive to cut your losses?

At the core of some people's inability to manage their portfolios is that certain feeling of detachment that occurs when you exchange cash for shares in a stock or mutual fund. For many people, this process is like putting a letter into the mailbox, assuming it will arrive at the proper address thanks to the collective competence of the post office. Many investors simply assume that once they convert cash into shares, the share price will begin to rise and will continue to do so automatically.

If you have done your research, identified the function of the investment within your portfolio, and established a reasonable investment horizon, this long-term "buy-and-forget-about-it" attitude may not be a bad strategy. After all, nothing can eat up your profits as fast (or make your broker as happy) as jumping in and out of a stock because you've defined your risk tolerance too narrowly. And in many instances, the price curves of thousands of individual stocks have shown conclusively that even a major bear market like the one we experienced beginning in April 2000 may cause temporary setbacks but not necessarily lasting damage.

But if you apply this strategic tolerance to tactical positions in your portfolio—those you entered to derive short-term benefits—you are playing with fire. The implicit assumption that playing the markets isn't work can cost you dearly, in real losses and opportunity cost. So while you manage and tweak the Tamagotchi portions of your portfolio, it also makes sense to pick up the laundry now and then, to organize the whole room, and to keep a broad view. Remember, those shares are real money.

Almost all the recommendations our editors make are tactical plays with an investment horizon of a few weeks or months, and in the case of many of our trading services, only a few days or even hours. These trades are dynamic by nature as they follow the dynamic movements of a dynamic market. It requires some work on your side to make your money work for you. Generally, we recommend you observe a trailing stop of 20 to 30 percent, depending on the degree of your individual risk tolerance.

Dynamic Market Theory, then, is simply a commonsense approach to handling your money and your portfolio. It recognizes the importance of remaining involved in your investments and in accepting ultimate responsibility for how that portfolio performs. Within that theory and investing philosophy, we have a specific understanding of value as part of a cyclical pattern. At various times in that pattern, the market and its participants develop and follow a series of perceptions about value. Some are realistic, but most are part of the bubble mentality in the market. Once you accept this, you are far ahead of most people. And you will be well equipped to begin controlling—and creating—profits on your terms, and not merely on the terms dictated by some unknown, unseen, outside force.

CHAPTER 3

A STORY IS JUST A STORY . . . UNTIL THERE'S A PROFIT

The market's precise position in the wave structure is always in question, and . . . one's interpretation of a pattern is only a probability until it is certifiably complete.

—**Robert R. Prechter, Jr.,** *The Wave Principle of Human Social Behavior and the New Science of Socionomics* **(2002)**

What ever happened to virtual sex?

Now that I have your attention, I want to make a point. Current thinking, at times, is going to be dominated by fads, passing ideas like the New Coke, the pet rock, Beta videocassettes, and the miniskirt. Some may pass out of favor forever, and we may wish that others would return—the miniskirt comes to mind.

What does this have to do with Dynamic Market Theory? Everything. When was the last time you thought about the famed "data glove," dusted off the fuel cells in your car, or had a spare part for your boat faxed to you in 3-D as you watched the sun set over Punta Cana?

Most technology stories of the past 10 years have by now played themselves out in the market's buzz machine—think Internet B2B, cell phones, and virtual reality. Chances are, most investors who bought into these stories and held on tight to their stocks are not much better off than they were before. Greg Eckler, co-author of the 20/20 hindsight treatise *Bull! 144 Stupid Statements from the Market's Fallen Prophets*, provides an idea of how the mainstream brand of "story" investing tends to work out for most:

> In 2000 Eckler discovers fuel cells, snapping up Ballard Power Systems at a bargain US$60 against his father's stern warning that companies with no profits in their history are not worth US$5 billion. Eckler Jr.'s brilliance becomes clear as the stock hits US$100. Less clear when it hits US$10. Eckler Sr. explains that "whether it's fuel cells or flying cars, until there's profit, it's just a story."[1]

We find the double entendre of "fallen prophets" in *Bull!*'s subtitle particularly apt for our discussion here. Given the cyclical (and unavoidable) nature of auction markets in every form, it only makes sense that profits and losses are going to occur—inevitably, eventually, and unavoidably.

GETTING OUT, AHEAD OF THE CURVE (AND STAYING THERE)

If you happen to be a long-time subscriber to *Taipan*, our flagship publication, you probably had a good chuckle reading Eckler's words. After all, *our* "story" hunter-gatherers began tracking Ballard Power Systems (BLDP:Nasdaq) in June 1998—fully two years before the story was discovered by Eckler, which means that *Taipan* subscribers had a fighting chance to get into the stock when it was trading below US$27. And with a trailing stop (any trailing stop) in place, the Ballard story at its height of hype would have netted between $90 and $100 in cold, hard, pragmatic profits. (And reader, let us not forget that pragmatic profits are always preferred over paper profits, especially the kind that evaporate if you wait long enough.) Just look at Figure 3.1: even Eckler had at least two chances to break even on his $60-a-share investment.

So what went wrong?

Applying Dynamic Market Theory, we can reduce the conundrum to a handy syllogism: *We bought the story. Eckler bought into the story.*

BLDP Weekly

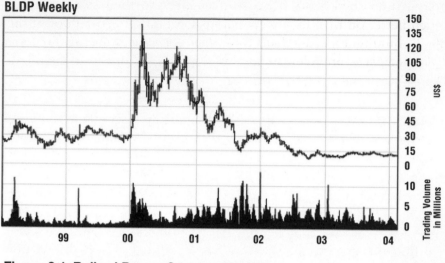

Figure 3.1 **Ballard Power Systems Weekly**

However, after that we diverge. Whereas we were following early indications of a dynamic movement, Eckler was making an emotional commitment.

The Point of Investing (Hint: It May Have Something to Do with Profits)

This pragmatic view of such things means the difference between making a mint and losing your shirt in the stock market. Over the years we have found that deviating from the strictly pragmatic analysis of dynamic movements is an expensive proposition. As soon as you allow your ego to get wrapped up in an intuitive, emotional, or overly dogmatic view of the markets, your chances of losing increase in direct proportion to the degree of your commitment to your worldview.

The point of investing is to end up with more money than you started with. For most of us, that means buying low and selling high (instead of the other way around)—or at least selling higher. I know it sounds simplistic, but you'd be amazed at the number of investors who come to see the market as a form of validation of their worldview and personal philosophy, when it is merely the soulless aggregate of dynamic buying and selling behaviors. Many investors are understandably mystified by the occurrences around them. They don't know why or how they lost money, where they went wrong, what they missed—because they have programmed themselves to lose. Amazing, isn't it?

The difficulty begins at the very onset, when you can't determine whether stocks are cheap. As a rule of thumb, stocks are never cheap if you look at them from the perspective of the present. For example, if you accept the efficient markets hypothesis, then you also accept its thesis: All stocks are fairly priced in the market given all circumstances known to all investors at this time. Prices are reasonable in the moment; otherwise, those astute investors who know more than everyone else (insiders) would be making all of the money. Does this sound familiar? Well, in fact, astute insiders are those following Dynamic Market Theory. Remember, stocks only become cheap in hindsight, after you know that they've gone up, when you are kicking yourself for not buying when you had the chance. While some investors are busy climbing the wall of worry and scolding themselves for past bad timing, others are sitting atop the wall, where they can see much farther. That is where you want to be, above the worry and recrimination, and able to keep a cool head.

MATTERS OF PERSPECTIVE

There is a story of an old man who, when asked what he regretted most about his life, responded that the worst thing that ever happened to him was finding a wallet in the gutter with a $10 bill inside when he was a boy. For the rest of his life, his eyes were drawn to look down at the sidewalk and gutters, in a less-than-rewarding mission to repeat the experience. How much, the old man mused, could he have seen and experienced had he not felt compelled to look down all his life?[2]

In many ways, the old man in the story spent his life doing what most investors do: looking for opportunity in the same places where once (and usually, once only) they were able to hit it rich by chance or premeditation. Over time, this tendency limits people and their focus; emphasizing the desire to repeat a positive experience, in the process they miss out on so many opportunities. Ultimately, this turns people bitter and they learn to think in small terms. We want to move beyond that human tendency and show you how to broaden your horizons.

Over the years in the financial investment advisory field, I've met plenty of people like the old man in the story: competent, highly educated and cultured financial editors and equally highbrow investors who've been looking for profits like those from past lucky strike years, when they came to believe they knew all the right places. There have been goldbugs who rode gold and bullion's heyday in the mid- to late 1980s, Internet stock pickers who can't let go of the glory that was the late and lamented Internet bubble of the 1990s, mining and exploration company investors who didn't strike it rich even in those decades the underlying commodities actually *rose* in price, or whose profits actually declined since they counted the cost of their operations in U.S. dollars, even while those dollars were declining sharply against the local currencies they pay their bills in.

What they all have in common is a compulsive shortsightedness, a hyper-focus on one particular asset or equity type, and, later, a near missionary zeal in proselytizing their view of a second coming of their respective favorite asset class.

This, my friend, is the death of profitable investing.

It is a self-destructive way of thinking, one that limits your ability to see beyond where you are today. It brings to mind another story:

A Russian farmer is visited by a genie who tells him he has one free wish, and that he can have anything he wants. The only caveat is, "Whatever you get, your neighbor will get twice as much." This creates a true dilemma for the Russian farmer, who hates his neighbor with all of his heart. He thinks and thinks and finally tells the genie his decision: "I wish to be blinded in one eye."

Focus, focus, focus. Opportunities *are* missed when your focus is on the wrong thing. Because so many investors remain focused on one particular asset class, life and profits pass them by.

All in the Mind?

I sometimes think that car dealers must wish they had a nickel for every time they've heard an elderly couple state that the new Camry costs more than the first house they bought in 1951. It's nostalgia, pure and simple: a sentiment gained with increasing maturity that drenches the past in warm hues of pink and gold.

We bumped into nostalgia recently reading the words of my friend and colleague Bill Bonner. He wrote back in early 2004:

> In the late '40s, you could buy an ounce of gold for US$35. Today it will cost you more than 10 times as much. And stocks? You could have bought all the Dow stocks for less than you'd pay for a single ounce of gold today.[3]

Reality, of course, is the nemesis of nostalgia. You know by now that the pragmatic wet blankets aboard the HMS *Taipan* can make the most luminous idyll look downright barren. And what's more real and barren than inflation?

A funny thing happens: Just by applying inflation rates, for example, that $35 you paid for one ounce of gold suddenly doesn't look quite as lustrous anymore. According to the U.S. Department of Labor's consumer price index, one dollar earned in 1949 corresponded to $7.78 in 2004. One 1946 dollar was the equivalent of $9.50 in more recent times. And if you go back to 1945, one dollar was worth $10.29 in 2004.

Let's see: Applying simple math, our 1949 ounce of gold would have cost us $272 in 2004 dollars; in 1946, we'd be out $332; and in 1945, it would have cost the 2004 equivalent of $360.16.

Pinch me: Didn't we see gold trade in exactly this price range in 2002 and 2003? In other words, had we bought an ounce of gold in 1945, we would have been up 50 bucks in horribly inflated 2004 currency. If we assume we bought at the equivalent of $350 in 1945 and sold that day, we'd have netted a profit of 14.28 percent.

In 1945 dollars, however, that's 35 bucks in very cold, hard cash. As far as returns go, don't mind me if I say that this appears to be a bit on the skimpy side, considering you've been paying safe-deposit box fees for that one ounce for two or three generations and almost half a century—and in all likelihood you would have paid retail dollars for gold but would have to settle for wholesale prices as you sell.[4]

Would it be presumptuous of me to point out that the Dow between 1945 and 1949 was trading at between 155 and 200? Adjusting for inflation occurring between 1945 and 2004, it would correspond to a Dow at 1,593. Today, as I am writing this chapter in July 2005, it's at 10,500 and change.

Stocks or gold? What would be the better asset to invest in, I wonder, provided you prefer being rich to being bearish?

Honestly, if we have to go back to the late 1940s to make a case for the profit potential of any given asset, it's probably not our cup of tea to begin with. When it comes to profits, we at the Taipan Group have cultivated short attention spans. And we've found that nothing gets our members through their workweek faster than taking a triple-digit profit before Joe Investor even finishes his first cup of coffee.

As I've pointed out again and again, it doesn't matter if stocks are in a bull or a bear market, or if the dollar is high against the euro or low against the pound sterling. It doesn't matter whether gold and precious metals are rising, or oil is on its way down. If you look at the market from the vantage point of Dynamic Market Theory, it matters little if a stock, asset, or index is going up or down, *because you can leverage either movements into profitable opportunities to make money.* You only need to know where to look for that opportunity. That's the beauty of the "Dynamic" part of Dynamic Market Theory.

Other investment advisers have developed systems that work sometimes and in certain markets. One fellow I'm thinking of is a well-known market bear. When the market does poorly, he makes money with his system and helps his readers avoid big losses. But in a bull market, his system just falls apart. In 2003, he was down 42 percent—making him the worst-performing financial advisory of the more than 160 financial newsletters rated by *Hulbert Financial Digest.* The problem with this system, obviously, was its inflexibility, its singularity of focus.

But the Dynamic Market Theory holds in every market and all the time. And with more than half a dozen proven systems based on it, we're always making profits, even when other investors are being devastated by losses. Systematic gains in the stock market seem almost too good to be true. Yet, for nearly two decades, we've used Dynamic Market Theory to help investors get rich regardless of what's happening on Wall Street. It works.

OWNING THE FUTURE

Since 1988, the Dynamic Market Theory team at the Taipan Group has made piles of profits by holding true to a single core belief about investing: that the truest and best investments are found where no one else can see value.

That sounds obvious enough, even fundamental. But believe it or not, the average investor can plod through a lifetime of investing and never wake up to this discovery.

When I joined Taipan full-time back in the summer of 1989, my hometown, West Berlin, was still surrounded by a concrete wall and barbed wire. Trains entering the city were stopped by East German border guards letting lose menacing-looking German shepherds to search the underside of the trains for potential defectors. The Soviet Union was still intact. And most investors weren't giving the Eastern Bloc a second thought.

The night the Wall came down in November 1989, it was nearly impossible to get through to Berlin on the phone—that is, if you tried dialing after the news had hit the wires. I actually spent the night tying up two phones simultaneously: My brother, on one line, kept me up to date on the German media coverage. On the other one was a friend whose apartment overlooked the Wall in a dingy part of town—who had originally alerted me that something was going on.

Later that month, our founding editor Bob Czeschin and I showed *Taipan* readers that all you had to do to profit when the Wall came down was buy the Germany Fund. The final take was $17,000 for every $10,000 invested. Then, thanks to more advance insights from within Germany, we were able to get out before the unification blues set in, with our 70 percent profits intact. I'm confident you could've done the same.

Back in the late 1980s and early 1990s, a lot of our research was still done "on foot." We had groomed and developed a neural network of researchers who tracked corporate news and reported back to us, often before the slow-moving media was able to respond to publicly known and important developments. We took advantage of inefficiencies in international communication by getting updated information in hand as rapidly as possible, and developing ways to react profitably.

Does this sound like insider information? The editors of this book actually were uncomfortable with the preceding paragraph. Who can blame them, with all the nonsense and misinformation about insider information and insider trading out and about in the press? But here's the rub: Insider information isn't illegal. Keeping it between you, your best friend, and the doorpost and trading on it is. Some of the information our editors and associates gather could indeed be considered insider information. When we get it, we publish it—because regulations prohibit us, or anyone else, from trading on insider information. We don't manage money, and we don't trade for anyone. We make our living publishing information we have gathered from various sources—and that includes company insiders as well as the tracks they leave in the market. (In Chapter 9, I'll let you in on how to obtain firsthand information on what exactly the insiders are doing in anticipation of major stock-moving events. That particular set of analytical catalysts is obtainable through almost all currently available financial web sites and portals that provide information on prices and trading volume. It's even better than getting tips from shady CFOs and corporate PR guys—who as a rule are as credible and unbiased as used-car salesmen. It's better . . . and perfectly legal.)

Every year throughout the 1990s, we invited select groups of individual investors to accompany our editors on their research expeditions to the Far East, Russia, South America, and the Middle East. The stories I could tell you from these expeditions could fill a book by themselves: One of our editors was attacked in the back alleys of Tel Aviv, and as he was recovering in his hotel room, a bomb blew apart his favorite café down the street. Another one witnessed a coup attempt in Thailand, and saw the lobby of his favorite hotel converted into an impromptu morgue as he was typing up his recommendation of buying select Thai stocks from the cast-iron bathtub of his hotel room. He then proceeded to fax to our home office via a hotel room telephone he had taken apart with his pocket knife.

I've watched our analysts call not just the markets, but every presidential election and most overseas elections since 1988, the Asian currency crisis in 1997, and the real estate collapse of 1989. I heard them talk about a "total information network" long before the Internet. Then I watched them show investors how to make as high as 341 percent profits on Free Markets, 515 percent profits on Interwoven, and 1,842 percent profits on Red Hat—far in advance, they revealed step-by-step how you could get rich on turmoil in South Africa, Turkey, and Indonesia.

From 1998 to 2001, just by following the advice of the analysts sitting at our editorial board table, and based on the principles of the Dynamic Market Theory trading systems that we have developed as a team and individually, you could have averaged 271 percent gains on your total portfolio. [5]

That absolutely clobbers the market performance of almost every broker and mutual fund in America. Incidentally, did you know that 80 percent of money managers and investment advisers and 95 percent of bond fund managers underperform the market? In fact, between 1984 and 1999, almost 90 percent of all mutual fund managers failed to outshine even the rather dim bulb of the Wilshire 500 index.[6] You'd be better off hiring a monkey to throw darts at a dartboard than paying managers' fat commissions and the hefty fees they charge for their so-called advice.

It doesn't matter if you missed out on these profits. You're better off with both of your eyes, trust me. Don't be like the Russian farmer of the fable. There are plenty of profits to be earned in the future, and we're going to show you how you can find them. Today. The strength of our Dynamic Market Theory is that it uncovers investments most other investors completely overlook. That's how you get in when you should be getting in—long before the mainstream coverage. And long before institutional investors move in and rocket stock values through the roof.

That's why you will rarely find the Taipan Group editors among the "irrationally exuberant" bulls or the permanently dyspeptic bears. We don't care to commit. More money has been lost in missed opportunities than was lost in the global market decline between 2000 and 2002.

So, in the absence of the hyped-up "next big thing," what are you supposed to do with your money? No matter where the markets are headed—an extended bull market such as the one predicted by Harry S. Dent Jr. or the ever-looming depression my colleagues in the financial advisory industry have been predicting since 1988—there will be plenty of opportunity here as the latticework of evolution progresses. So far, it's been working just fine for us.

While the Chicken Little crowd has been predicting since 1995 not only a stock market crash but also the unceremonious demise of the U.S. real estate market, we have been riding the dynamic waves for years. Thus far, we're quite happy with the results. So are our subscribers. *Taipan* reader Warren B. wrote to us in March 2004:

> I bought 1,000 shares of Impac Mortgage Holdings about nine months ago for about US$15.00 and have reaped the huge dividend as well as a very good appreciation in price. I wish I had bought a lot more of Impac. Thanks for your good advice on other stocks, especially the Chinese companies you recommended. I have done very well with them.

We had recommended Impac Mortgage Holdings (IMH:NYSE) as a yield play on the U.S. mortgage and real estate market in the July 2001 issue of *Taipan*, when the stock in Chapter 7 was trading at $7. In late 2004, it reached $29 a share, not to mention the regular double-digit cash dividends. (We'll be revisiting this particular stock to illustrate one of the Dynamic Market Theory tricks of the trade.)

Of course, pragmatists that we are, we don't expect trends to last forever: As the real estate bust in the early 1990s proved, no asset is safe from downward pressure. This is why we recommended a generous trailing stop of 25 percent to 30 percent on that IMH position.

Other than gut feeling and comparative analysis, you have a few hands-on facts to go by in weighing the upsides and downsides of U.S. equities. Many actually trade at less than their cash holdings and have a great deal of insider buying. As far as we at the Taipan Group are concerned, if you can find a company that has more dollars in the bank than the amount at which the stock market values its entire assets, and the smartest people in said company are buying shares, well then, that's a no-brainer. You buy. Put in a bit of sweat equity, dig a little deeper, seek out historical precedent, study the charts, or discover little-known new technologies whose stories have yet to make their way through the media-driven phases of investor interest.

What Big Money Knows That Joe Q. Investor Doesn't

We believe—and act upon—the philosophy that there is no magic, secret insider information, or tricks of the trade that someone else knows. All of us can and should act pragmatically and realistically to maximize the spirit of profitability. That ideal, the logical and justified pursuit of *profits*, is what defines our free market. As Max Weber once said:

> The investigation into what the driving forces of capitalism are is primarily not a question into the origins of the money supplies that can be used according to Capitalist principles, but a question into the development into the Capitalist spirit.[7]

But this ideal is far from simplistic. It is a path characterized by twists and turns and by a few pits of quicksand along the way. Anyone with a computer can see, just by going online, when a stock's price has moved—say, from $20 to $25 on a given day. And anyone with any imagination can see that they could have made a quarter for every dollar they put down. That's how it begins. And that's usually about the time average investors make their first mistake.

As soon as you start looking for a particular stock whose price could rise, you then introduce the idea of valuation—that a stock's price is somehow linked to the prospects of the company. But this is true only in the most general understanding of valuation. This is a problem, because there are so many momentary and short-term forces affecting price movement and having absolutely nothing to do with value itself. The market operates not on value but on the *perception* of value, and that is the key to the whole thing.

We've already spent plenty of time talking about value as a concept. So I will spare you a repeat of this discussion. But indulge me for a moment longer as I share the following observation:

If you watch stocks trade on options expiration days, you'll realize that valuation takes a backseat to the infinitely more powerful forces of *money flow*. The only question is, who's going to be left holding the bag?

Watch a stodgy old New York Stock Exchange stock as options expiration day (the third Friday of every month) approaches. Pay particular attention to the open interest on puts and calls in the vicinity of the current stock price. Like clockwork, the greatest number of people who can be squeezed out of their money at expiration will be. Whether that means selling down a good stock or pumping up a bad one, the trend is observed predictably.

Want to know where the S&P 500 and Nasdaq are headed? You could listen to bulls or bears or stock analysts. You could track unemployment, follow earnings trends, and pay close attention to market gurus and the financial media. But if you really want to know, you should check the "Commitments of Traders" (COT) report released every Friday by the Commodity Futures Trading Commission. The COT measures three entities: commercials, large traders, and small traders.

The COT report is more valuable than all the economic or technical analysis known to man. Why? Because it tells you what the big money, the money that literally moves the market—the commercials and the large traders—is doing.

Following the big money is where you'll get your first clue about what's really behind value, and why we prefer to use the realities of Dynamic Market Theory rather than traditional valuations of companies and their stocks.

You see, you'll usually find that the big money is doing the exact opposite of what the herd is doing. In general, it is the small trader who gets fleeced in the market. The investors looking for steady-growth, low-P/E stocks in which to park their $100,000 individual retirement accounts (IRAs) have no idea what they're up against.

Think Big and, Well, Think Bigger

The big money, the guys with billions upon billions in buying and selling power, *will* have their way. And if that means dropping a low-P/E stock even lower, then so be it.

For example, eBay traded in early 2005 at 22 times sales, had a P/E above 100, and had a 50 percent premium to its growth rate. It was richly valued, to say the least. Eight million shares of eBay were sold short. And the open interest on options was about 2-to-1 in favor of the puts (investors betting the stock will go down). A lot of people were betting the stock was overvalued and were expecting it to fall.

It's not that they were wrong. It's that they were asking the wrong question.

The single most important question you need to ask about any stock is not whether it's overvalued, but who's going to make money?

When you know the answer to that question, you can make a fortune. That's how the richest people in the world make their money.

Here's what I mean: The top three institutional owners of eBay in early 2005 had about $3.5 billion in the stock. Add in the next three institutional owners, and you're talking about $6 billion. So, will the investors who have approximately $800 million in shorted stock ever turn a profit?

Not likely. The big boys—that is, the top institutional owners— are going to keep the price up in a stock until the shorts call it quits. Or they'll run the price up and squeeze the shorts[8]—handing them bigger and bigger losses—until they give in. And the situation is usually going to be even worse for the vast number of put options holders.

Another example: Barclays, State Street, and Fidelity owned 613 million shares of Cisco at the beginning of 2005. Cisco averaged 50 million shares traded a day. That's less than 10 percent of its total holdings. If these institutions want to support the price of Cisco, they certainly can, though it can work only on a short-term basis; they can't keep buying forever.

The stock market is a game, pure and simple. And there's only one rule: money always wins. In other words, a lot of that money that disappeared from stocks (equity funds) simply moved into bond and money market funds. It changed pockets, as Gertrude Stein would say.[9]

As I have indicated earlier, the money didn't disappear—it just moved. Add to that the moves into gold and real estate, and you begin to see that, allowing for fluctuations in the value that we love to assign to the market, money tends to move around more than it appears and disappears. Of course, those who bought Internet shares at the top of the market only to watch their valuations plummet actually did lose money, much as those investors who sold real estate in the past three years actually made money. In that situation, many of the Internet companies had been so blown up, out of proportion to any definition of value, that the losses were inevitable.

In the spring of 2005, money began flowing back into stocks again. Actually, it had been flowing quite steadily since the presidential election in November 2004. But beware: The market is set to fool investors and separate them from their money yet again. Between now (any point in time) and the peak of the "next big bubble market" that has been forecast by Elliott Wave theorist Harry S. Dent Jr. there are plenty of snares and pitfalls to trap the unwary.

The Stock Market Is Just There to Make Trading Convenient

If you follow Dynamic Market Theory and keep your eye on the dynamic movements of markets, indexes and individual stocks, you're much better positioned to profit, no matter what happens in the stock market. It's a new and different way of investing that takes into account volatile market conditions and the many factors stacked against the individual investor.

Many stocks exhibit certain predictable behaviors before they make a large move—that is, before the money moves toward or away from them. Over time, this behavior, shown by indicators, gets recognized, and everyone begins to look for those indicators and act on them. At that point, the significant factors evolve into something else.

To turn this action into profits, you need a set of methods for looking at the dynamic market action of stocks (in other words, price action) to arrive at decisions about how to invest. These individual methods, or systems, for looking at price action are explained in detail later in the book. They enable us to predict developments in stocks in any market by interpreting the different indicators.

It has become obvious that static theories or traditional views of the markets can't and won't work in the long run, because there is no one set of principles—like value investing—that will always work. Since the market is dynamic and constantly changing, following one investing principle dooms you to failure. It may work for a short period of time, but once the market factors change, then so must your investing philosophy.

If everyone looked for value and bought value based on certain criteria, there would be only buyers for stocks one day, and only sellers another day. Markets just don't work like that. There have to be both buyers and sellers to maintain equilibrium in the markets.

Anyone concentrating on only one sector or one style of investing is going to fail. Money flows from one stock to another, and from one sector to another. This dynamic action is what you must read to be successful—and you will learn to read it in this book.

SAFE, PREDICTABLE PROFITS WITH DYNAMIC MARKET THEORY TRADING

Profiting regardless of market conditions is a habit you'll come to love when you master Dynamic Market Theory trading. Over the past two decades, we've helped investors stay head and shoulders above rocky markets time and time again.

For instance, while the rest of the world shrank from South Africa at the end of the 1980s, our readers tucked away triple-digit profits on South Africa's ESKOM bonds. In 1990, we told investors to short the Nikkei in Japan. They tripled every dollar invested. Just before the 1997 Asian currency crisis, our team of Dynamic Market Theory analysts smelled danger and yanked our readers out with 232 percent, 271 percent, and 289 percent intact.

Do you see what I'm suggesting? Triple-digit profits appeal to everyone, so I urge you to find a comfortable chair, throw a log on the fire, and settle down with this book, a pencil, and a cup of strong coffee. In Part III, we begin to explore some of the myths about how investing works, and show you how it *really* works.

But before we do, let us examine the nature of the bubble and what it means. Once you come to realize how this whole market works, you will change your view of markets completely. You will realize that bubbles are not the end of the world, but merely a part of the natural economic cycle. Read on, and you will see why.

PART II

CRISIS AND OPPORTUNITY IN THE GLOBAL MARKETS OF 2006–2009

CHAPTER 4

THE LAST PHASE OF THE BUBBLE MARKET (2006–2009)

The stock market will probably remain the single best indicator of social mood and change.
—**Robert R. Prechter, Jr.,** *The Wave Principle of Human Social Behavior and the New Science of Socionomics* (2002)

Based on the research of Ralph Nelson Elliott, Laurence Kotlikoff, Robert Prechter, and other wave theorists, the financial markets, long-term price trends, and larger economics move in predictable wave patterns. Each of the major macroeconomic waves may last as long as an entire century. Currently, according to technical experts, we are approaching the end of the final wave in an important multi-decade wave trend.

The following chapters outline for you exactly what this means for the economy and the equity markets of the United States; how inescapable demographic developments will shape our fortunes and lives; and why these trends trigger some of the most dramatic and long-lasting shifts in the global balance of power. Of course, I will also show how you can use this foreknowledge to your advantage, to allow you to not just survive but prosper in the turbulent period we're entering.

CRISIS AND OPPORTUNITY

Each of these developments constitutes an acute crisis in its own right. But each crisis in turn holds the seed of opportunity, the opportunity to harness trends for your own financial gain and long-lasting benefit. In the coming years, great fortunes will be lost and won, and those who read the trends right and act with courage and foresight will be able to lay the cornerstones of great wealth.

Pundits and politicians alike are having a field day with the concept of "privatizing Social Security." No doubt this debate will last for many years to come. President George W. Bush kicked off his second administration with an ambitious reform plan, and the fight is on.

Consensus appears to be as elusive in Washington, D.C., as it is on Main Street USA. Now, this is not a political book. And if you're counting on Social Security checks as a financial mainstay of your retirement, I think you should put this book down right now and enroll at a community college to acquire some extra skills that may feed you in your old age, as you will probably need to work until you drop dead. Even Wal-Mart can hire only so many greeters.

The Social Security crisis, as it has been analyzed and described by hundreds of commentators for the past 15 years, is simply the tip of a demographic iceberg that appears set on a collision course with the American way of life as we know and love it. As of July 2004, Americans aged 65 and older total 36.3 million, or about one-eighth of the total population. By 2030, this percentage will have increased to 20 percent (one-fifth), according to estimates by the U.S. Census Bureau. Studies and official reports hold that the Social Security system is approaching a major financial catastrophe: by 2018, the program will be paying out more money to retirees than it will be taking in from workers.

Already, the annual statements that the Social Security Administration supplies you with around the time of your birthday clearly state that:

> Your estimated benefits are based on current law. Congress has made changes to the law in the past and can do so at any time. The law governing benefit amounts may change because, by 2042, the payroll taxes collected will be enough to pay only about 73 percent of scheduled benefits.

People get this statement every year. They even got it in 2000, a few months after the end-of-the-world crowd milking Y2K for all it was worth had forecast that the Social Security Administration's legacy mainframe systems would unleash Armageddon on all those who hadn't moved to the Ozarks with a truckload of dried fruit, laundry detergent, rolls of quarters, and a trusty AK-47.

That's plenty of warning, if you ask me. And every year, the benefits you can expect in a best-case scenario are tallied up as well, down to the penny. Now, I've been gainfully employed in the United States since 1990. According to my 2004 statement (which summarizes my earnings through 2003), I have exceeded the maximum wages on which Social Security is levied, and this has occurred eight times. Still, the maximum benefit I can calculate is a Social Security payment of $2,553 a month, based on my working until I am 70 years old. For the year, that would total $30,636.

Here's my question: could you live off 30,000 bucks a year? More importantly: would you want to? If you depend on paying off a mortgage or paying rent from that amount, I suggest you develop a taste for Spam and government cheese, because that's about what you will be able to afford.[1]

Still, "When the future comes," write Kotlikoff and Burns in their book *The Coming Generational Storm*, "Washington will discover that everyone is 'rich.' Our tax system will work to put people with very pedestrian incomes into fat cat tax brackets."[2] This may eventually apply even to those with a measly $25,000 in Social Security income each year. Accordingly, after you deduct taxes (and believe me, you will be paying plenty of income taxes on your Social Security checks by the time you retire) and account for inflation, you'll be left with a paltry sum you may remember from the beginning of your career.

Count on your 401(k) or 403(b) to bail you out? Consider this fly in the ointment: You spoon-fed these accounts with pretax dollars for decades in the hope that you'd be pulling money out of them when you retire at a far lower tax rate. But chances are that by the time you think you can afford to retire, politicians will be as keen on this reservoir of untaxed income as the states are now on Internet sales taxes.

If nothing is done to reform it, the Social Security system will begin to see annual cash flow deficits in 2018. Those deficits are predicted to grow significantly over time as the system becomes more and more strapped, and are estimated to reach about $72 billion in 2020, $275 billion in 2030, $429 billion in 2050, and $719 billion in 2070. That's a lot of burden to place on the Social Security system, and a huge load to place on the coming generations of American workers. Add in the exponentially growing implicit debt that an aging population places on Medicare and other entitlement programs, and you arrive at a sum so large it seems impossible to bankroll with a pay-as-you-go scheme, where current workers pay for retiree benefits from their income.

Truth be told, there is not a whole lot that can be done to reform the system. Personal accounts that you can use to invest some of your payroll deductions are not a bad start, despite the current media hubbub. The chances of coming out ahead are quite good.

In the April 2005 issue, *Money* magazine asked New Frontier Advisors of Boston, Massachusetts, to figure out how you could beat the average 3 percent return (annualized and adjusted for inflation) that would be required to outperform existing returns. Calculating stock market and bond returns and market volatility for the period from 1978 to 2004, New Frontier Advisors determined that a mixed portfolio consisting of 50 percent stocks and 50 percent bonds has a 15 percent chance of being worse off after 15 years. On the upside, it has a 50 percent chance to earn close to 5 percent.[3]

But even personal accounts bankrolled by a part of your payroll contributions won't fix the underlying problem: Politicians can raise payroll taxes or scrap the maximum. Neither will do anything for their chances to remain in office. Increasing income taxes on individuals and corporations will choke off economic growth at a time it is most crucial to maintain, triggering an exodus of capital to low-tax countries. And since there will be plenty of countries suffering from the same syndrome, there will be plenty of competition for expatriate dollars.

There's only one thing we can be almost sure of in regard to Social Security: The politicians will royally screw it up. If you belong to the generation left holding the bag, you will have to get used to the thought that you will be keeping less of your income and will also have to accept a lower standard of living.

That's the bad news.

The good news is that you can do something about it.

THE LAST BIG BOOM

Luckily, you've been granted a bit of a reprieve. For one, as an American, you may not feel the full brunt of the age bomb. Kotlikoff and Burns wrote:

> The entire planet is aging, much of it faster than we are. Most of the developed world is aging faster for two reasons. First, Americans aren't contenders in the Life Expectancy Olympics, so we aren't increasing our elderly population as fast as other countries. Second, our birthrate, while flagging, isn't so low that our population will shrink over the next fifty years.[4]

The second reason is that demographically, you still have an ace up your sleeve. Between now and the onset of the great wave of retirement there is a period that the market analyst Harry S. Dent Jr. calls the "next great bubble boom."[5] He writes:

> The demographic wave of earning and spending of the largest generation in history, the baby boomers, never stopped during the downturn of 2000–2002 and will continue until 2009 or 2010.[6]

This last big boom will be fueled by three main factors: the telecommunications revolution, changes in the spend trend, and the echo effect.

A Revolution

The first is the Internet and telecommunications technology revolution, whose spectacular collapse after April 2000, according to Dent, merely represents a shakeout and consolidation phase that will be followed by a last and unprecedented push of global market permeation. It has happened before with the automobile and radio technology revolutions. Whenever a revolutionary new technology hits 50 percent market penetration, problems begin. This occurred in auto manufacturing in 1914 when more than 200 companies were in business. It also happened in 2001 in the mobile phone industry. The broadband revolution—growing at twice the rate of the Internet itself—will accelerate voice activation, speed video communications, give a new look to the whole Internet and communications industry, and achieve a 90 percent penetration by 2009. (Think about it: there's a billion single Chinese males waiting to discover Internet porn!)

Changes in the Spend Trend

The second reason is that the baby boomers, to quote a *Monty Python* character, aren't "dead yet." In fact, a large chunk of those born before 1964—yours truly included—are only at the cusp of their prime earning and spending years: Data derived from the Consumer Expenditure Survey of the U.S. Bureau of Labor Statistics indicates that there is a double peak in spending that occurs at age 50 and at age 56.[7] The economic boom that began in the 1980s, according to Dent's research, will be over only when the last group of baby boomers is done spending and its productivity cycle declines, probably by 2010.

The Echo Effect

The last reason why the age bomb will not punish the United States as badly as other industrialized nations is closely correlated with the spending patterns of the baby boomers: their children, the so-called echo boomers.

If you're a parent, you were able to follow the echo boom based on the amount of toys scattered on your living room floor. First came the Disney videos that you bought throughout the 1990s. Then there were the happy meal toys from McDonald's and Burger King, who merchandized the heck out of every new movie release and rerelease by issuing incredibly intricate action figures and games. (Of course, more elaborate versions were sold at Toys 'R' Us.) Then, right alongside the Internet boom years, came Beanie Babies, cheap limited edition (that were, in fact, not really "limited" at all) plush animals people bought for $5.95 and sometimes were able to resell for hundreds of dollars. Then came Pokemon, a card game with—you guessed it—toys and video and movie tie-ins. (The stock of its US license holder, 4Kids, soared in late 1999.) Then came the Tickle Me Elmo and Yu-Gi-Oh!

Each mini-boom in the stocks associated with these trendy toys today looks like a classical stock bubble. And yet, each movement was pushed up by honest-to-goodness demand, and the pent-up spending of youngish parents willing to open their wallets to shut up their whining offspring.

They still do. It's just that the spoiled four-year-olds from 1994 today are teenagers—sometimes called Generation Why—whose spending focuses on other soon-to-be-outgrown items, iPods. And pretorn jeans from Abercrombie & Fitch. And it's not just toys and clothes. It's minivans, SUVs, and finally, houses.

Take a drive through southern Maryland, the suburbs of San Francisco, or Seattle, and you see how baby and echo boomer consumption behavior has changed the landscape. Homes built in the 1950s to 1970s tend to be quite modest by comparison: ranches and Cape Cods with snug bedrooms, small bathrooms, and lots of yard. Their 1990s counterparts have inverted the ratios: The footprint of the house takes the major part of the property: bedrooms, kitchens, and bathrooms are huge; formerly snug dens are designed around wide-screen TVs whose dimensions exceed those you just got used to at your local cinema multiplex. And most new houses are constructed with one side entirely windowless, an indication of enormous storage space for toys, sports equipment, clothes, and more toys.

Look at the recent real estate boom from the perspective of generational life-cycle spending patterns and you get an inkling of its enormity. And that boom isn't done yet. There is still an enormous section of the echo boom that has yet to incur some of life's major expenses: college tuition, first cars, starter homes.

This generational expense cycle will be reflected in the U.S. equity indexes. Estimates for new record highs in the Dow Jones Industrial

Average range from 18,000 up to 40,000 by 2009.[8] By the time this book is published, in January 2006, the current levels of 10,000-plus may appear like grand opportunities to have bought.

Wave analysis is, of course, just one way to analyze the market for potentially profit-rich patterns. And as Benoit Mandelbrot pointed out, it can be a "very uncertain business":

> It is an art to which the subjective judgment of the chartist matters more than the objective, replicable verdict of the numbers. The record of this, as of most technical analysis, is at best mixed.[9]

That may be right. Forecasting according to patterns is a matter of probabilities, not of certainties. Chance may produce deceptively convincing wave patterns, just as slime mold on an old refrigerator or mineral seepage on a concrete wall may produce weeping apparitions of the Madonna, Elvis, or Carl Sagan. But underneath the wave patterns of the markets are correlating patterns of human demographics, behavior, and history. It's not all that far-fetched. Robert R. Prechter, Jr. wrote:

> Except for the timing of the recession of 1946 . . . all economic contractions came upon or after a downturn in aggregate stock prices. In not one case did a contraction or recovery precede a like change in aggregate stock prices, which would repeatedly be the case if investors in fact reacted to economic trends and events.[10]

In a worst-case scenario, this means that you have less than five years of a strong bull market to get your house in order, to get ready for the tough decade and a half that will follow the collapse of this last great bubble boom sometime in late 2009 or 2010.

Use the strong upside moves to build the foundation of your financial survival: Get rid of debt and pay off your mortgage, free up the income and effort required to service both, and channel them into wealth-building strategies. Get in shape and eliminate health risks that will otherwise drain your wealth at a time when you can least afford it. Look for income-generating investments, producing rent, interest, dividend, or yield income that you can use as "wealth engines" that will substitute for income generated by your current work.

Most of all, once you've covered your bases, set aside an amount of speculative capital that you can use to learn the ins and outs of the trading secrets I'm going to share with you starting in Chapter 7.

No bull market lasts forever. And the end of this one will be or-chestrated by global forces that have already embarked on a course that will shatter our profitable little bullish idyll by the time the first decade of the new century is wrapping up.

CHAPTER 5

STAGNATION AND DECLINE: THE INEVITABLE IRRELEVANCE OF THE EUROPEAN UNION

The reality is that Europeans inhabit a post-Christian society that is economically, demographically, but, in my view, above all culturally a decadent society.

> —Niall Ferguson, in an AEI Bradley Lecture published on March 1, 2004

As we have seen in the preceding chapter, demographic trends make for an explosive mix for the American equity markets in the years ahead: In the medium term, the U.S. market is entering the last stretch of a long-term bubble market, followed by a protracted decline that may last a decade or longer. And, as Chapter 4 outlined, a major part of this decline is based on the way that technical waves work.

Between now and then you have many opportunities to profit

from these ever-emerging conditions. But by the end of this decade, your investing strategies will need to change dramatically. To adapt in time and to prepare those strategies for the changing market environment, you need to know what lies ahead. Time is short. And current opportunities require fast action to make stock market gains—and keep making them despite changing market conditions!—and not just to defend your portfolio against losses.

The demographic changes outlined in the previous chapter apply not only to the United States. In fact, due to its work ethic, its flexible labor market, its immigration and integration policies, and its traditional emphasis on family and procreation, the United States may in fact be sheltered from the worst fallout of demographic booms and busts.

Other regions will not be so lucky. Here, demographic trends have already set the tracks for a slow decline . . . a decline that will be precipitated by the most explosive economic event of the twenty-first century by 2010.

Here's how we at the Taipan Group are seeing history unfold in the coming decade:

Back in the early 1990s, when I was a young assistant editor at *Taipan*, I interviewed two American businessmen who were about to embark on a daring venture: they were getting ready to launch a business magazine in Eastern Europe that bore the name *Profit*.

As far as I recall, their ambitious venture did not succeed. After more than 70 years of Marxism-Leninism in Russia, and almost 50 years of communism in Eastern Europe, the very title was a dirty word to the inhabitants of the region, so vulgar indeed that few advertisers wanted to be associated with it.

DIRTY WORDS

Even today, among certain circles in Europe and the United States, the word *profit* is synonymous with greed, ruthlessness, selfishness, and other mortal sins. You tend to find this attitude prevalent at colleges and universities, where academia has established tenured reservations for those who seek to make a comfortable living without ever getting their hands dirty.

This ideological aversion against the concept of profit is part and parcel of the nineteenth-century class struggle legacy of Karl Marx and Friedrich Engels at the close of the industrial revolution. Implementing the abstract theories cooked up by these well-to-do scions of property-owning classes, totalitarian systems like the Soviet Union and East Germany identified the capitalist as the enemy of the state and enemy of the working class, although their economies, too, relied on capital to keep going.[1]

Much has changed in Eastern Europe since the early 1990s. When it comes to implementing free market theories, countries like Poland and Estonia today are far ahead of Germany and France, where institutionalized corporatism and an unhealthy commingling of state and business still aim to limit competition and preserve entitlements and kickbacks for an ever-expanding cadre of functionaries and political mandarins.

Interestingly, even the Soviet Union employed typical capitalist concepts to perpetuate its grasp on Europe and Asia throughout the Cold War: The very concept of outsourcing was practiced in the Soviet Union, where industrial espionage substituted for research and development in large segments of the military-industrial complex. Documents related to the French in the early 1980s by the renegade Soviet colonel Vladimir Ippolitovitch Vetrov—code-named "Farewell"—indicate that the KGB was giving to the Soviet Politburo "the precise amount of money saved by Line X through stealing this or that piece of Western technology."[2] (And according to Kenneth Timmerman, state-capitalist France has been keeping up the tradition of industrial espionage by planting agents in U.S. technology firms since the 1980s.)

In modern Europe, socialist and communist political ideologies are now again gaining in influence under the auspices of antiglobalism, despite the spectacular failure of Eastern Bloc communism. The city of Berlin, the new capital of reunited Germany, is being ruled by a coalition of Social Democrats and the Party of Democratic Socialism (PDS), the shameless and unrepentant successors to East Germany's ruling Socialist Unity Party (SED). (In fact, a former SED bigwig who was heavily involved in hiding and channeling ill-gotten party assets now poses as Berlin's economic secretary.)

It shows. Visiting German relatives in April 2005, I was struck with how run-down and decrepit entire districts looked . . . districts I remember as vibrant parts of old West Berlin. There was block upon block of empty apartment buildings. Roads and city streets were rutted like private driveways in rural Appalachia or downtown Baltimore after the first thaw. And opening the newspapers and listening to private conversations was like tuning into the *Schwarze Kanal*, East Germany's Monday night anti-Western propaganda show hosted by the late Karl-Eduard von Schnitzler, a gloating goateed bear-baiter with Coke-bottle glasses. I felt myself wondering just who had won the Cold War: to me, it seemed the East had successfully colonized the West.

Of course, dilapidated buildings can be fixed or torn down. Potholes can be filled when the signs warning of "pavement damage" have rusted away. But the damage done to the public psyche and culture is far more grave. In Germany, a deeply rooted distrust against capital and knowledge-based progress remains: Campaigning in the late 1990s, German Chancellor Gerhardt Schröder was able to gather brownie points with his electorate by stressing repeatedly that he himself did not own stocks. In February 2005, Schröder and French president Jacques Chirac again exploited this populist aversion to capitalist institutions by calling for a worldwide tax on "speculation"—speculating being the archetypical pastime of the capitalist class enemy and communist code for the concepts of "investing" and "trading." In April 2005, one Franz Münterfering, chairman of the German Social Democrats—the senior government coalition partner—embarked on a campaign of anticapitalist rhetoric, calling investors "locusts" and entrepreneurs who put profits before mass employment "irresponsible." He was eagerly celebrated by the German chancellor and other high-level government officials.[3] This in itself would have been sad enough were it not for the fact that online polls by major German newspapers registered two-thirds of those responding in favor of the old proto-Marxist chestnuts.

This old-fashioned bipolar ideology of capital versus labor—one greedy, ruthless, and inhuman, the other supposedly compassionate, humanistic, and noble—tries to obfuscate that capital and labor have always been in a symbiotic relationship: Without capital, there is no work. If there is no money to pay for a particular job, the job will remain undone.

WATER FROM THE WALL

The endemic European ignorance of financial matters that has been fostered by this ideology has created a pervasive entitlement mentality that encompasses claims on retirement, education, and health care.

A perennial European (and American) favorite is the misconception that health care in Europe is free. It is so widespread that the recent introduction of a 10-euro co-payment for doctor's visits in Germany created what Chancellor Gerhardt Schröder characterized as "prerevolutionary conditions."

This particular incident reminds me of an anecdote my mother used to tell from the time her hometown of Stendal was occupied by the Red Army after World War II. Plundering Russians were very fond of water faucets, which were removed from walls and sinks to be shipped wholesale back to Russian villages. It seems the rustic Russki draftees had reduced the concept of indoor plumbing to *Wasser aus Wand* (a kind of pidgin German, that translates into "water from the wall"), assuming that if only a stolen faucet were pounded into a wall, babushka back home would be able to enjoy free running water out in the Russian boondocks.

Of course, if you've ever spent a month working for your living, maybe even running a business, you come to realize pretty quickly that nothing is ever free . . . not "water from the wall"—which requires the construction and maintenance of a water and sewer system—and certainly not health care, where 10 bucks paid at the receptionist's desk may cover part of that particular month's water bill, but doesn't make a dent when it comes to paying for nurse, doctors, receptionists, or colostomy bags. (What Europeans usually don't volunteer to tell you is that the contributions to that supposedly free health-care system are taken out of their paychecks each and every month. In Germany, for example, an average 13 percent of your gross salary disappears this way before you've even registered that you have a headache!)

There is a certain irony to the fact that the European entitlement mentality—which really is nothing but complete financial ignorance—has spread and grown over a period that is characterized by an unprecedented democratization of finance.

Let's take a step back here: European post-communists calling for the democratization of the financial markets (like Messrs. Schröder, Müntefering, and Chirac) have soundly slept through the fact that the democratization of the world's equity markets also democratized capital. As columnist Thomas Friedman wrote in 1999,

> The democratization of finance actually began in the late 1960s with the emergence of the "commercial paper" market. These were bonds that corporations issued directly to the public in order to raise capital. The creation of this corporate bond market introduced some pluralism into the world of finance and took away the monopoly of the banks. This was followed in the 1970s by the "securitization" of home mortgages.[4]

In the United States, this democratization of capital also expressed itself in increasing ownership of stocks by private households and consequently in the emergence of a booming financial and brokerage industry that established itself not as an integral part of but as a competitor to the traditional banking industry. The average American household keeps 13 percent of its assets in cash and 33 percent in shares. In Europe, at 28 percent cash and 13 percent shares, the ratios are inverted. In Japan, it's 53 percent cash and only 8 percent in shares.[5] Which ratio, I ask you, reflects a more thorough democratization of capital?

THE NEW LABOR

With the democratization of capital and the shift from traditional manufacturing or farm work to knowledge-based production of added value, we arrive at an expanded understanding of labor. This new understanding incorporates the capitalists' prerogative to live off the "work" of their capital—by creating added value in the form of regular revenues in the shape of interest, dividends, yields, and good, old-fashioned capital gains. There is no magical water from the wall here, just the rewards of productivity, risk, and investment.

Americans have already implemented the concept in the creation of self-managed individual retirement accounts (IRAs) and 401(k) and 403(b) retirement plans. The Bush administration—I've mentioned this previously—has proposed allowing younger workers to invest part of their Social Security in the stock market. To these individuals, this is an opportunity to supplement and, eventually, replace their personal traditional compensation-based labor with the labor of their *capital*. This may further explain why so many politicians—especially those who see and cultivate a certain intellectual kinship with Europe—are so vehemently opposed to the plan, even without having any details to complain about.

The replacement of compensation-based labor with capital labor is also a power shift. The concept of having capital work for you rather than depending on your ability to perform compensation-based labor (as a blue-collar worker or a white-collar executive) becomes of paramount importance in economic environments where the supply of workers exceeds the availability of labor, or, more generally, when an economy is in an extended downturn—a downturn like the one we will be facing a little less than four years after this book hits the bookstores!

It is the further progression and democratization of capital labor that accounts for many of the discrepancies of the U.S. and European savings rates that published opinion has been citing as the cause of the low dollar exchange rate from 2002 to 2005. The lower and decreasing savings activity of private households in the United States has been partially rooted in the lower risk to income generation via traditional compensated work: more flexible labor markets offer higher chances of employment and reduce the perceived necessity to provide against the risk of prolonged unemployment. However, wealth is being built not only out of current compensated labor income, but also via the appreciation of other assets—such as stocks and real estate. If wealth grows based on appreciation of assets and income is supplemented by yields and dividends, the need to increase savings from compensated labor income diminishes: a larger segment of this income can be diverted for consumption, which in turn drives the economy and reduces the risk of unemployment.

This has resulted in an interesting development in household net worth: According to a study by Hubertus Bardt and Michael Grömling published in October 2003 by W-Trends,[6] the net worth of private households—bank accounts, life insurance policies, equities and private pension plans minus debt—grew by 77.5 percent in Germany in the period between 1991 and 2002, when it totaled 2.195 billion euros, or 159 percent of the spendable income. In the United States, net worth increased by 73 percent. But the wealth ratio (net worth as a percentage of spendable income), at 276 percent, was considerably higher, despite the effect of the post-2000 decline in the equity markets.

The savings rate of a country can be interpreted in two ways. In the Neo-Classicist approach, savings are considered the foundation of investment, a positive indicator for short-term growth and long-term capital base. In Keynesian terms, however, growing savings slow down economic expansion, as saving represents a reduction in demand and consumption. Look at European GDP growth rates today and you see Keynes vindicated!

In both cases, savings follow the prevalent demographic and life cycle trends: they are accumulated during prime earnings years to be spent in retirement. And this bodes ill for the financial future of Germany in particular, and Europe in general.

SILENT SPRING, PART II

Strolling through downtown Bonn, the former capital of Germany, in the spring of 2004, I felt oddly out of place. Now, generally speaking, that is not a novel experience for me: Immigrants like myself every now and then feel out of place even if they've spent more than 15 years in their residence of choice. Upon returning to the old homeland for visits, they come to admit that they wouldn't fit in back there at all.

But Bonn was different. It wasn't me, for a change. (I'm sure of it!) The former West German capital felt like a newly renovated suburban home after a major wedding celebration: The fancy-dressed guests have left, leaving the shell-shocked parents of the bride sitting in slightly used finery in front of a fridge full of leftover hors d'oeuvres and half-empty bottles of champagne, as the mailman rings the door-bell to deliver the bills.

With the German government and foreign diplomats all safely relocated to Berlin, Bonn apparently is slowly reverting to its "small town in Germany" status, to cop a phrase from John Le Carré. Huge office buildings that corralled the pencil pushers of a dozen government agencies when I last visited in the mid-1980s are empty and for rent. And in the shopping area, fly-by-night stores hawking Chinese health and folklore junk have taken over where highfalutin boutiques once catered to pampered diplomats.

Most remarkable is the small number of children and adolescents out and about on the first sunny afternoon in March. Were they all at school? (Unlikely, considering schools in Germany tend to close at around 1 p.m.) Playing computer games at home? (I thought only lazy American kids were supposed to do that!) Practicing the accordion? Or are there really much fewer young people around in Germany?

(The new-old German capital, Berlin, provides quite a different story: If you were wondering where all the hillbilly cousins had gone who spiked the punch at the reception and absconded from the motel with the contents of the minibar and the towel supply, look no further than the Kurfürstendamm!)

Demographics have the answer: In the years between 1991 and 2002, the population of Germany grew by 3 percent. In the United States, it grew by 13.5 percent. In Germany, the segment of the working-age population (aged 15 to 64) increased by just 1.1 percent, while those 64 and older increased by 19 percent. In the United States, however, thanks to the echo boom, the 15 to 64 age group increased by 15.1 percent, while the number of people aged 64 and older increased by only 11.8 percent.

These demographic developments go into the savings behavior. The savings rate—that is, the segment of your spendable income you put to work by investing—has receded not only in the United States but in Europe as well, especially in those countries clamoring the loudest that Americans should start saving more. If the German savings rate was around 14.5 percent in the mid-1970s, it shrank to 13.1 percent in the 1980s and to 11.5 percent in the 1990s. Since 1999, it has been below 10 percent.[7]

Almost all of these assets are invested in low-yield savings accounts, bonds, or life insurance policies. (After briefly peaking at 18 percent, only 9 percent of German households own stocks, much the same rate as in 1995.) But even these savings are threatened. Germany currently has an unemployment rate of over 12 percent, a postwar record. To get a handle on unemployment compensation, a reform package called Hartz IV (after a Volkswagen executive) went into force in 2004, which mandates that long-term unemployed are required to deplete their savings before qualifying for full assistance. With domestic demand already at rock bottom and both the German workforce and the economy depending on external buying to keep a minimum of growth alive, what do you think the long-term effect will be on the economic role of German savings?

EINE TRAURIGE GESCHICHTE (A SORRY TALE)

Budget deficits in violation of the Maastricht Stability Pact may be the smallest of Europe's problems: Recent population growth projections peg the number of Germans at anywhere between 25 million and 50 million by 2050, down from 80 million today. Currently, pensioners make up about 35 percent of the population, a ratio expected to grow to 75 percent by 2050. And since pensions are currently paid out of current tax revenue, working Germans are already paying 29 cents of every euro they make into the pension system—in addition to their sky-high income tax and health care contributions and, not to forget, a 16 percent sales tax. (German sales taxes, however, are a downright bargain compared to those levied in France!)

The same is happening in Italy, France, and, to a smaller degree, Spain. The *Economist*'s Charlemagne in 2003 arrived at the conclusion:

> So Europe will probably try to muddle through its demographic problem. There will be some pension reform, a bit more immigration, more family-friendly policies, higher taxes, growing fiscal problems for many governments and slower economic growth. With luck, the European Union will avoid or postpone a really huge economic crisis. But the political and economic renaissance of Europe at the European convention is likely to be stillborn.[8]

Boasting the world's third largest economy, Germany is already a country wilting into history: "Whole towns are turning into retirement homes," reports Radio Netherlands[9] as Germany's population undergoes one of the biggest demographic changes in history. Some impressions from the German and international media speak volumes:

> A typical example, central Germany's Wolfen North, has become a ghost town . . . empty apartment blocks now silent as the town of 33,000 shrunk by half. The sound of playing children replaced by the drilling of jackhammers ripping down empty apartment buildings.[10]

> The few young people around are moving to bigger cities, leaving much of Germany nearly deserted. In the Ruhr Area, some cities have lost tens of thousands with the city of Gelsenkirchen losing 130,000 residents over the past few decades.[11]

In other cities across the country, housing vacancies as high as 30 percent are typical and in many cases residences are left abandoned and dilapidated.[12] Even in the once bustling city of Berlin, some 100,000 apartments now lie empty.[13] For the first time, the country's population is shrinking, and is expected to drop another 15 percent in the next 25 years.[14] During this same period, the number of retirees will increase by 150 percent to make up half of the country's adult population.[15]

> What is true for Germany holds true for other European nations as well. Demographically speaking, the European continent is undergoing an unprecedented and irreversible change. It has a birth rate that's been below replacement levels for 25 years.[16] And with the number of seniors growing 60 percent faster than the overall population,[17] the portion of working-age adults will shrink by 10.4 percent to 14.8 percent[18] over the next 20 years. This will be the first time since the Black Plague in the 1340s that Europe's working population will shrink. According to the United Nations Population Division, by the middle of the century, seniors will outnumber children for the first time in history.[19]

This will have deep economic effects. According to the French Institute of International Relations, Europe's GDP will grow at half the rate of North America's, taking it towards a "slow but inexorable 'exit from history'."[20]

By Organization for Economic Cooperation and Development (OECD) estimates, immigration into Europe would have to increase by five to 10 times to offset the current demographic and economic trends.[21] This, of course, is unlikely since even current immigration levels are already meeting strong political opposition from anti-immigration politicians such as Italy's Umberto Bossi or France's Jean-Marie Le Pen.[22] Even in Germany, which in typical and late overreaction to the Third Reich has probably the most open attitude to immigration in continental Europe, a government-sponsored effort to attract Indian software engineers (to make up for all those socially conscious young Germans studying deconstructivist politology well into their thirties) was a complete failure, due mainly to the fact that the German system is not set up to culturally integrate newcomers—and a popular backlash that called for *Kinder statt Inder* (kids instead of Indians).

HEALTH CARE COSTS

If the European Union wasn't already facing a challenge in meeting health care costs, the addition of the new member states has made matters even worse, as they weigh heavily on the economy of the EU as a whole. (As I am writing this, the European Parliament in Strasbourg is about to embark on a bitter debate about increasing the 2007–2013 budget by more than 10 percent in view of the integration cost of the new member states—a move highly unpopular with the greatest net payers, Britain, Germany, and France.) For one, the new member states, despite amazing economic progress, bring with them the same "gifts" as East Germany did back in 1990: double-digit unemployment and a tattered economic infrastructure. Eastern European cultures thus far have not developed the same widespread popular health consciousness as those in the rest of the modern world. Alcoholism, smoking, and lack of exercise have all contributed to a population that is generally in worse shape than their Western European counterparts. As a result, they have a higher incidence of the main killer diseases such as cancer and cardiovascular disease. This is further aggravated by those countries' health care underfunding, which averaged around 5.8 percent of gross domestic product. By comparison, the Western European member states spend from 8.6 percent[23] to 15 percent[24] of GDP on health care.

Yet even there, the money flowing in is not enough to keep up with the costs. For instance, the treatment of one illness—lung disease—is costing over a hundred billion euros per year, while costs associated with care for cardiovascular disease, another largely avoidable disease, are even higher.[25]

UNDERFUNDED PENSIONS

Meanwhile, European pension systems are creating growing deficits that threaten to destroy the economy of a whole continent. European governments have made promises to today's retirees that they are unable to fulfill. Today, Europe still has 35 pensioners for every 100 workers. And according to the *Economist*, by 2050 the average ratio will be 75 pensioners per 100 workers.[26] In some countries it will be much worse. These problems make the U.S. Social Security debate seem almost insignificant in comparison.

Though the exact estimates vary from one study to another, the picture they paint remains dismal. According to other studies, over the next 15 years the number of European workers supporting their pension systems will be cut by half, from four workers per pensioner to only two.[27] Comparable numbers in Spain and Italy are expected to reach a ratio of one to one in the next 45 years.[28]

In economic terms, the unfunded pension liabilities of some European countries are as high as two and a half times their economies.[29] To put that in perspective, the United States' unfunded pension liabilities are $10.5 trillion,[30] slightly less than its $10.99 trillion GDP.[31]

THE ENVY OF THE WORLD . . . UNTIL YOU LOOK AT THE NUMBERS

Steeped in the welfare mentality that took hold in Europe in the 1970s, many European countries have government pension systems that strike their American contemporaries as overly generous and enviable: Spaniards continue to receive 94.7 percent of their average paycheck at retirement, while Austrians are guaranteed 93 percent.[32] As a result, 90 percent of Europeans rely completely on government pensions to see them through retirement.[33] (Americans expecting similarly generous income streams from the yield of their private retirement savings as that enjoyed by your average middle-class retired European government employee would have to command portfolios of several million dollars.)

This causes a problem beyond the obvious number crunch. Most European countries use a pay-as-you-go pension system. Pension funding comes out of current tax revenue, so, in order to maintain the current pension system, taxes will have to escalate each successive year in order to meet the government's obligations.[34]

A generational struggle seems almost inevitable. Pensioners will demand higher taxes to fund their pensions and social security, while workers will protest against the rising taxes. This will put further pressure on government to keep workers from leaving, while remaining obligated to care for the aging population.

Even with the picture clearly in sight, European governments have their hands tied, unable to head off the inevitable. Trade unions brought Italy's and France's economies to a standstill at the threat of any change to their pensions.[35]

THE DEMOGRAPHICS OF DECLINE

While European demographic trends paint a bleak outlook for the EU economy—Niall Ferguson once called the process unfolding in Europe an "impire," which he describes as a political entity that instead of expanding outward toward its periphery implodes—it is German demographics that may hold the key for the economic prospects of the entire European Union.

In terms of population, the European Union already was a slightly larger entity than the United States—even before the 10 new member countries joined it on May 1, 2004. With its current population of 450 million people, the EU is one and a half times larger than the population of the United States.

Despite this demographic parity and much to its chagrin, the EU economy has grown at a slower rate in real terms than that of the United States in every year of the past decade but one. In seven out of the last nine years, productivity has grown faster in the United States than in Europe. Average unemployment rates in the European Union have been twice those in the United States over several decades.

(The inclusion of the 10 new states, mostly located in central and Eastern Europe, may also turn out to be a new drain on EU resources, much like the integration of East Germany into the Federal Republic post-1990 remains an ongoing process that has exponentially increased government obligations, unemployment, and economic stagnation in what used to be West Germany.)

The gap between Europe and the United States most likely will grow wider still. And there may be some truth to the general assumption in the United States that Europe is "too tired, too old, too lazy, too inward-looking to compete in the rough, tough world of globalization."[36]

A paper presented to the Royal Economic Society in March 2005 cast doubt on whether Europe will be able to compete at all. Rocco Huang, of the World Bank, notes that a cultural shift toward statism and economic conservatism has been under way in Europe since the 1970s. Part of this cultural process may be due to an aging population's becoming ever more averse to risk uncertainty. Larry Elliott wrote:

> Capitalism, as Schumpeter explained, is all about occasional episodes of wrenching change in which an old set of technologies is replaced by a wave of innovations. Clinging onto the old delays the arrival of the new. . . . The fact that cultural attitudes change only slowly suggests that it will be an uphill struggle for the EU to turn itself into a centre for technological innovation (even assuming that such a transformation can be achieved by acts of political will, which is highly dubious). To the extent that Europe is changing, it is becoming older and more averse to uncertainty.[37]

TEUTONIC TRIGGER

Historically, Germany has paid the lion's share of Europe's bills. In the days of the Montanunion,[38] it was the German taxpayer who bankrolled the coal and steel community and literally shored up the inefficient, unprofitable coal mines of Belgium. German taxpayers paid the development aid for France's crumbling colonial empire throughout the 1950s and 1960s. German taxpayers also footed the bill for the Common Agricultural Policy, the single largest item in the European Community's budget.

The total of all those "unrequited transfers" made by Germany since Chancellor Konrad Adenauer first took the tentative steps of integrating Europe in the aftermath of World War II actually exceeds the amount that the Weimar Republic was to pay in reparations after World War I, more than 132 billion marks. This is the sum Germany insisted would bankrupt the country back in the 1920s. Niall Ferguson summarizes: "Well, they finally did pay it. They paid it not as reparations, but as net contributions to the European budget."[39]

Germany, with just over a fifth of Europe's population, still accounts for a little less than 25 percent of the EU's combined GDP. But in terms of net contributions to the European budget in the years 1995 to 2001, Germany contributed a whopping 67 percent.

Even so, Germany is in decline. Its main growth industries are unemployment—over 12 percent as of the beginning of 2005—and government debt, which will exceed the economic straitjacket defined and imposed by the Maastricht Stability Pact again in 2005. It is worthwhile to consider that German economics professor Peter Bofinger (who is one of the "Five Wise Men" advising the German government) speculates that

some of the authors of the Maastricht contracts may have hoped that those numbers were prohibitive enough to prevent a currency union from the get-go. . . . With Italy and Belgium, two founding members of the EU were so far removed from the 60% limit [of debt to nominal domestic product] that their membership could hardly be considered probable from the 1991 point of view. Without those two countries, the European currency union as a whole would have been hard to realize politically.[40]

Domestic demand is stagnant. Tax revenues are recessive. The only viable sector—exports—might seem to depend on profligate Yankees spending money on Beck's beer and Volkswagens.

Due to the German government's commitment to keep up its lavish package of entitlements—retirement, social, and health spending—the implicit liabilities of the German social security system currently are 270 percent of GDP, and chances are that Germany will be unable to keep up the level of its financial contributions that has made the EU possible. So who will be paying for all the "maximum enlargement-related commitments" made to the 10 new Eastern European member states, nominally capped at 40 billion euros?

As European economic power contracts throughout the first decade of the twenty-first century, we have to come to grips with new facts of life:

First, Europeans may have already reached—and passed—the apex of their post–World War II wealth and standard of living. For growth and capital-derived income, they will need to focus on those cultures whose work ethics, flexible labor markets, and economies still provide a fighting chance for growth. (This would be mainly the United States, China, and India.) European (and particularly German) companies will increasingly relocate their production facilities, not only into low-cost labor countries such as the Czech Republic, but follow the path defined by German car manufacturers BMW and Daimler, who transplanted manufacturing capabilities to the United States in the 1990s.

Second, the United States economy will have to increase its economic and political focus on Asia and the Pacific Rim for exports and outsourcing of labor, and to provide a preferred target haven country for the emigration of Asian capital, wealth, and prosperous individuals. This is true because trouble is brewing in Asia as well.

The impending economic changes triggered by demographic forces are not unique to the United States, and in the coming future economic situation many areas of the globe will be shaken up. Some people believe that Europe is immune from the economic conflicts between the United States and Asia, and point to the strength of the euro as evidence of their position. This is simply self-delusional. The currently high valuation of the euro versus the dollar may be rooted in part in the American current account deficit. But that in turn is already reflecting European decline: If Europe were economically and demographically in better shape, European imports would be higher due to healthy domestic demand. America's trade deficit in turn is not just an indicator of profligate American consumer spending, but a reflection of Europe's endemic stagnation and decline. And Europe's recent outbreaks of reform actionism paradoxically are bound to inflict further harm on the growth of domestic demand by creating an oppressive atmosphere of forced savings for an inevitable rainy day that further will drain money from an economy that is already suffering from its consumers' age-defined tightfistedness.

The numbers don't work, and they are not likely to recover miraculously in the future. The feeding tube has been pulled, and it's now only a matter of time until the body of Europa begins to wither.

European criticism of American economic policy should be taken with several shovels of rock salt. Yes, the United States are running current account deficits as well as budget deficits that appear to be downright suicidal and threatening to global economic growth. But where did this growth originate? Peter Bofinger writes:

> Apart from the very expansive policy of the USA one should remember Japanese fiscal policy, which for the budget year of 2004 shows a deficit of 7%, while its lending rates have been near zero for years. Have the people in Frankfurt thought how the global economy would be doing right now if Japan and the USA had acted like Euroland? Would Mr. Trichet really welcome if those two countries had had interest rates of 2% and limits on new debt had been below the 3% mark of the stability pact? Macro-economic policy in Euroland thus lived up to its global responsibilities in a very unsatisfactory fashion over the last few years. By allowing itself to be pulled out of its stagnation by the rest of the world, Euroland is at the same time responsible for the high imbalance in the American current accounts deficit. Because this number reflects—apart from currency exchange rates—the very strong domestic dynamism of the United States and the concurrent anemic development of domestic demand in Euroland.[41]

Against this highly combustible economical backdrop, a new threat is arising that might provide the spark that will trigger the great depression of the twenty-first century. Ironically, this spark will issue from the one global economy that is well on its way to giving both Japan and Germany a run for their money when it comes to sheer size: China.

CHAPTER 6

DRAGON OUT
OF FIRE

The only thing that stands between the Chinese financial system and utter ruin is citizens' confidence that the state can, and will, fully back the banks.

—Stratfor, 2005, at www.stratfor.com

In 1930, Rafael Trujillo, chief of the Dominican national police force and head of the army, managed to leverage his power to get himself elected president of the Dominican Republic. Being "very hardworking, a superior administrator, a shrewd judge of people, a clever politician, and absolutely ruthless,"[1] he made himself dictator. He eliminated the opposition, established a totalitarian police state, and proceeded to modernize the Dominican Republic's economy along the lines of a private family business. Trujillo usurped some of the country's export monopolies, laid claim to a portion of prostitution earnings, and charged state employees 10 percent of their salaries in exchange for the privilege of working for him. He also built the region's largest army, navy, and air force.

His family business—the Dominican Republic—prospered, at least when compared to that of his Haitian neighbor, dictator François (Papa Doc) Duvalier. In the 1950s, however, "the economy deteriorated through a combination of government overspending to celebrate the 25th anniversary of the Trujillo regime, overspending to buy up privately owned sugar mills and electricity plants, a decline in world prices for coffee and other Dominican exports, and a decision to make a major investment in state sugar production that proved economically unsuccessful."[2]

Weakened, the Trujillo regime was barely able to fend off a Cuban-backed invasion of exiles. In 1961, the dictator himself fell prey to an assassination plot involving a high-speed car chase and a gun battle that would have done Ian Fleming proud.

Trujillo's history provides a cautionary story for centralist, nominally capitalist economies in specific and for banana republics in general. And I'd be the first to admit: on the surface, it may seem a stretch to compare the economy of the Dominican Republic in the middle of the twentieth century to major global economic powers today. And yet, I believe that similar development will trigger the spark that will precipitate the first big global economic crisis of the twenty-first century: the collapse of the Chinese *Wirtschaftswunder* (economic miracle) within 18 months after the Olympic Games of 2008 in Beijing.

ECONOMIC CRISIS TRIGGERS THE NEXT BIG COLLAPSE IN GLOBAL EQUITY MARKETS BY 2010

Are there indeed thunderclouds on the Chinese horizon? This prediction may seem to be a bit of a stretch to you. After all, our Chinese stock picks have been doing quite well. Indeed, ever since we recommended you buy stock in Hong Kong & Shanghai Bank back in 1989—even before China became the byword of economic pundits—*Taipan* has been on the forefront of capitalizing on China's exponential profit potential. We recommended Chinese stocks and their American depository receipts (ADRs) even before the tidal wave of foreign investment began flooding mainland China after 1994. We were invested in Hong Kong almost a decade before it reverted to the People's Republic. And we've identified triple-digit gainers even as the Asian currency crisis in 1997 was redefining the economic roles of the Pacific Rim countries.

But if you watched the mainland Chinese stock indexes in late 2004 and early 2005, you probably noticed an interesting trend: the

Shanghai Composite, for one, looks like the track of a downhill skiing competition. In fact, it has been declining since 2001.

This might come as a surprise to those who have modeled their views of China's economic prowess mainly on Chinese gross domestic product (GDP) growth rates and that country's bulging trade surplus with the United States. But stock markets are the reflections of how a people really see its immediate economic future. And a yearlong decline in the mainland Chinese indexes might be a better indicator of trouble in the making than any consumer confidence indicators in the world.

BATTEN DOWN THE HATCHES

Japan, the economic engine of East Asian economic growth for the latter half of the twentieth century, continues to languish in the clutches of the severe economic decline that it entered in the aftermath of the Nikkei's collapse in the early 1990s. This economic decline was brought on by the severe financial mismanagement endemic in the traditional Japanese business and banking culture. A semblance of stability has been retained by Tokyo's willingness to go deep into hock (running budget deficits of around 7 percent of GDP), keep money dirt cheap at interest rates around zero percent, and actively play the currency markets to keep the yen from appreciating too fast, too much against the currencies of its export customers, who provide what little growth the overall Japanese economy has been able to chalk up in recent years. Because of the country's demographics, there is little chance that the Japanese economy will be able to duplicate its meteoric rise from 1950 to 1989, simply for lack of domestic demand and changing spending habits, which are exacerbated by the country's demography.

Since the 1970s, however, China has been evolving into the economic and political center of the region. And yes, the GDP growth rates of China are currently the envy of the world: compared to the 8 percent growth Beijing is aiming to reduce its economic expansion to, Germany—whose 2005 GDP growth rate just has been downgraded to 0.8 percent by the European Commission—looks like an ice cream stand in Novosibirsk. China's ever-increasing export volume and its surging current account surplus with the United States provide a never-ending supply of arguments for bears to predict the downfall of the U.S. manufacturing base and the American way of life. But below the surface of an exploding GDP growth and record-breaking exports, not all is well in China: industrialization and urbanization may be proceeding at a helter-skelter pace, but we might be well served to remember that there still is a vast, nominally communist bureaucracy underneath the dazzling capitalist trimmings that is as inefficient as it is both corrupt and wasteful.

Some of the most aggressive and influential businesses are owned either directly by the state or by the armed forces. This "distinct" ownership has provided a perfect screen behind which Chinese business has armed regimes from Baghdad to Tehran to North Korea. After all, who's the Chinese government to tell army-owned NORINCO with whom it should do business?

Since 1994, the People's Republic has turned into the world's top investment destination, attracting the majority of the world's direct foreign investment. China's main attraction is its low labor cost. Unfortunately, the Chinese system is so opaque that it is almost impossible to obtain reliable data on what exactly those labor costs are, and on how much of this attractiveness is owed to shady subsidies.

In the medium term, we see trouble brewing. China already borrows more as a percentage of GDP than the United States under the second Bush Administration. China's banks—much like Japanese banks in 1991—are buckling under a heavy load of non-performing loans and are being "undermined by an institutionalized misallocation of capital with little regard for international norms of risk management and the extension of credit," as a Bloomberg correspondent put it recently.[3]

The Chinese government is currently attempting to overhaul the Big Four state-owned banks. It has no choice in that, because it made a commitment to the World Trade Organization (WTO) to open the country's financial markets to foreign competition by 2006. The business intelligence service Stratfor opines:

> If that happened today, most Chinese depositors would flee the government banks for the foreign banks, where they could receive higher rates of interest for their deposits. Foreign banks, after all, do

not subsidize their loans. The loss of depositors would kill the state banks and leave the government footing the entire bill for sustaining the country's industrial non-sector—an obligation that likely would bankrupt the government within a year.[4]

The Big Four—the Industrial and Commercial Bank of China, Bank of China, China Construction Bank (CCB), and China Agricultural Bank—are the foundation of China's financial system, holding a combined $1.8 trillion in assets. That's 55 percent of China's total banking assets. But the Big Four are weighed down with more than $500 billion in bad debt owed by ramshackle state-owned enterprises (SOEs) and corrupt bank officials.

Stratfor indicates that since 1999, Beijing has transferred more than $200 billion in dud bank assets to other institutions to clean up balance sheets:

> In late 2003, the government provided the CCB with $22.5 billion to recapitalize the gap. When even that was not enough, in 2004 the government allowed the CCB and the Bank of China (another of the Big Four) to move another $33.7 billion in non-performing assets off their books.[5]

The core problem, according to Stratfor, is that none of these banks is really a bank proper; they merely are dispensing agencies for the Chinese Ministry of Finance, "a means of allowing the government to extend credit to its herd of white elephants, the state-owned companies."[6] And despite some halfhearted attempts, the Chinese government has not managed to make any meaningful change to its lending policies.

Part of the problem China is already having to deal with is the influx of foreign capital. In 2004, China's foreign reserves reached a record $609.9 billion, up from $403.3 billion in 2003. China now ranks second only to Japan in the amount of dollar reserves held. (In the spring of 2005, Japan's dollar reserves are estimated to be in excess of $820 billion.)

And just like Japanese banks in the 1980s, Chinese banks are at the core of a highly speculative real estate bubble. On April 20, 2005, AFP reported that Guo Shuqing, director of the State Administration of

Foreign Exchange and thus China's foreign exchange chief, had publicly criticized massive fund inflows, warning of "excessive speculation" in the property market:

> Indiscriminate support of exports and foreign capital influx has created short-term economic problems, excessive speculation in the property market and the economic decoupling of the fast-growing coastal areas with the rest of China.[7]

Guo's administration has repeatedly spotted foreign funds entering China disguised as money for trade or direct investment purposes but used to buy financial assets and property. In one case, a single foreign person was buying up to 100 houses in coastal cities for speculative purposes.

A large part of this speculative money is betting that China will have to raise the value of its currency, the yuan, uncoupling it from its peg against the US dollar. The floating of the yuan against other world currencies is something the Bush administration has urged China to allow since 2001. Chinese government officials may actually use the prospect of unlinking both currencies as part of their standard rhetoric when pointing at the U.S. current account and budget deficits. But this is mainly bluff: The Chinese yuan will depend on its peg against the bargain-basement dollar to keep the export economy humming and China able to borrow to feed its growing class of unemployed. Beijing will do what it takes to come out ahead in the looming struggle to take business away from competitors such as Cambodia, Vietnam, or Thailand. For Western consumers, that means prices for Chinese imports will get even lower.

HUNDRED-MILLION-MAN MARCH

Despite the booming manufacturing sectors (or maybe because of them), China is already suffering from one of the world's worst unemployment problems. Experts estimate that there are more than 200 million unemployed and underemployed at large in the People's Republic. There are also tens of millions of unregistered migrant workers pouring into the cities every year from the agrarian north.

It could get even worse as the government, pushing economic reform, has laid off tens of millions of laborers from inefficient state-owned enterprises. China's ecological and health problems are also magnifying exponentially. Large areas of China's agricultural heartland are suffering from severe human-induced water shortages, followed by flood catastrophes that wash away arable soil. The air in some of the sprawling metropolitan areas is so polluted that just breathing it has the same effect as smoking two packs of cigarettes a day. (Chinese health spending on problems cause by air pollution is estimated at 8 percent of GDP.) Lead levels in the blood of Chinese city dwellers are almost twice as high as the levels considered dangerous elsewhere in the world.

The age bomb is ticking just as loudly in China as in Japan and Europe. China is in the same situation as most industrialized nations when it comes to demographics. The number of retired people in cities is expected to more than double, reaching 100 million by 2020. Due to its rigorous one-child policy, 10 Chinese workers will have to support three Chinese retirees by 2025. That may be comparable numerically to the United States and is far less burdensome than the ratios of Japan and Germany. But Japan, Germany, and the United States have had a half-century of prosperity, enabling them to create a fiscal backlog, however deficient it may be. The Chinese national pension system, in comparison, already covers only 20 percent of workers. *BusinessWeek* reported in 2005:

> The national pension system has a shortfall of $6.2 billion, which could reach $53.3 billion by 2033, according to the Asian Development Bank. Most provincial pension plans are also in deficit.[8]

Only about 20 percent of China's population is even modestly covered by the pension system. And the government's social security program promises to cover medical costs through unemployment insurance, welfare, and living wages for unemployed former SOE workers.

It remains to be seen whether this is practical. How do they intend to pay for this? Actually, according to state-run Chinese media, China plans to use money tied up in state-owned assets to deal with the boom in retirees that is expected to begin in 15 years: State-owned assets, such as stock in large companies, would be converted into funds that can help fill China's 2.5-trillion-yuan ($300-billion) pension shortfall, according to a 2005 article in *China Daily*.[9]

There is one enjoyable irony in this: While Democrats in the United States are vociferously campaigning against privatizing parts of Social Security as proposed by the Bush administration, the Chinese Communists are planning to scrap the pay-as-you-go system underlying the current arrangement entirely, replacing it with a new system in which each individual saves money for himself or herself in a personal retirement account. (History's just funny like that!)

ECONOMIC PROGRESS WRAPPED IN FERVENT NATIONALISM

But the ideological turnaround has come at a price. The attractiveness of communism and the draw of the Communist Party are fading rapidly. The Chinese people are readjusting their values toward consumerism, and increasingly the Chinese government looks to fill an ideological vacuum. It has embraced a variety of ultranationalistic trends focusing on technological, economical, and military superiority.

Beijing's defense budget has increased by more than 10 percent every year for 13 years in a row. For 2003, official numbers pegged military spending at $22.4 billion. Including arms purchases, research and development, and other line items associated with quasi-independent business run by the Chinese army, some foreign estimates calculate totals closer to $65 billion. This amount may even increase: France in particular—having lost its best arms customer with the capture of Saddam Hussein — is eager to provide modern weaponry, nuclear technology, and global guidance systems to any cash-laden totalitarian dictator it can find. Jacques Chirac in particular has been bullying his European colleagues into agreeing to lift the EU's arms embargo against China. As in the buildup of the Second Gulf War, Germany's Gerhardt Schröder is acting as the wagging tail to French commercial aspiration, even against the objections of peace-espousing coalition partners, the Greens. If and when this dynamite duo succeeds in reopening the Chinese weapons market to their industries, we predict

Chinese military expenditures will increase exponentially alongside the technologies that are coming up for purchase.

At the same time, the People's Liberation Army has focused on expanding China's space technology capabilities. China launched its first manned space flight in 2003 with great nationalist fanfare. It sent up a record six satellites the very same year, with 10 additional launches attempted in 2004. Given China's manifest military ambition, Japan's recent moves to abandon its constitutional post–World War II pacifism appear quite reasonable.

But there's another money pit opening up for the Chinese government: the Olympic Games of 2008. Much as the Olympic Games of 1936 in Berlin were orchestrated to showcase the achievements and superiority of the Nazi regime, the Beijing Games are China's way of convincing the world (and its own population) that it has arrived as the world's other superpower.

Hosting the Olympics costs money, lots of money—so much money indeed that the previous host of the Olympic Games, Greece, was forced to run budget deficits exceeding 7 percent in some years, in blatant violation of the Maastricht Stability Pact underpinning the European single currency. (To still qualify for participation in the euro, the government underreported its new debt levels to the European Commission for several years, a deception that conveniently came to light only after the Athens Games of 2004 had concluded.)

China's budget deficits are already exceeding 5 percent of GDP a year—more than the level incurred by the Bush administration—despite the enormous amounts of foreign cash flooding the market. Chances are that China's new public debt may reach or exceed 8 percent by 2008.

CASH MIGRATION

Capital flows out of China are also increasing: China, like Japan in the late 1980s, is purchasing foreign assets like there is no tomorrow. (The most spectacular was the recent purchase of IBM's computer division for $1.75 billion.[10])

During the 1990s China's investment outflow increased to $2.3 billion a year. Based on the United Nations Conference on Trade and

Development (UNCTAD) World Investment Report for 2002, the top 12 transnational corporations of China now control more than $30 billion in foreign assets. In addition, capital flight from China from 1997 to 1999 was estimated at $52 billion, a high percentage that ended up in the pockets of corrupt officials. While actual amounts are difficult to ascertain, outflows in recent years have been estimated to average $40 billion to $50 billion.

Stratfor sees reason for concern:

> If China's economy is really expanding with annual growth rates of up to 10 percent and the nation's market is the hottest thing since instant noodles, the amount of money leaving the country illustrates a startling lack of confidence in the future. China's behavior is eerily reminiscent of Japan's in the 1980s and early 1990s, when Japanese investors bought everything and anything they could find overseas. At the time, Japan's yen for anything not Japanese was mistaken for strength, but eventually it was exposed as a bet against the country's economic future. The very same trend already might have begun in China.[11]

CRISIS AND OPPORTUNITY

Here's what we see occurring in China in the near future: China will continue on its aggressively expansionist economic course, becoming the low-cost manufacturing center of the world. This will include an aggressive trade policy toward its competitors in the region. This process is already well under way: Two months after import quotas on Chinese-made textiles were lifted, countries such as Thailand and Cambodia registered drops of 20 percent or more in their textile export volumes. To remain competitive and safeguard the only viable industries of their economies, these countries have little choice but to compete on price, creating a competition-driven damper on global inflationary trends at the cost of domestic quality of life.

Under the terms of the WTO, China's banks will face stiff competition starting 2006. There will be additional pressure on the Chinese financial system caused by the triple strains of hosting the 2008 Olympics, speeding along its space program, and continuing the military buildup while footing the bills for increasing social costs.

Throughout 2008, Beijing will be able to handle these pressures, which will be alleviated by a booming global economy. The first cracks in the system will appear by mid-2009, when Beijing's public debt levels will set new records. A spectacular bank crisis will rock China by late 2009, involving a collapse of the property boom and equity markets, whose effects will be felt all over the world. By 2010, domestic pressure on the Chinese government will have built up to a degree that Beijing will feel forced to stage a "wag the dog" incident, possibly involving Taiwan.

For investors, this also means keeping a clear and critical eye on how the mainland Chinese indexes perform: as in Japan a decade and a half earlier, they may provide the early warning system that signals when things are coming to a head. After all, they always do. Luckily, our Dynamic Market Theory thrives on just this kind of volatility. When the Nikkei started to buckle in 1990 and 1991, the Taipan Group was riding its epic decline to triple-digit profits with Kingdom of Denmark Nikkei put warrants. Since then, however, our analytical tools have improved dramatically. Our WaveStrength team spent the better part of a year developing and back-testing an analytical tool that harnesses the WaveStrength predictive system to chart the immediate future of the Chinese market.

The effectiveness of this new system remains to be seen. We believe it will serve as an excellent predictive tool. But independent of how it works, there is one thing that appears certain to us: the four years of the last phase of the great bubble market (2006–2009) will set the stage for a gigantic and seemingly sudden fall. That fall in the global finance markets will be triggered by an event emerging in China: the popping of the speculative real estate bubble may be triggered in late 2009 by the collapse of one or more of China's Big Four banks in the aftermath of the Beijing Olympics. Public unrest fed by large-scale unemployment and the sudden devaluation of Chinese assets and currency may result in a Tiananmen-style crackdown on civil disobedience and ultranationalist military adventures aimed at subjugating Taiwan. The inevitable confrontation with the United States—whose capitalist philosophy will be blamed for the crisis yet again—may lead to a protracted military standoff that could trigger a second phase of the Cold War.

Any crisis, however, contains the seeds of opportunity. As in the established American and Western capital markets, each crisis can be played for gains on the upside *and* on the downside—both in view of entire markets and in view of individual stocks.

Consider yourself warned: The ability to recognize, read, and exploit these micro and macro trends by harnessing them into your financial survival strategy will be make the difference between losing your shirt and living in comfort in the postcrisis years. But one thing is certain: If you're reading this book in early 2006, you have a little less than four years left to learn the ropes and practice these techniques in the safe (relatively speaking!) environment of the bull market. Make good use of this grace period the market gods have granted you. Mastering the analytical concepts and tricks of the trade that the Taipan Group's team of analysts and editors have prepared for you in the following section may be the best thing you've done this century!

PART III

THE TRADING SECRETS

CHAPTER 7

TRADING SECRET NUMBER ONE: HOW TO PROFIT FROM CYCLICALITY

Seasonals can be defined as the up and down trends that occur at approximately the same time each year. These market trends reflect the normal change in the fundamentals of the supply/demand equation.

—John L. Momsen, *Ultra-Reliable Seasonal Trades* (1999)

To survive and prosper in the changing market climates that are lying ahead, you will need to understand one essential concept:

Markets are the compound reflection of human attitudes and desires and as such as much a part of nature as man himself. They are subject to certain recurring patterns that are as predictable as natural cycles of growth and contraction.

This insight is the ultimate secret of seasonal cyclicality trading.

Let me ask you: If you knew there was a publicly traded book retailer's stock that gains an average of 50 percent every August and 48 percent every December, or if you knew about a takeover play that's jumped 58 percent every January for the last four years, or a small health technology company that has gained 35 percent every February for the past six years, or a shoe retailer that has shot up 12 percent every May for eight of the past nine years, or a sportswear maker that has gone up 20 percent for four years (and just jumped 120), or a clothing chain for oversized teens that has soared 32 percent for the past five years . . . you would buy these stocks, wouldn't you?

I know I would. In fact, I'd ask a team of my most experienced analysts to come up with a timetable, a kind of *Farmer's Almanac*, to tell me exactly when to buy and when to sell these seasonal profit engines.

Which is exactly what I did. But before I spread this smorgasbord of profit opportunities out in front of you, give me a minute to explain exactly what kind of thought went into our research:

You see, when I was in middle school back in the 1970s, my parents used to send my siblings and me to spend a week or two with relatives in East Germany over the summer. We would have preferred a somewhat more exotic location to brag about to our schoolmates than little sand-blown Borstel in the Altmark, a village near my mother's hometown of Stendal. After all, the other kids at school went to Mallorca or baked on the "Teuton griddle" beaches of the Côte d'Azur. But in retrospect, I have come to regard these excursions into *Realsozialismus* as priceless experiences.

East Germany was a throwback in time, a run-down, decrepit, soot-stained throwback at that. Technological progress—at least to the degree it was enjoyable by ordinary people—had simply stopped in the early 1940s. In big red letters, signs of all sizes proclaimed unbreakable friendship with the Soviet Union and the relentless advance of the "people-owned" economy.

But that people-owned, planned economy was in poor shape. Department stores (a generous description at best) were stocked with unattractive and mostly unneeded merchandise you'd buy only because you had to spend your money on something, such as a neon green polyester sweater two sizes too big.

Grocery shopping was no different: If you wanted beef for lunch (*Mittagessen* was the main meal of the day), you had to be on good terms with the butcher, or know someone else who was, like the doctor, because supply was depressingly out of step with demand. In

1980, during the Olympic Games in Moscow, not even your connections were worth much: It was impossible to scare up a single scrap of meat at all, even in East Berlin, the capital. Everything had been shipped to the "Great Friend of the Working Class" in Russia to impress those foreign visitors who hadn't joined the American boycott of the games.

To the Amberger kids, who had been brought up in capitalist West Berlin, it was not apparent that there could be times when fresh apples were not readily available at the supermarket. When we requested pancakes with apple slices for dinner one day, we were surprised to watch our old Aunt Elsie go into her pantry and bring out glasses of homemade apple preserves. After all, in Northern Europe, apples used to be seasonal fruit. If you wanted to eat one in July or August, you had the choice of chewing a rock-hard, sour little appling the size of a walnut or dipping into last year's cooked crop, kept in tightly sealed glasses in every respectable housewife's pantry alongside cherries, pickles, and pears with curled rolls of cinnamon bark.

Nowadays, apples are available year-round in the Western-style supermarkets that sprang up all over what used to be East Germany after the Berlin Wall came down in 1989. But to the older generation in Germany, plenty of culinary occasions still revolve around the seasonal availability of produce, from the harvest of new asparagus in the spring to the first issue of fermenting white wine or *Federweisser* in the fall. You may remember similar seasonality of produce in the States—the first crop of Silver Queen corn in the summer or the availability of crabs in coastal Maryland and along the eastern seaboard. And if you're unlike me, you even remember if you're supposed to devour crustaceans and filter feeders in months with an "r" or without.

CONSUMER BUYING CYCLES

In consumer terms, we still find cyclicality all around: The time to buy Christmas decorations is the week between December 26 and December 31 of any given year. Every hairdresser's apprentice can tell you that. According to Lorene Yue, staff reporter on money matters for the *Baltimore Sun*,[1] December, January, and February are also great months to buy winter clothes, rugs, linoleum, carpeting, and linens.

March to May are good months to get bargains on furniture (as furniture manufacturers introduce their new lines in April and October at the International Home Furnishings Alliance in High Point, North Carolina). It's a good time to book summer travel arrangements, and to buy wedding gowns (sample sales usually take place in April).

Between June and August, you can stock up on cheap menswear (before and right after Father's Day) and beach gear. And between September and November, in the model changeover period, your chances are good for finding a favorable price on a new car of last year's vintage.

Indeed, each holiday creates its own micro-environment of consumer spending that follows very predictable patterns: a slow buildup in the weeks preceding it, with massive sales (and often, price increases) the week prior, with a sudden reversal in volume and pricing on the day of the holiday, which in turn is followed by discount sell-off of surplus stock.

The money changing hands is not inconsiderable: just look at Table 7.1, which illustrates just how much money U.S. consumers spent on each holiday in 2004. Honestly, it ain't rocket science.

MARKET SEQUENCES

The concept of seasonal trades is nothing new in the commodity futures market. Quite simply, in industry and especially agriculture,

TABLE 7.1   TOP SPENDING HOLIDAYS
(Total Holiday Spending in Billions)

Winter holidays (Christmas/Hanukkah/Kwanzaa)	$219.90
Valentine's Day	$12.79
Easter	$10.47
Mother's Day	$10.43
Father's Day	$8.04
Halloween	$3.12

Information source: The *Baltimore Sun.*

there are specific seasons of the year when certain functions have to be performed within a particular and often clearly defined time frame. This includes sowing, planting, growing, and harvesting of crops. In other cases, season-specific weather patterns create predictable seasonal demand for resources, such as heating oil and gasoline. It's inevitable. John L. Momsen, in his book *Superstar Seasonals* (2004), writes: "[Seasonal conditions] exist because man has not yet conquered nature as far as growing cycles and weather cycles [are] concerned."[2]

Technical analysis includes recognition of the principle that markets, being compound entities reflecting human behavior patterns, are based on growth patterns, just as are crops or harbor seal populations. In Chapter 4, we looked at economist Harry S. Dent Jr.'s correlation between the demographic and life cycle developments of the United States—birth rates, spending patterns, social cost, and revenues—and what lies ahead for the U.S. equity markets.

At the bottom of this predictive science is the phenomenon of *cyclicality*. Markets and populations move according to long-term cycles, each of which can span decades and even centuries. (In Chapter 17, I will introduce you to a man who has taken this concept and turned it into a predictive system that allows us to anticipate and profit from impending market moves with commendable reliability.)

But let's take a step back to consider how you can make trading cyclicality a cornerstone of your financial survival strategy: Market seasonality features a number of catalysts creating opportunity with predictable recurrence. In fact, Sy Harding, in his *StreetSmartReport*, wrote:

One of the main advantages that we always point out about trading on the market's seasonal patterns is that it is basically mechanical. And by being so, it totally ignores surrounding economic and political conditions. . . . The market's seasonal tendencies have nothing to do with surrounding conditions and concerns. Seasonality is created by the extra chunks of money that flow into investors' hands beginning in the Fall, much of which finds its way into the stock market, driving it higher. The sources of that extra money dry up in the following Spring, depriving the market of that extra fuel and leaving it vulnerable then to any selling pressure that takes place because of concerns about surrounding conditions.[3]

(On the downside, of course, there is also a time of the year when your average mutual fund manager goes on a spree of numerical window dressing, selling off losers and taking profits to make his annual portfolio performance look good.)

Where does this extra cash come from that creates this sizable wintertime spike? Well, in November and December of each year, mutual fund distributions, holiday and year-end bonuses, year-end corporate dividend disbursements, and bonus payments to top executives all contribute to the spike. In April, tax season with its income tax refund checks and the seasonal resolution to pay more attention and invest more prudently in the following year have a similar effect. (This, by the way, is the financial equivalent of New Year's resolutions—joining a fitness club and losing the two buckets of lard that have been adorning your midriff, for example.)

Each year, the cyclical spikes add up to a sizable amount of cash entering the market, independent of the interest-rate environment or economic cycle.

But it doesn't end here. What goes for the market as a whole also holds true for individual stocks, and this is the key to cyclical trends. If you track equities, you will identify and recognize similar seasonal patterns in prices and volume.

For many stocks, quarterly earnings and dividend timing are easily recognized: Take, for example, Impac Mortgage Holdings (IMH:NYSE). This REIT has been raising its cash dividend almost every quarter since July 2001, when it traded at $7 a share on the American Stock Exchange.

Over the past four years, quarter after quarter, every time Impac Mortgage Holdings has announced a dividend we have also seen a pattern unfold: the stock rises up from a quarterly low, only to fall off the cliff days after the dividend for more gains on the short side.

Profiting from this cyclical phenomenon as a trader takes a total of about 30 minutes a year, simply because the timing is predictable. If you know the events leading to these price patterns, you know when to buy and when to sell.

According to the company, the projected dividend payout schedule for 2005 was:

Declaration Date	Record Date	Pay Date
March 29	April 8	April 15
June 28	July 8	July 15
September 27	October 7	October 14
November 29	December 9	December 30

Figure 7.1 shows what the stock price did throughout the past few years. How could you have profited from this? The question should be, how can you *not* profit from this cyclically occurring opportunity? Buy IMH on the date of the dividend declaration. Exit after the run-up. Short it or buy puts two days after IMH pays the dividend. Use puts and calls if you feel particularly frisky.

And while you might think that these market price changes work predictably under the popular efficient markets hypothesis, it's usually not the case. Here's a short synopsis of seasonal profit opportunities that are offered by the markets almost every year.

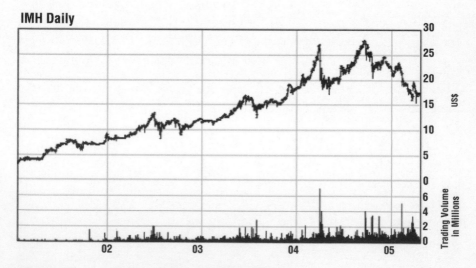

Figure 7.1 Impac Mortgage Holdings Daily

The January Effect

Take the well-known January effect, for example. It is based on a simple observation: In more than two-thirds of all Januaries since 1926, the stock market has gained in value. In fact, academic studies have shown that especially small-cap stocks achieve almost 50 percent of their price growth for the entire year in the first month of the year. The reason is simple: Investors tend to sell off their losing stocks near the end of the year to take advantage of tax write-offs. Then, in January, they buy them back. (We assume that savvy investors know to wait at least 30 days to avoid canceling out their tax benefits under the wash sale rule.)

In 1942, Frederick Wachtel wrote the first academic study documenting the January effect on stocks. Years later, Michael S. Rozeff and William R. Kinney reintroduced the January effect to modern finance, and Donald B. Keim reported that virtually all of the return advantage that small-company stocks hold over large-company stocks is earned in the first four trading days of January.

St. Patrick's Day Green

Even a minor secular holiday such as St. Patrick's Day can create a disproportionate effect based on consumer spending. We observe an upswing in holiday shopping, with estimates of consumer spending for 2005 expected to reach $1.94 billion on the holiday. According to the National Retail Federation's *NRF 2005 St. Patrick's Day Consumer Intentions and Action Survey*, 84.5 million consumers celebrated St. Patrick's Day that year, spending on food, drinks, and decorations.

The average person, according to the survey, planned to spend $27.65 on the holiday. That's a lot of cardboard shamrocks and green beer! Many others planned to travel out of town, and 19.8 million planned to go to bars or restaurants. Another 12.7 million people across the United States planned to have parties. Decoration spending was expected to be hot as well, with more than 15 million people decorating their homes or offices. The stocks to buy during St. Patrick's Day season are retailers. They have typically packed their shelves with Irish tunes, books, and shamrock clothing in anticipation of this holiday.

The Monster Index

The New York–based Conference Board's Help Wanted Advertising Index is usually considered a strong indicator of labor demand, measured by the volume of job ads placed in major U.S. newspapers. Another index that works as a great indicator of things to come is the Monster Employment Index, which measures the volume of job ads placed online.

The Monster index culls its information from web sites posting job openings. And employers have been diverting their Help Wanted advertising dollars from newspapers to web sites such as Monster.com. The only drawback: the Monster Index goes back only to 2003.

Monster.com (MNST:Nasdaq) has demonstrated a seasonal history as well, taking a plunge from late each year to the beginning of the next year. In November and December, online job postings have a seasonal history of falling because of the holiday season. By timing decisions based on this cycle, you can create profits. We bought MNST puts late in 2004, for example, and took a three-day 165 percent gain. The goal with MNST should be to short the stock or buy puts late in the year as online job postings fall, and then buy shares starting at mid-March when job postings begin to pick up again.

For example, the predictable seasonal interest in online job searches in mid-March 2003 helped move MNST share value from a low of $20 to more than $30 in late April, a neat 50 percent increase in approximately one month! So if you had put $10,000 into this stock, by the time you sold you would have had $15,000.

Back-to-School Seasonal Profits

Every year from 2001 through 2004, Varsity Group (VSTY:Nasdaq) rose from mid-December through January, and from mid-August through September—and by an average of 75 percent. There's a simple reason for it. Varsity Group is a clearinghouse for used course books. American students are heading back to colleges and universities in those particular months. Faced with the choice of spending several hundred dollars on brand-new course books or beer, they use Varsity as a cheaper alternative. Investors familiar with this pattern buy VSTY stock in December and August and sell—at a profit—a week or two into the respective summer or winter semester.

Conference Season

Specific times of the year are characterized by big conferences and trade shows. You will see a pattern here, too: Earnings announcements slow down as conference attendance picks up. Watch for companies making presentations at the big conferences. Before and during these investor conferences and trade shows, these companies' stocks are especially susceptible to moves based on conference-related news. A good source for conference data is www.fulldisclosure .com/conference_full.asp?client=cb.

THE LONG AND SHORT OF IT

A host of seasonal patterns have been studied by trading professionals and ivory-tower academics. A study published in 2004 by the Federal Reserve Bank of Atlanta produced compelling evidence that seasonal patterns turned up in the stock exchanges of several different countries. This highly detailed report can be downloaded at www.frb atlanta.org/filelegacydocs/wp0408.pdf.

Once you know which stocks will move and when, all you have to do to make money is invest ahead of that move. These bankable stocks are the ultimate secret of professional investors. Cycle research is key to finding these hidden gems. The beauty of using a recurring pattern that has been tested and proven over time is that chances are excellent that it will be there for you as reliably as clockwork.

A team led by the Taipan Group's veteran analysts Christian De-Haemer and Ian Cooper has managed to come up with a handy resource for such cyclical trades. They call it their "Year of Profits Calendar." Chris told me:

"I managed a run of 15 winners out of 16 picks with the likes of Kana Software and Internet Capital Group. During the heyday of the Internet bubble, at one point, my readers saw gains of 176 percent on Art Technology Group, 91 percent on Versata, and 206 percent with Navisite, not to mention the 206 percent and 118 percent gains with Kana and Internet Capital. And, because cycle research played a big part in helping me discover some of these profitable opportunities, I decided to create an all-in-one-place calendar so that you would have all the seasonal patterns at your fingertips."

The result of the project, Chris and Ian's "Year of Profits Calendar," is something that you can just flip open in the morning, know exactly what to invest in and when, and have the rest of the day free. Cycle research is the key.

For example, in July 2004, the Year of Profits Calendar told you to buy gambling and casino stocks as summer vacations kicked in. But of course you can't buy just any gaming stocks. The four companies detailed in your Year of Profits Calendar have a history of returning huge gains for investors. But to make those gains, you would need to sell shares in August. Remember, the cycle indicated not only when to buy, but also when to time the sale.

Another recommendation from the Year of Profits Calendar was to buy shares of a certain automotive company on January 21. This company's stock price has risen an average of 22 percent every year as people begin repairing and getting their cars ready for moving to a warmer climate. Buying this company at this time on average means a gain of 22 percent.

Seasonal stock trades included in the Year of Profits Calendar are the very opposite of buy-and-hold investment strategies. These are your typical in-and-out opportunities. You'll buy and then sell them in days, or weeks at the most.

Consider the case of tax preparer H&R Block (HRB:NYSE). This is a great example of a stock that is hit with a predictable surge of buying every year. Millions of people visit H&R Block during tax season. And a percentage of these satisfied customers get the idea that it would be great to own a piece of this obviously successful company, so they buy the stock. Predictably, this drives up the price every February and March. In 2005, everyone who followed the advice in the Year of Profits Calendar and bought H&R Block earned 44 percent. That means if you put $5,000 into this stock when it was recommended, you'd have ended up with $7,200.

What's more, H&R Block was an in-and-out trade. You wouldn't necessarily hold it for the long term. And that is an essential feature of the magic in tracking seasonal profits: Within the grand overall market climate, seasonality creates micro-pockets of opportunity. It doesn't matter whether the market is going through a pronounced bull market or the bears are on the prowl. As long as life is ruled by the calendar, as long as crops are planted and harvested, and as long as taxes have to be paid and students shipped off to college, seasonal profits are there for those who know where to look for them.

And that is a message of optimism given the prospects of a major and protracted market decline in the very near future. Rather than trying to anticipate market movements in total, you can and will profit in *any* type of market if you know how to read cycles and how to identify the signals you are going to need.

CHAPTER 8

TRADING SECRET NUMBER TWO: THE PERFECT VALUE TRIFECTA

Breakout Signal, Dividend Discount Model, and Forward Earnings Forecaster

In a market there is, I believe, a spontaneous internal life, an inherent activity that comes from the way people come together, organize themselves in banks or brokerages, and exchange assets.

—**Benoit Mandelbrot,** *The (Mis)Behavior of Markets* **(2004)**

Let me introduce you to a quiet young man named William Bradley Colburn. Brad, as he prefers to be called, joined us a couple of years ago to help our micro-cap maven Brian Hicks with his research. When Brian left to start his own business, Brad had already taken over running his trading services Value Edge (now called BreakAway Investor) and Volume Spike Alert.

Deep down, Brad is a minimalist: "I look at my trading approaches as simple," he says. "The less complicated the system, the easier it is to realize profits."

He may be onto something: If you rely on a system that revolves around placing a dozen geographic images on a chart and deciphering barely discernible numbers, can you really grab an easy profit? (The answer, as you may have guessed, is: of course you can! But it is a lot of work.)

Instead, Brad uses what he calls his "trifecta of breakout indicators" that form the pillars of this chunk of the Dynamic Market Theory.

BREAKOUT SIGNAL

The bread and butter of the breakout signal is the moving average.

I know what you're thinking: Moving averages are one of the most widespread and easiest tools available to investors. (In fact, many online resources provide them free of charge.) Moving averages smooth out a data series and overall make it easier to spot trends, which is especially helpful in volatile markets. They also form the building blocks for many other technical indicators and overlays.

And that's the key.

Sometimes we all need to get back to basics, to what is important. The building blocks almost always show the greatest strength.

A simple moving average is formed by computing the average or mean price of a security over a number of days, months, or quarters. While it is possible to create moving averages from the open, the high, and the low data points, most moving averages are based on the closing price. For example: a seven-day simple moving average is calculated by adding the closing prices for the prior seven days and dividing the total by 7.

$$13 + 11 + 15 + 21 + 19 + 16 + 12 = 107$$
$$107 \div 7 = 15.3$$

The calculation is repeated for each price bar on the chart. The averages are then joined to form a smooth curving line, the moving average line.

This highlights the fact that all moving averages tend to bring up the rear and will always be below the rising price or above the declining price. Moving averages are trend *lagging*, or following, indicators.

When prices are trending, moving averages work well. However, when prices are not trending, moving averages can give misleading signals.

Fine-Tuning the Averages

One way to provide more weight to the most recent data is to use what is called an exponential moving average (EMA). This allows you to compute a moving average using a formula that, while complex, can be easily reduced onto a spreadsheet.

The first step is to divide 2 by the number of periods in your EMA calculation. We will use the example of 7 values:

$$2 \div 7 = 0.2857$$

Next, compute the simple moving average for the values. As we showed earlier, the values are added together and then divided by the number of values:

$$13 + 11 + 15 + 21 + 19 + 16 + 12 = 107$$
$$107 \div 7 = 15.3$$

The third step is to subtract the next value periods from the previously computed moving average. For example, if we assume that the eighth period has a value of 9, we would compute a revised total of 6.3:

$$15.3 - 9 = 6.3$$

Fourth, multiply the new value by the exponent from the first step:

$$6.3 \times 0.2857 = 1.80$$

Finally, add the value in the previous step to the previously computed moving average:

$$1.80 + 15.3 = 17.1$$

This is the exponential moving average.

The formula is easily reduced to a simple spreadsheet calculation, so that you can simply plug in the latest value and find an instant EMA. Using the earlier example, the calculations on an Excel spreadsheet are:

Address	Cell Value	Calculation to Use	Explanation
A1	7		Number of fields
A3	0.2857	=SUM(2/A1)	Calculation of exponent
A6	13		Value #1
B6	11		Value #2
C6	15		Value #3
D6	21		Value #4
E6	19		Value #5
F6	16		Value #6
G6	12		Value #7
A8	15.3	=SUM(A6:G6)/7	Simple moving average
A10	9		latest entry
A11	6.3	=SUM(A8-A10)	Prior moving average less latest entry
A13	1.8	=SUM(A11*A3)	Multiply by the exponent
A15	17.1	=SUM(A13+A8)	Add to prior moving average to find new moving average

We can also summarize the formula for exponential moving average:

$$\frac{P_1 + PV_2 + \ldots P_f}{N} - L \times \frac{2}{N} + \frac{P_1 + P_2 + \ldots P_f}{N} = \text{EMA}$$

P = Values in the selected periods
$_{1,2,\ldots f}$ = First, second, remaining, and final values
N = Number of values in the field
L = Latest entry
EMA = Exponential moving average

Applying the formula to the previous example:

$$\frac{13 + 11 + 15 + 21 + 19 + 16 + 12}{7} - 9 \times \frac{2}{7} + \frac{13 + 11 + 15 + 21 + 19 + 16 + 12}{7} = 17.1$$

EMA *weights* the moving average to give more value to the latest entries. Other weighting methods would include double-counting the latest period. For example, in a seven-period calculation, the latest period is counted twice, and the sum divided by 8. Using the same values as earlier:

$$13 + 11 + 15 + 21 + 19 + 16 + 12 + 12 = 119$$
$$119 \div 8 = 14.9$$

Note that in this downward-moving trend, weighting the latest value brings the moving average down as well. In the straight moving average, we arrived at 15.3. This method reduces the average to 14.9. These methods—notably EMA—are valuable when dealing with larger numbers of entries, when any type of calculation will tend to be complex. Using a simple spreadsheet formula, EMA is easily and quickly computed.

BACK TO BASICS

In its most simple form, a security's price can be doing only one of three things: trending up, trending down, or trading in a range.

An *uptrend* is established when a stock forms a series of higher highs and higher lows. A *downtrend* is established when a stock hits a series of lower lows and lower highs. And a *trading range* is established when a security cannot establish a clear uptrend or downtrend. If a stock is caught in a trading range, the uptrend is technically started when the upper boundary of the range is broken and a downtrend begins when the lower boundary is broken.

Once a security has been established as trend-worthy, the next task will be to select the number of moving average periods and type of moving average. The number of periods used in a moving average will vary according to the security's volatility and trends.

The more volatility in the range of prices being studied, the more smoothing that will be required and hence the longer the moving average. An alternative method would apply if and when the range of prices includes exceptional and atypical price spikes. For example, if a stock is trading in the $25 to $35 range and at one point the price rises to $45, that is an exception, a spike away from the normal trading range. Spikes can be removed from the calculation altogether, given this important qualification: To count as a true aberration, the price range should return to its normal levels and remain there. If that is the case, then leaving in the spike price would only distort the moving average.

Even so, for situations where the trend is unclear, not bold and specific, we recommend extending the period of study. Stocks that do not show trend strength are more reliably studied with longer moving averages.

Perspective Adjustment

Short-term traders may look for evidence of two- to three-week trends with a 21-day moving average, while longer-term investors may look for evidence of three- to four-month trends with a 40-week moving average. For our purposes, we'll stick primarily to the easier-to-grasp 20-, 50-, and 200-day moving averages. This, of course, doesn't mean that we won't delve into other areas, but we can easily sink our teeth into these three types to start.

Now, just crossing the 50-day moving average isn't a rare feat. A stock has to cross the 50 and stay over it for a decent period of time before we can call it a reliable trend.

Usually some form of company news or earnings announcement is at the origin of specific price moves. (Other times, however, they're not: the movements almost appear to be spontaneous.)

Here is where Brad's breakout signal comes in to pick and choose the cream of the crop. In short, Brad is screening for those stocks that have broken away from their previous trend to crack their moving averages.

DIVIDEND DISCOUNT MODEL (DDM)

The second tool is equally revealing and interesting.

Sometimes you find inspiration in the oddest places. Brad confided in me that one of his moments occurred during a recent trek through an economics textbook, where he came across an analytical tool that he instantly glommed onto.

Using a maze of mathematical formulas that would make even Stephen Hawking scratch his head, this tool is able to churn out a stock's future price.

The end result—a future stock valuation—may be similar, but this tool is different. It uses dividends.

There is a traditional way that old-school investors and analysts look at their long-term holdings. To them, any stock's worth is based on what it will provide investors in current and future dividends.

This is a solid and proven view. After all, dividends are by definition the cash flows being returned to the shareholder. They provide income on top of capital gains, which, using dividend reinvestment plans (DRIPs), can be converted into more dividend-paying shares, thus creating a compound return on dividends themselves.

But while I believe stocks of solid companies that consistently pay good dividends are an integral part of any long-term investment portfolio and retirement strategy, the purpose of this book is to uncover how to use market phenomena for short-term trading profits.

The dividend discount model (DDM) has consistently beaten the market over five-year time periods. The main reason is right in line with our Dynamic Market Theory: it couldn't care less what the market is doing.

The DDM allows investors to determine the absolute value of a particular company without the influence of current stock market conditions. (In contrast, most analysts' price targets are set on a relative basis, based on the valuation of comparable companies.)

There's another thing I like about the DDM: you can meaningfully compare stock valuations. Most of the time, analysts will gather a pool of stocks from which to make their selections. They have so many considerations to make that a winner may be lost in the shuffle.

The dividend discount model is concerned only with what investors could rake in from a company in future cash flow. Using DDM, an analyst can look at three companies. If the DDM churns out a value for one stock that is 97 percent higher than its current price, that will be the stock to pick.

There's no pussyfooting around with the DDM. That's why I like it.

Results Are All That Matters

So how do we get results like this from the DDM? Multiple formulas are involved, and each is applicable to a different situation. For the purpose of this book, allow me to focus on the primary DDM formula, called the Gordon model.

Here is an example. Stain Resistant Ties Inc. pays a $1.50 annual dividend. To formulate the future value of Stain Resistant Ties, we divide the annual dividend by the company's discount rate, and then subtract its dividend growth rate.

Let's say Stain Resistant Ties' dividend grows at 3 percent annually. Using a discount rate of 6 percent, we can figure on Stain Resistant Ties trading for $50:

$$1.5 \div (6\% - 3\%) = \$50$$

The end figure will be Stain Resistant Ties' full future valuation with dividends considered.

Now, what if Stain Resistant Ties' dividend payment hasn't been steady? How could we calculate the company's value then? We'd apply the multistage DDM and figure it out.

See, the DDM isn't just a one-tier system. Different stocks pay dividends on different schedules. As Brad likes to say: "If you sit and think about it for too long, blood may start shooting out of your eyes!"

The Two-Stage DDM

The two-stage model assumes that the company will experience a period of high growth followed by a decline to a more stable growth period.

The first thing when using the two-stage model is to estimate how long the high growth period should last. Should it be five years, 10 years, or maybe longer? The second issue is that the model makes an abrupt transition from high growth to low growth.

In other words, the model assumes that the firm may be growing at a 30 percent rate for five years, only to grow at 6 percent (stable growth) until eternity. Is this realistic? Probably not. Most firms experience a gradual decline in growth rates as their business matures.

Since the model is highly sensitive to the assumptions made about growth rates and discount rates, performing a sensitivity analysis would be appropriate. Sensitivity analysis allows the investor to view how different assumptions change the valuation using the dividend discount model.

The dividend discount model is a good starting point to begin thinking about the valuation of a company.

Need more proof? Here you go . . .

Take a look at Anthracite Capital Inc. (AHR:NYSE). AHR has a 9 percent annual dividend, which equals $1.12 per share. Assuming AHR's dividend will continue to grow steadily, we can crunch a few numbers and come up with a future value of AHR.

After throwing AHR's figures into the DDM, we come out with a future AHR price of $56. We simply divided AHR's $1.12 dividend by the net of the 11 percent discount rate less the dividend growth rate of 9 percent:

$$\$1.12 \div (11\% - 9\%) = \$56$$

Now for this calculation, I used a discount rate of 11 percent. The average discount rate is from 4 percent to 6 percent, but AHR is in a strong sector. To account for future growth, we'll use a discount rate of 11 percent. This shows you the power of this system—but it's not scientifically perfect.

The model is sensitive to the assumptions made about growth and discount rates. Sensitivity analysis allows the investor to view how different assumptions change the valuation using the dividend discount model.

FORWARD EARNINGS FORECASTER

Brad's system has yet another ace up its sleeve. This indicator is called the forward earnings forecaster (FEF) and was developed in collaboration with Brian Hicks.

The FEF uses a series of stock screens to filter out junk stocks, pinpointing the strongest growing stocks (according to the stock's estimated growth rate) trading at the best price.

What a Stock Screen Does

A stock screen, in a nutshell, consists of a database of stocks that can be analyzed according to selected criteria. The screen Brad uses focuses on all domestically traded equities, all 8,000-plus of them. The FEF finds the best value stocks there are. It runs a series of screens on stocks to find the very best value stocks with the highest potential for capital appreciation.

Typically, these are small-cap stocks—companies with a small stock market capitalization—that are excellent targets for accumulation by institutions. This is the kind of stock that can return 8 to 10 times your investment . . . *very quickly* (if you pick the right one, that is).

Brad explains how he proceeds:

> To locate the stocks with the biggest potential, I begin with the universe of all publicly traded stocks. Theoretically, they're all candidates

for investment. There are over 8,000 in all. But I don't want just any stock, so I put them through a series of screens to get only the ones I want.

Step 1: Get rid of the huge companies. Accordingly, the first screen I apply screens out all big-cap stocks. Why?

Because stocks with market caps over $2 billion are too big to move fast. I want only those stocks having market caps under $500 million. They may be good long-term investments (and then again they may not), but either way, it's highly unlikely that they'll produce the kind of returns we want. *The highest growth is almost always found in small-cap stocks.*

This first screen yields about 5,200 stocks. But it's only the beginning.

Step 2: Get rid of fully valued stocks. Once we have our pool of small-cap stocks, the next thing I do is to screen for stocks that currently trade at a price-to-earnings (P/E) ratio of less than 10.

Again, this may strike you as very old-school. After all, the traditional definition of value strives to quantify value by bringing it into relation with the price of the stock. If the price of a stock exceeds its earnings by a long shot, it is an indicator that the current price is a result of speculation on potential increases in price, and not based on the amount of earnings an investor can reasonably expect to make based on the profits a company actually generates for its shareholders.

There are two reasons for me to use this traditional measure of value for a dynamic market trading strategy. For one, a stock with a P/E of less than 10 is a good buy just on the face of it. You're likely to get a good return on your investment even if the stock price stalls.

Number two, if a stock is way below the average P/E ratio of the market, it is a top candidate for growth. Stocks tend to move toward the average. Look at it this way: If you're way above it, you're a top candidate for a fall. If you're way below it, you're a top candidate for a rise—especially since a large number of investors will always look to value.

So if the Dow is trading at an average P/E of 25, as it currently is, I don't want to buy stocks that trade over that. In fact, I want stocks that are *way* under it. That's why I look for stocks with a P/E of less than 10.

Here's what this step looks like:

This second step of the process yields about 1,500 stocks. All of these are small-cap stocks with a solid price-to-earnings ratio.

But P/E multiples are really meaningful only if they're compared to something—something that suggests that the stock is indeed *very* undervalued. *And that "something" is called profit growth or earnings growth.*

You see, many stocks that trade at low P/E multiples trade there for a reason. Sure, they might be very profitable, as indicated by the very P/E multiple. But it frequently means that a company may have stopped growing as a business.

But for our purposes, we want just those stocks that will give us significant capital appreciation—and we want our money to grow rapidly. That means finding stocks that are undervalued and growing their profits. These are the small-cap stocks that are most likely to be targeted for accumulation by institutions—which would place them in a position to skyrocket as millions of shares are gobbled up. The way I find them is to run another screen on the 1,500 stocks that my P/E screen produced.

Step 3: Get rid of stocks that aren't growing fast enough. I screen these stocks for companies that have grown earnings by 25 percent or more for at least three years. Now we're getting down to the *real* value stocks—the cream of the crop; the ones with real strength; the best values out there, stocks that are going to grow like weeds in a vacant lot.

Here's what this step looks like:

Believe it or not, if it's done correctly this process reduces the field—the entire field of 8,000-plus stocks—*down to about 30 stocks.* That's right: 30!

Now we're in what I call the sweet spot, down where the P/E-to-earnings growth (PEG) ratio is of critical importance.

The PEG ratio measures whether a company is fully valued or undervalued based on its own earnings growth. To get the ratio, you divide the P/E by earnings growth.

For instance, if a stock is growing its earnings per share (EPS) by 20 percent per year or so, the stock should trade at a P/E multiple of 20. That would be a PEG ratio of 1.

A stock that is growing its EPS 20 percent per year but trades at a P/E below 20 is said to be undervalued. So if the PEG ratio is less than 1, it's undervalued.

This last screen reduces the field further, to about one or two stocks a month. But these two stocks represent the best and most solid chances for rapid price growth at that moment.

TOP OF THE LIST

Applying Brad's perfect value trifecta, we end up with stocks that are the cream of the crop when it comes to profit potential. Time and time again, Brad has been pulling winners applying this particular constellation of catalysts.

One such example is Top Tankers (TOPT:Nasdaq). TOPT is engaged in the worldwide transportation of liquid and petroleum cargoes through the ownership and operation of a fleet of tankers, consisting of four Suezmax double-hull tankers (for crude oil), 10 Handymax double-hull tankers (for petroleum products or crude oil) and one Handysize tanker (predominantly for edible oils).

Across the board, the water transportation sector has been fundamentally sound over the past few years. That means all the damage the Organization of Petroleum Exporting Countries (OPEC) may do to oil prices will just seem like a small hunk of driftwood to tankers. And especially to TOPT: Top Tankers is a fundamental Hercules.

Here's what our screens latch onto: For starters, TOPT had a P/E ratio of 9 when analyzed at the beginning of 2005. That's the top end of the spectrum of the usual forward earnings forecaster allowance. In general, Brad doesn't like stocks with P/Es greater than 10. The low ratio shows that, even as an initial public offering (IPO), TOPT is bursting at the seams with profit potential. Now for the second factor: TOPT had a 17 percent return on equity (ROE). Return on equity (a measure of a company's management effectiveness) gives us a good idea of the kind of return investors can expect when investing in a certain stock.

With this kind of strength, do you think TOPT will hit its 52-week high of $24.14? You're darn right. In fact, TOPT was poised at the start of 2005 to blow that high out of the water. TOPT was recommended in January that year. Based on his value trifecta analysis,

Brad came to the conclusion that the stock could hit $30 by the end of 2005. Figure 8.1 shows that by February 28, TOPT had already hit $22. TOPT was well on its way to fulfilling the $30 forecast.

But wait, there's more.

Shortly before TOPT was recommended, another forward earnings forecaster pick had fulfilled its prediction. Back in May 2004, our forward earnings forecaster placed a trade on DHB Industries (DHB:AMEX). According to numbers at the time, DHB had the potential to be a $20 stock by the end of the year.

According to those same numbers, DHB was an undervalued company: its PEG ratio was 0.83. That's right under the magic PEG of 1. But its forward PEG was just 0.30.

DHB was expected to grow its EPS between fiscal year 2003 and 2004 by 55.9 percent. (This growth rate is calculated by taking fiscal year 2004's estimated EPS of $0.53, subtracting the 2003 EPS of $0.34, and dividing the net difference by $0.34.) This calculation is similar to the simplified calculation of price volume based on the range of prices, but applied to EPS.

What exactly does this mean? If the stock traded at a P/E of 55.9 on last year's EPS of $0.34, the stock would trade for $19 a share. Figure 8.2 shows what happened.

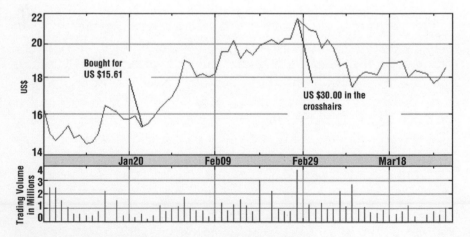

Figure 8.1 Top Tankers Inc. as of 31-Mar-2005

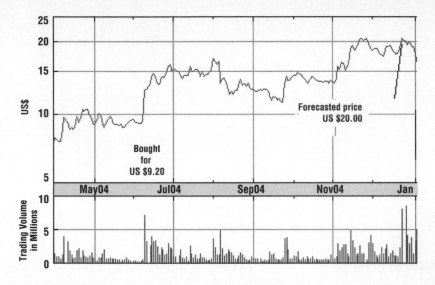

Figure 8.2 DHB Industries as of 31-Mar-2005

Here's another example of how Brad's evaluation factors come into play: In early 2003, the forward earnings forecaster ran a screen and picked up Audiovox (VOXX:Nasdaq), which traded for about $10.50 a share. The stock had a whole lot of room to grow. But let me give you a brief analysis of the fundamentals at the time.

VOXX did more than $1 billion in annual revenue. Yet the stock's market cap was about $250 million. Here's where it got interesting: For fiscal year 2003, VOXX was expected to post an EPS of $0.55 a share. VOXX was forecast to post an EPS of $0.96 in 2004. This would be an EPS growth rate of almost 75 percent.

If the stock traded at a P/E ratio of half its expected EPS growth rate, the stock would have traded for $20.63 a share. That's not bad in my book. (See Figure 8.3.)

SURVIVAL OF THE FITTEST

Brad's analytical strategy is based on a very basic idea: use stock screens to eliminate all but the strongest companies that are temporarily at the verge of a price breakout. It's not new, and it is not unique. There are a number of online tools that you can use for this

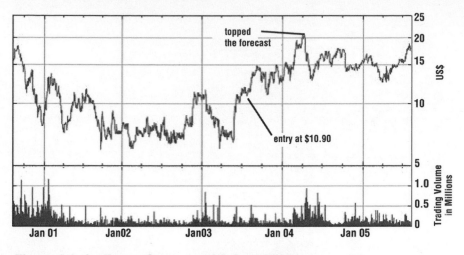

Figure 8.3 Audiovox Corp. as of 8-Aug-2005

process. Some are free, while others run upward of $99 a screen, payable every month for the duration of your subscription.

Still, this system works in both up and down markets. Even in the worst periods of a bear market, there will be a company that the market is overlooking for one reason or another. (In fact, a bear market tends to punish even those companies that have solid fundamentals.)

Practice how to use these screens, or develop your own, and you will have a survival tool kit for your trading portfolio at your fingertips once the markets start heading south for good. We like to think of these tools as useful for creating profits. Realistically, they also help you to get out before losses begin, too.

Useful Information

If you want to put Brad's value trifecta to the test, I recommend that you subscribe to his free daily e-letter *Fear & Greed*, where he applies, improves, and follows up on his theories each trading day. Simply point your browser to www.dynamic marketreport.com/fearand greed.

For his service Value Edge/BreakAway Investor, check out the following web site: www.value-edge.com.

CHAPTER 9

TRADING SECRET NUMBER THREE: FOLLOW THE MONEY!

(This Trading on Insider Information Is Completely Legal)

Pecunia non olet. (Money doesn't stink.)
—Caesar Augustus

In the past chapters, I have tried to convince you that market movements—both upward and downward—are products of collective human activity, activities occurring according to patterns with analogies in nature. As such, they can be monitored and (to a certain degree) predicted with reasonable accuracy.

If you apply this concept to single stocks rather than entire markets, this human behavior leaves its traces in the daily data flow, data that can be collected, compiled, and collated. Daily, weekly, monthly prices can be analyzed using Japanese candlesticks (more on that later). Applying mathematical formulas, you can manage your analysis of long-term trends using moving averages. Putting earnings and dividends into the equation, you can obtain P/E ratios and other standard analytical goodies that are the foundation of all the typical indicators.

The most obvious track human behavior leaves in the daily data flows of a stock is *trading volume*. Low trading volume typically signals modest public interest in a stock, which means that expectations for a gainful move on the upside (or a loss-generating move toward the downside) are low. If trading volume is high, there are plenty of people around buying and selling a stock. Major moves typically accompany volume spikes: If lots of people are buying and the demand to own a stock is high, the price typically goes up. If multitudes of investors are selling and the supply of their stock exceeds the demand from new buyers, the price takes a dive.

Everybody knows that.

But in the mid-1990s, my former associate Brian Hicks noticed something odd. In a handful of cases, stocks exhibited a different behavior. Trading volume in some stocks increased dramatically, seemingly without reason. And the price remained fundamentally the same until it suddenly took off a few days or even weeks later.

Take Harvard Scientific (VGENQ), for example. Brian and his team—among them an even more youthful Brad Colburn—had been monitoring this company for some time. Then, one day, something unusual caught their eye.

There was no earnings report released and none due for several weeks. In fact, there was no announcement, no news of any kind. Oddly enough, though, the company traded more than 88,000 shares that day. (Figure 9.1 clearly shows what happened!)

Big deal, you say. But what was most interesting was that the company's trading volume typically was in the 20,000-share range daily. Suddenly, in one day, volume more than quadrupled.

Why? My associates did some digging and found out that the company had been sitting on several patents pending for a topical and noninvasive drug delivery system to treat impotence. And approval was scheduled to arrive any day now.

The spike in volume told us that two things were highly likely: First, a decision had been made, and second, approval was imminent. As word leaked out, people close to the situation—insiders—began snapping up shares.

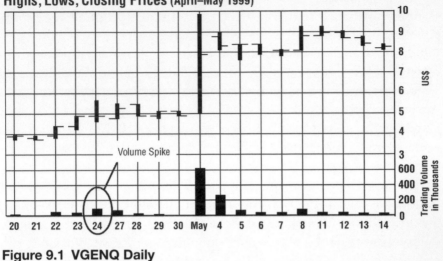

Figure 9.1 VGENQ Daily

READING BETWEEN THE INSIDER LINES

Unfortunately, none of us were in that insider loop. But actually, we didn't mind. Neither did the members of Brian's Volume Spike Alert trading advisory. To us, this volume spike was as good as insider information. Even better. It was based on publicly available information and as such, trading on the information was perfectly legal.

You can probably guess what happened next. Three days later, Harvard Scientific was officially handed its long-coveted patent. Once that became widely known, shares soared. In one week, six million shares traded hands.

Harvard Scientific is a perfect example of how you can profit following insider trends with this volume spike indicator. Sometimes, you'll be rewarded with 400 percent gains in a matter of hours. Other times you'll make 100 percent in a few weeks or 1,000 percent in a month, as you will see in a moment.

Please understand: There's more to picking a winner than just volume. And I'll explain the other factors in a moment. But first, let me give you another example. It is one of our vintage track record trophies, but it beautifully illustrates how this particular constellation of indicators works.

Zi Corporation is a small-cap language translation company. For years, its stock traded in the $1 to $3 range. Volume was generally low, averaging a few thousand shares a day. But on June 23, 1999, our tracking system alerted us that volume had spiked from 9,000 one day to 171,600 the next. We did a quick check. You can guess what we found: No news to speak of. No earnings reported. No announcements.

Over the next nine trading sessions, more than 633,000 shares traded hands, more than triple the volume of the previous nine sessions.

But why? Again, we dug deeper, and discovered the company had been actively courting the Ministry of Education in China, trying to put its language translation products in more than 975,000 Chinese schools. But that's not all. We also found out that Zi was working with several Chinese government agencies, trying to embed its language translation chips in everything from television sets to cellular phones.

This was clearly a case of someone on the inside knowing something was about to happen. In fact, it had all the hallmarks of classic insider activity: Stock changed hands in irregular blocks, 5,000 shares here, 12,000 shares there; small blocks were bought over several days in an attempt to keep the stock price low and not draw too much attention.

Sure enough, on July 8, 1999, Zi Corporation announced that a deal had been struck with China Huaya Development Corporation to embed the company's translation chips in educational products destined for schools nationwide. Over the next five days, eight million shares traded. But it got even better: There was yet another volume spike! (See Figure 9.2.)

On July 15, 1999, 2,690,000 shares traded in a single day. This was our signal to get on board. Obviously, more news was coming. More deals would be announced. Insiders had been merely warming up with the earlier buys.

Brian sent out an alert to his subscribers,[1] telling them to buy Zi Corporation at under $5.25 a share. In the days that followed, three more announcements were made. The company announced licensing agreements with two of China's largest electronics manufacturing companies—the Konka Group and Xiamen Overseas Electronics Company—to embed Zi Corporation's products in cell phones and

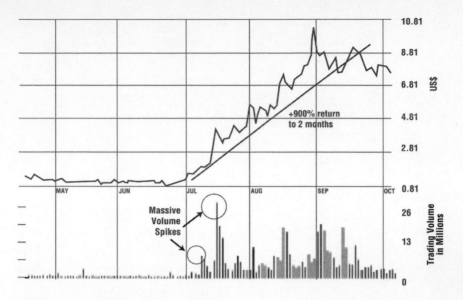

Figure 9.2 Zi Corporation Daily

other handheld electronic devices. As a result, Zi Corporation shares soared to over $10 in less than a month. Brian's subscribers saw up to 100 percent in easy gains.

TRIPLE-DIGIT RETURNS

And if you think doubling and quadrupling your money is fun, imagine making over 10 times your original investment following the same surefire insider signals. That's exactly what happened with LCA Vision, a chain of laser vision correction clinics that came out of nowhere a few months back. LCA Vision is a company that was on Brian's radar screen for the better part of two years.

Look closely at Figure 9.3. As you can see, there was very little price movement in the stock from September 1998 through January 1999. Yet along the way there were some interesting volume spikes that caught our eye. These included action in late October/early November, and more in late November/early December, plus a substantial spike in early January.

Our research revealed that these spikes clearly occurred in advance of some major news, and news that was very positive indeed.

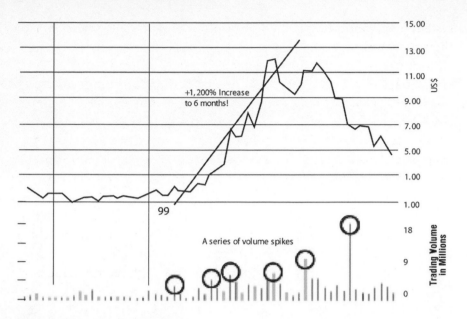

Figure 9.3 LCA Vision Weekly

Laser vision correction was becoming a hot industry, and LCA Vision was quickly establishing itself as one of the leading players. Profits were steadily rising, and the number of laser vision correction procedures was growing at the phenomenal rate of 100 percent per year.

We first recommended buying LCA Vision in late 1998, and kept recommending it through January 1999 once our research confirmed that the volume surges were very likely insider activity.

Within seven months, LCA Vision soared from a low of $1.06 to over $14 per share on the strength of what many insiders no doubt knew: that the company was about to turn a profit for the first time since its inception, and that its procedure rate was growing by leaps and bounds.

Our $1.75 stock grew to $13.50 before we issued a sell recommendation just a couple dollars short of the high. Volume spike indicator traders who followed our earliest recommendation turned $5,000 into $60,000 in a little over seven months, a remarkable 671 percent gain.

Now, the trades I've just told you about are incredible. But they were generated in what I like to refer to as the learning curve of the system. You would be justified in blaming "irrational exuberance" for their successes.

But even in the deadbeat markets we experienced between 2001 and 2004, the volume spike indicator proved to be outrageously useful. That's exactly what was happening with Midway Gaming (MWY) back in early 2004. (See Figure 9.4.)

I've circled the volume spikes so you can spot exactly what our analysts were looking for. In this case, the spikes look small because of the massive volume that followed. But those spikes were precursors to coming rallies in the stock.

On February 4, 2004, our team—headed by Brian Hicks' successor, Brad Colburn—sent out a Volume Spike Alert to readers telling them to buy MWY at $4.10 per share.

Midway took off a short time after this buy recommendation. Four months later, our team decided it was time to sell. On June 17, 2004, Brad issued a sell on half of the MWY shares at $12.85.

Volume Spike Alert readers who took his advice pulled in 213 percent in just four months. Those are awesome gains. Making 213 percent in a few months is a tremendous feeling.

But in some cases, you don't even have to wait months for gains to materialize:

In late March 2003, Alpha Pro (APT), a manufacturer of medical

Figure 9.4 Midway Gaming Daily

equipment, began to experience a series of volume spikes. (See Figure 9.5.)

On March 28, the stock's trading volume increased to 170,000 shares. To give you an idea of how dramatic an increase that was, the day before only 4,600 shares were traded; this makes it a classic volume spike.

On March 31, over 792,000 shares traded, and on April 1, a million shares changed hands. Brad and his team began to do some digging and discovered that insiders were buying stock because the company's surgical masks were being bought to stem the spread of SARS. The team issued a buy on April 8 at $1.45 a share.

Now, in reading the preceding paragraphs, you may have stumbled over the repeated use of the terms *insider* and *trading*. But before you go out and call the Securities and Exchange Commission (SEC) to check out this Amberger character who seems to be taking liberties with the law, let me emphasize that insider trading is illegal in the United States. But one thing is sure: it happens all the time. And just to keep the lawyers and editors reviewing my manuscript from fidgeting, let me stress that I'm not talking about doing anything illegal ourselves. We do our homework and spot what insiders are doing with the stock and then draw our own conclusions—*without access to any information that is not also available to the general public.*

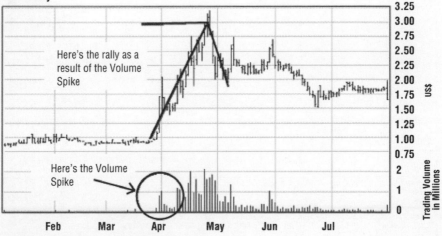

Figure 9.5 Alpha Pro Daily

THE MIND-BOGGLING CASE OF SAM WAKSAL

It is considerably different when true insiders make decisions based on something they know that is *not* available to the average investor. Take the case of Martha Stewart's buddy Sam Waksal, the former CEO of ImClone. If you watch CNN, you probably saw Mr. Waksal being carted off to federal prison on insider trading charges. He got seven years for using inside information to profit in the stock market. (For the gains he made on that particular deal, he would have been better off holding up a few blue-rinsed old ladies for their Bingo money and shaking down a few banks: chances are he'd have gotten off with anger management classes and a few hundred hours ladling soup for the homeless.) The big difference between what Sam did and what we do is defined by that line in the sand, the legal versus the illegal. Sam had access to information the public did not, and that's why he's cooling his heels in the Graybar Hotel. In comparison, all we do is study the data and perform research based on what's published and known.

By any measure, Sam Waksal qualified as loaded, a multimillionaire many times over. Why would he take that risk? If you ask me it's because inside information can be a surefire ticket to simply outrageous profits. It's simply irresistible! Corporate insiders who know what a company is going to do before the rest of the world can make enormous sums of money. Unfortunately, average investors usually get stuck with equally enormous losses. The combination of greed and stupidity is a dangerous one.

The advantage insiders have is access to information not yet made public. That's why true insider trading not only is unfair, it's also against the law. And that raises the question: Would you be comfortable using this kind of unfair advantage to get rich yourself?

But you don't have to break the law to get a real advantage over most investors. Imagine yourself using *legal* information generated by our first trading secret, and raking in enormous profits of 50, 100, or even 500 percent, while your neighbors and associates get eaten alive by Wall Street sharks and corporate thugs. The volume spike indicator does, indeed, give you a rare advantage. And it's legal.

This presents you with a choice. You can whine about corporate insiders using inside information to get rich. Or you can find a way to use the inside information yourself, without breaking the law. That's what the volume spike indicator is all about: following the trail of the insiders—and using it to make a profit—*without breaking any laws*. Volume spike trading is for people with guts and vision, those savvy traders who aren't afraid to take profits and who don't feel guilty when they outperform their neighbors. It's for people who are willing to stand up and stake their own claim to the riches available at this very moment, rather than sit by and let corporate thugs walk all over them. When it comes to making money in the markets, you're either on the inside or the outside—and I can assure you, the only way to guarantee your opportunity to accumulate substantial wealth is to be on the inside or be able to read how and when the insiders work.

HOW THE SYSTEM WORKS

Let me tell you more about how the system works.

First of all, our research team focuses on roughly 1,000 lesser-known small-cap high-tech and biotechnology companies with the most potential for breakthrough deals and announcements. These typically are young companies whose energies are focused on new products and new discoveries. But these are just the kind of organizations where information leaks are most likely to occur—since they're typically small companies with relatively loose corporate structures. And because volume is generally light, any sudden surges are very noticeable.

As I said before, this kind of insider trading happens all the time. It's not supposed to. But information has a way of leaking out. Confidential memos get seen. Printers read prepress reports. A friend helps a friend. A PR jockey shoots off his mouth in an unobserved moment. A needy in-law gets a hot tip. Next thing you know, there's unexplained volume activity surrounding a once-quiet stock. We never profit from insider information, but we *are* observant. When we see a change in volume, we look for reasons.

But as I said earlier, there's more to it than just watching volume. At the first sign of unusual volume activity, we look to see if there's any current news on the company—earnings, product announcements, coverage, upgrades, downgrades.

If everything seems to be normal—like during the days with low trading volume—and absolutely nothing appears to be going on, that's when we know something big is up.

One of the first things we do is check out the company's transaction log. If it's made up of a lot of small in-and-out trades, this usually means day traders are driving the stock. We stay clear. After all, the companies best suited to volume spike trading tend to be smaller-cap stocks. That means it doesn't take a lot of volume to drive the prices very high, very quickly. That's not the way we want to profit. We want to get in with the insiders at "controlled" prices—and let the market take the stock upward when imminent news goes public.[2]

Again, when we see a handful of 5,000-to-10,000 block trades, this usually means that some big hitters are trying to accumulate shares quietly and without pushing up prices through large block orders. That's a sign something's stirring. So we look deeper into the company to find out what's happening behind the scenes.

Interpreting the Changes in the Trend

Does the company have a new product? Does it have any patents pending? Is it up for any special licensing agreements or FDA approvals? Has it been in any long-term negotiations concerning major deals? You have to do some footwork to get these answers. You can't just call up the publicity director of the company: These guys are as reliable as used-car salesmen and will do anything that benefits the company (and of course, the insiders). You knowing ahead of the general public is *not* on their priorities list.

A "yes" to any of these kinds of questions—combined with any unexplained volume spikes—usually means something's about to break. That's when profits are close at hand. And that's when Volume Spike Alert members can expect an instantaneous e-mail alerting them to the opportunity ahead. Once we discover insider movement signaled by the telltale volume spike on a stock, it is absolutely crucial to act quickly. This activity usually means stock prices are ready to take off—usually in a matter of days.

The same holds true when it's time to get out. The kinds of stocks that create insider activity are also the kinds of stocks that can fall in a flash. It's absolutely important you get out when the profit run is over. Don't get greedy. Don't try to squeeze every last dollar out of the trade.

The average holding time for Volume Spike Alert positions is less than six months. That means following the volume spike indicator is purely a trading strategy. It's not a buy-and-hold portfolio decision. When a volume spike arises—and the research checks out—ride it until you see signs that the fervor is fading. Then get out with whatever profits you may have. Trading on volume spikes requires you to employ a stock trader's most powerful weapon: discipline. You're in only for the ride up. Usually it's a quick one. But it's never a buy-and-hold situation. This kind of trading using the volume spike indicator system is never passive. It's fast-paced. It's exciting. And the potential for big, speedy gains is tremendous.

The system we developed around the volume spike indicator allows us to catch anywhere from 35 to 75 opportunities each year. And I'm happy to report that we're right on the money with most of them.

In the past bull market phase, it was especially biotech companies whose proverbial volatility played right into our hands. Prior to the 1990s, the Food and Drug Administration (FDA) approved an average of three biotech products a year. In 1995, that number grew to 23. In 1997, 59 products gained FDA approval.

Over the following three years, more than 125 biotech drugs were scheduled to gain FDA approval. Did that mean there were 125 opportunities to profit? Actually, there were many more. Each one of these drugs had to pass through Phase II and Phase III clinical trials. And each time they do, it's a huge milestone for the drug—and a boon for the company. Each time one of these milestones is reached, word has a way of leaking out before the official announcement. That's when the mysterious volume spikes typically occur. And that's when our opportunity to profit comes—not from any real insider scoops but simply from (1) observing the otherwise unexplained change in volume and (2) investigating the timing and the cause of the change.

Biotechnology stocks may well be at the cusp of a new, powerful wave of profitability in the coming last phase of the great bubble market: Due to public pressure, there has never been a more favorable FDA environment when it comes to approving new drugs quickly.

Once a bastion of inefficiency and red tape, the FDA's approval process has become much more streamlined and much more interested in seeing that these worthwhile drugs are brought to market in a timely fashion.

And believe it or not, biotech companies are again tremendously undervalued. In fact, the market cap of all the major players in the biotechnology sector put together is less than that of Microsoft. But that may be about to change. If you're a trader, it's very possible that you can double your money riding volume spikes. In my opinion, the profits in the biotech sector will match or outperform all the profits made in the high-tech sector over the past 10 years.

The high-tech boom of the late 1990s was a proving ground for the volume spike indicator strategy. And judging from the profits we made, it has proven itself a valid, viable, and valuable trading tool. Along the way we've fine-tuned and perfected our volume spike indicator system. We quickly learned how to tell when volume is up on true insider activity, how to tell when a company is ripe for an important announcement, and how to anticipate jumps before they happen.

There are literally thousands of opportunities in the coming years in the biotech industry alone as drugs and medical products work their way through the five stages of FDA approvals—the lengthy pre-clinical phase, Phase I, Phase II, Phase III, and final approval.

As sure as the sun will set, as these products approach each FDA milestone, leaks will occur, resulting in some unexplained volume spikes—spikes worth investigating inside and out. And it's not just in any single sector that this can occur. There's still a lot of kick left in high-tech, too. Between these two very hot, very active, and very profitable sectors, there will be opportunities for many years to come. Some of our competitors seem to think so, too. I've counted two services that are now unabashedly offering the

> **Useful Information**
>
> For the recent scoop on Brad's volume spike indicator, check out www.roguetraderonline .com.
>
> Brad updates open and emerging positions in his daily e-letter *Fear & Greed,* which is yours for the asking at www.dynamicmarket report.com/fearandgreed.

same system under a different name, and that's just within our mother company, Agora.

Make sure you don't miss out on any of these opportunities. You see, once a stock trading system gets rolling, it doesn't matter which way the market goes—up or down. It makes no difference. If you follow the proven system, you're going to make money. The volume spike indicator is just getting warmed up, and the really big money is coming down the pike at this moment.

CHAPTER 10

TRADING SECRET NUMBER FOUR: "PROFITS AT THE SPEED OF NEWS"

Trading Extreme Volatility

New technology is rapidly democratizing securities markets. The costs of gathering information and executing trades are being driven to negligible levels. These changes allow a rapidly growing base of investors to participate in the financial system.

—Harvard Institute of Economic Research[1]

Gaining 33 percent a day for several days in a row surely beats that annual 1.5 percent return you get on a money market fund these days, wouldn't you say? But in fact, one of our Dynamic Market Theory specialist teams has done even better, generating 41 percent and 253 percent gains in just four days and on just one single play (Monster.com puts). The key to returns like this is what we call extreme volatility.

Of course, our team doesn't do that every day. But they've nailed 131 winning trades out of 202 trades over the year (2004).

Their biggest winners have included 246 percent gains on Ipix Corp. (IPIX), 150 percent on Energy Select Sector (XLE) puts, 79 percent on Altair Corp. (ALTI), and 138 percent, 270 percent, and 100 percent on On2 Technologies (ONT). Our biggest losers have included a 45 percent loss on Roxio (ROXI). Even better, in 2003 alone, our extreme volatility trading system generated 108 winners and only 30 losers. That's a 79 percent win rate. As of July 6, 2005, our extreme volatility team has already nabbed winners like 83 percent on Adobe calls, 99 percent on Archipelago Holdings, 252 percent on Taser puts, 225 percent on E-Trade calls, and 133 percent on Schwab.

While you don't have to play every extreme volatility trade detected by the system we're about to show you, it's still fun to think about the money you could make if you did. Investing just $10,000 in each of these trades would have given you a pure profit of $257,558.03 in just one year.

With profits like that, you could quit your job and become a full-time trader. In fact, I know people who have done just that, like A.L.G., one of our Dynamic Market Theory readers. A.L.G. is 56 years old. After falling victim to the wave of layoffs in Silicon Valley, he had this to say about trading on extreme volatility:

> I looked around back there in September at the economy and the local job market, and decided my household was history unless I could make the market work for me. I was in trouble. I subscribed to newsletters, of which I find yours to be a definite "keeper," only wishing there were more out there!
>
> Long story short, I had $24,000 in my trading account in September . . . and at this minute I have $138,000. This is after taking a couple pretty significant paper losses (missed the "correct" sell window), car repairs, two laptops, house payments, and household expenses. My finances are probably small potatoes compared to your usual contacts, but to me, it's stay here or move on.[2]

In a way, extreme volatility works a bit like the volume spike indicator of the preceding chapter: it revolves around inside information that moves stock prices, without incurring Sam Waksal's legal liability.

What is extreme volatility trading? In short, the system involves buying a stock—or options on the stock—shortly before it makes a quick move in price, then selling quickly to lock in the gains. *Being able to accurately predict these price moves requires advance receipt of news or information likely to affect the stock price in a positive or negative way.*

Take American Airlines (AMR:NYSE), for example. You may remember the company's flirtation with Chapter 11 bankruptcy. In the spring of 2003, AMR was engaged in tough negotiations with its unions to persuade them to take pay cuts. On April 15, 2003, the flight attendants' union was poised for a vote that could save or kill AMR.

Just how would the vote turn out? You could sit at your monitor all day waiting for the news to percolate through the system. Or you could have gotten advance notice simply by asking one of the airline's flight attendants. We did, and were told that the vote would go through. Confirming our belief that the attendants would rather take pay cuts during a recession than give up their jobs forever—especially since they were the highest-paid workers in the industry—meant the vote would be favorable for AMR and its shareholders.

All of this was perfectly legal. The flight attendant simply told us what happened that day at work. No insider secrets were being spilled behind closed doors, and anyone could have asked the same questions—but didn't. Basing our buy recommendation solely on the flight attendant's information, we issued a buy on AMR shares at $3.28 on the market open, and waited. A few hours later, when the union vote for the new deal was made official, we issued a sell at $4.22—a 33 percent gain within hours.

And there's more to the American Airlines story. You may remember the company's top executives cut themselves sweetheart pay deals while demanding pay cuts from the employees. Once the workers found out what was going on, the manure hit the ventilating system. The union cried foul and pulled out of the reduced pay contract, agreeing to a new vote set for April 25. Not even 20 minutes after the vote was tallied we issued another buy on AMR.

But here's the kicker: The voting results didn't hit the news for almost two and a half hours, allowing us to profit from the time it took for the decision to reach the mass media audience. We recommended a buy at $4.20 and sold a few days later for $7.02—a 67 percent gain.

That was on top of the 33 percent we had already made off the first union vote.

Chance? A stroke of luck, unlikely to be repeated? Maybe. But do you remember the SARS scare of 2004? At the height of the SARS scare, a biotech company filed a patent application for the treatment and prevention of this deadly new infection. Better yet, the company announced it had scored a huge new distribution deal in Hong Kong, the very center of the SARS epidemic. While it took time for this news to trickle to cable news and the newspapers, we were already in position and boasted a 64 percent gain in five days.

LITTLE GEMS . . . THERE FOR THE READING

We learned this by searching several regular health-related web sites that are open to the public. Using them is free. You could have gotten the same information about this biotech company that we did. That's because *getting in on the ground floor is easy—there is no special intelligence network needed!* In both the American Airlines and the biotech moves, we aggressively pursued the story and got a jump on the market. How could we do this? Well, it makes the point: Analysts and most of the investment markets are lazy, slow-moving, and even slower to react. If we can act quickly—at least more quickly than most others—we surely are able to capitalize on public information.

It isn't that simple each and every time. The gains in the American Airlines trade were indeed the exception, not the rule. We had a connection that legally fed us the information. With 99 percent of our extreme volatility trades, we don't have such connections. Instead, we rely on publicly available information, often found on free media, easily accessed and read by anyone who knows how to do a Google search. That's why you can duplicate our system on your own, at home—that is, if you have the time and patience.

A recent study from Harvard Business School Publishing states:

Information is the raw material for any investment or trading strategy, and technology can radically alter the information landscape. Recent years have witnessed the creation of new means by which information, opinion, and analyses can be shared among investors.[3]

According to the study, "information friction"—the delay disseminating news to investors—has been dramatically reduced, thanks in large part to TV and the Internet. As a result, information affects prices much faster, meaning that the influence of either positive or negative news finds its way into stock prices more efficiently. Whereas a company's press releases used to be read almost exclusively by business editors, they're now available to hundreds, even thousands of retail investors as well. Through the Internet, even the local business sections of local or regional newspapers can reach a global readership that not only peruses this instant news over morning coffee, but is ready to act on the information instantaneously. And where discussions about stocks took place between broker and client, or maybe among a few people gabbing at the watercooler, Internet newsgroups and message boards are now frequented by increasing numbers of small investors—some with astonishing degrees of sophistication and knowledge.

Benoit Mandelbrot writes:

> The news that impels an investor can be minor or major. His buying power can be insignificant or market-moving. His decision can be based on an instantaneous change of heart, from bull to bear and back again. The result is a far-wilder distribution of price changes: not just price movements but price dislocations. These are especially noticeable in our Information Age, with its instantaneous broadcasting by television, Internet, and trading-room screen. . . . [Investors] can act on it, not bit by bit in a progressive wave, as conventional theorists assume, but all at once, now and instantaneously.[4]

Mind you, it is not the passive dissemination of knowledge that extreme volatility trading aims to harness. Academic debate, neighborly chitchat, and the peacocklike display of technical argot practiced by your average report-writing analysts are but the backdrop: it is the willingness of the predominantly silent readership to turn this information into action that creates opportunity.

Take, for example, NEI WebWorld Inc. (NEIP:PK). The company was close to filing for bankruptcy, with its stock trading at a scant penny and a half, when suddenly, seemingly out of nowhere, its stock price rocketed 106,600 percent within a few days. This gain was caused by the posting of several bullish comments on Internet message boards by two UCLA students. Both were indicted for manipulating the stock in what's known as a pump-and-dump—chatting up the merits of a stock to drive up the price and get out with a big profit.

Of course, disseminating false positive news about a company with the intent to boost its share price is illegal if the individual or organization promoting the stock holds shares in the company. But the NEI WebWorld example illustrates beautifully how effective the Internet has become in the permeation of actionable information, whether it be true or false: An old-fashioned pump-and-dump scheme would have required a long list of gullible investors, a skilled telemarketer, and several hours of long-distance calls. Two students were able to achieve an infinitely faster and greater result with a handful of targeted message board postings. The whole scheme could take place at a Saturday night keg party in the frat house.

The extreme volatility trading system uses the Internet (and other sources) to access the information affecting the market early in the distribution curve. Knowing where to look for it and who the key gatekeepers are, you can analyze and act upon that same information earlier than most people, who will eventually read about it in traditional sources such as business web sites, print newspapers, and much later—magazines.

But what type of information do you look for to trade extreme volatility? That, too, isn't exactly rocket science. There is a limited type of news that can make a stock jump or plummet:

- Insider buying.
- Buybacks (repurchase agreements).
- Stock splits or dividends.
- Disseminated rumors.
- A big new product or major contract award.
- Food and Drug Administration (FDA) approval for a new drug.
- Successful clinical trial for a drug.
- A license granted by the Federal Communications Commission (FCC).
- Big order from a government.
- Joint venture.

- Commercialization of new technology.
- Spikes in volume, message board chatter.
- Senseless stock or sector sell-offs.
- Bidding wars.

Let's use bidding wars as an example. From one of our most reliable extreme volatility information gatekeepers, we learned that Savvis Communications, a telecom company, had beaten out other bidders and bought Cable and Wireless America before this information had percolated through the standard media channels. The acquisition would immediately add $400 million to Savvis's bottom line, doubling the size of the company. Solely on the strength of this news, we recommended our extreme volatility traders buy Savvis. They stood to make gains of 43 percent on the stock in less than a week.

Or take the news category of senseless sell-off. On February 26, 2004, in an alert titled "Educational Gap Down Overdone," we recommended that readers buy call options on Career Education Corp. (CECO) and Education Management Corp. (EDMC) based on oversold conditions brought about by the federal investigation into ITT Educational Services. Less than a month later, we were up 59 percent and 50 percent, respectively.

Everybody knows stocks eventually go up following events like this. But average investors don't move fast enough. Sure, they'll learn about it on the evening news or next day in the newspaper, but by that time they've left money on the table. Fortunately, it's quite easy for us to get in on the ground floor time and time again.

LIKE STEALING CANDY FROM A BABY

There are a couple of surefire news catalysts that can bring about the sudden surge in a stock. One of them is the guru factor. We have found that when a news release includes mention that big shots like Warren Buffett or George Soros are buying a particular stock, investors will pile into that stock upon learning that a sage is putting down his dollar first. It has happened so frequently that I can't really call that a secret.

What *is* a rather well-kept secret, however, is that you can be one of the first to know when Buffett or Soros has made a move. Using the extreme volatility trading system, you can make a mint off the totally predictable run-up that follows important news and information announcements. And you can do it early, before others even know about it, and in time to pocket the big profits from each trade.

There's a little company called Bluefly (BFLY:Nasdaq) that we watched for a couple of years. The extreme volatility team generated double- or triple-digit gains at least four times using exactly this technique. In fact, every time billionaire George Soros buys the stock, we make a bundle—just by buying right after he does and before the chatterboxes on CNBC take up the story. It's so easy, it's shameful. Any monk in the monastery Soros announced he'd retire to if George W. Bush won the 2004 presidential election could do it between hymns at morning mass.

Ian L. Cooper, a member of our Dynamic Market Theory trading team who developed the Extreme Volatility Speculator service, knows how to get the news first because he was a reporter himself and understands how they do it. All he has to do is go to the same sources and exploit the time gap before journalists can get their stories on the air or into print.

His interest in how information travels through the different layers of news disseminators was awakened in journalism school, where Ian wrote two academic studies on the dissemination of news and its manipulation by the gatekeepers in corporate America, the government, and the media. In the course of his pioneering work, he collected over 500 pages of charts and tables and reams of documents devoted to the question of how news reaches the public and how it's shaped before it gets there.

In short, he is one of America's leading experts on news media and is known to many as the originator of the News Evaluative Matrix. That sounds fancy, indeed, but as with anything contained in our Dynamic Market Theory, the basic idea is pretty easy to explain.

You see, when Ian wrote his groundbreaking studies on how news spreads, he found out it's a lot like the flu. First a few people catch it, then hundreds, then thousands. If you chart the news dissemination process, you can see the process. It actually resembles a viral epidemic.

Even more interesting, there are news manipulation specialists who act like germ warfare experts. They can create a story that resembles a news-germ and manipulate the way it spreads. These people, the gatekeepers, work for the government, for big corporations, for the giant news conglomerates—for any organization that has a vested interest in telling the public what to think.

Eventually, millions of people "catch" the news story just as they do a virus, but it takes time. (This technique has recently been adapted by Internet marketers using e-mail as their predominant vehicle. Not surprisingly, this is known as "viral marketing.")

The markets move in response to all kinds of announcements: a buyout, a new product, a court decision, you name it. But they don't move until the news is out. That's why you can be sure that the first people to get the news make money on it.

The time it takes for a story to be fully disseminated may be a few hours, or days, or even weeks, depending on the type of story. There is *always* a window of opportunity when just a few people know and before millions of people find out.

REMEMBER "PICKLEGATE"?

A perfect example of how this process works was provided during the early phases of the 2004 presidential campaign.

One day, our information technology (IT) department issued this warning: "Drudgereport.com, a popular news site, may have viruses today: you may want to stay off that site for a few days."

What are the chances, I thought to myself. Not quite 24 hours had passed since the Internet's own Nancy Drew, Matt Drudge, had opened a potential can of worms with "Picklegate," the rumor that presidential candidate John Kerry had a Clintonesque affair with an intern, and suddenly inquiring minds were getting infected with Internet viruses?

While we were watching "Picklegate" develop with rapt interest since news broke on the Drudge Report web site, it provided us with a great, real-time opportunity to illustrate one of the aspects of our Dynamic Market Theory, which we like to call "Profits at the Speed of News."

Report a rumor, an innuendo, a juicy "fact" that attracts massive media attention, and what was once a trickling brook of information to a select few becomes an unstoppable tidal wave of news picked up by all major sources of news dissemination—all looking for the next hot, profitable story that can make or break a career, a business, or even a country.

How many outside of Democratic insiders knew about the rumored John Kerry intern infidelity prior to that Thursday morning? My guess is less than three dozen people. But that changed at exactly 11:45 A.M. on February 12, 2004, thanks to the Drudge Report. This was the starting point of "Picklegate" news dissemination. And, like clockwork, the rumor rapidly began to spread. Here's a brief dissemination time line:

Phase One: Rumor Dissemination

11:45 A.M., 2/12/04: Initial Drudge Report posting.

11:55 A.M.: WorldNetDaily.com reports on rumor.

12:30 P.M.: First message threads found on Yahoo! message boards.

1:00 P.M.: Drudge Report posts responses to initial report.

1:00 P.M.: Rumor found circulating on StreetInsider.com.

Approximately 2:00 P.M.: News radio is abuzz with the rumor.

Phase Two: The Rumor Itself Becomes News

Afternoon: ABC news radio.

5:07 P.M.: *Editor & Publisher* posts news about Drudge Report posting.

6:00 P.M./11:00 P.M.: Nightly news reports.

Local TV:

    WSYX-TV Columbus, OH (5:05 P.M.).

    WBTV-TV Charlotte, NC (6:00 P.M.).

    KABC-TV Los Angeles, CA (6:00 P.M.).

    KDAF-TV Dallas, TX (9:28 P.M.).

    KTBS-TV Shreveport, LA (10:00 P.M.).

    KRQE-TV Albuquerque, NM (10:00 P.M.).

    WTTE-TV Columbus, OH (10:11 P.M.).

    WBAL-TV Baltimore, MD (11:11 P.M.).

Phase Three: Commentary on the Rumor

Morning of 2/13/04: Don Imus Show, featuring a live interview with candidate Kerry.

Morning of 2/13/04: Morning national news programs report on Kerry.

Morning of 2/13/04: Newspaper reports in Philly.com, *London Times*, *Chicago Sun-Times*, *The Sun* Online, *The Independent*, BBC, and so on.

10 A.M., 2/13/04: Yahoo News, "Kerry Says He's Ready for GOP Onslaught."

As you can see, the news story about the rumor traveled in a predictable, systematic way—starting with a few people and eventually reaching millions.

THE NEWS EVALUATIVE MATRIX

That is how news in general behaves. It holds true for partisan innuendo on extramarital dalliances the same way it plays out in the process of stock news dissemination:

Rumor or News

- Statements circulated to shareholders or those on mailing lists.
- Press releases to major news providers such as Yahoo!, *Smart-Money*, CNN, MSNBC, CNBC.
- Rumor or news picked up by message boards and other sites, where it spreads like wildfire.
- Massive increases in volume activity and mentions in lists of best daily performers, and on and on.

The result is the potential for massive gains—provided you know how the game is played. Let's revisit the American Airlines trade.

The news: AMR was engaged in tough negotiations with its unions to get them to take pay cuts. On April 15, 2003, the flight attendants' union was poised for a vote that could save or kill AMR.

Speculation, rumor, hot news: We got word from an AMR employee confirming our belief that the vote would go AMR's way. The attendants would rather take pay cuts during a recession than give up their jobs forever, especially since they were the highest-paid workers in the industry.

Action: Based on these tips, we put out a buy on AMR at $3.28 on the market open.

News dissemination: Web site, print, radio, television reports began to surface.

Profit taking: A few hours later, when the union voted for the new deal, we put out a sell at $4.22—a 33 percent gain within hours.

The concept is not new and not at all original. Mark Twain, in his 1897 book *Following the Equator*, relates the story of a young Cecil Rhodes, who retrieved a copy of a London newspaper from a shark's stomach while in Australia in 1870. That particular issue had not arrived in Australia yet, as it took several weeks for the mail to reach Australia by ship. Based on the information in this "advance copy," Rhodes managed to buy the rights to the wool crop: He knew before any Australian knew that France had declared war on Germany, and that wool prices in London had risen by 14 percent. Twain writes: "The deal went through, and secured to the young stranger the first fortune he ever pocketed."[5]

Trading the News

Academic studies support the validity of trading on the news and information flow. In 1973, University of Chicago economist Eugene Fama developed the efficient markets hypothesis, which states that when news is released, it is immediately reflected in the price of stocks. In other words, markets efficiently and instantaneously process new information. In its hypothetical pure form, all stock prices would be assumed to have discounted all known information at any given time: the market is efficient.

If the theory is true, then it suggests that it is impossible to make money in the stock market by trading on news. Unfortunately, the financial community accepted this theory. The efficient markets theory was the rule that could never be broken—that is, until the theory was reexamined.

Dozens of high-level studies suggest that a news-driven approach to locating trading opportunities is indeed valid. In fact, during his stint at academia, Ian made important, original contributions to this growing field. Here are a few quick samples of what other academic researchers say:

> I examine returns to a subset of stocks after public news about them is released. I compare them to other stocks with similar monthly returns, but no identifiable public news. There is a major difference between return patterns for the two sets. I find evidence of post-news drift, which supports the idea that investors under-react to information. . . . There is a large amount of evidence that stock prices are predictable.[6]

> Arguably, the most important process affecting price movements is the news arrival process. For example, in Ross (1989) the volatility of stock price changes is directly related to the rate of flow of information to the market. . . . On days no news arrives, trading is slow and price movements are small. When new information arrives that results in a change in expectations, trading becomes vigorous and the price moves in response to the impact of the news. . . . In addition to price movements, news arrivals can affect the time between trades, number of transactions, and volume of trade."[7]

> Periods of good news are followed by periods of unusually high returns relative to natural benchmarks, with the reverse for bad news. . . . Post-event drift is the tendency of individual stocks' performances following major corporate news events to persist for long periods in the same direction as the return over a short window—usually one to three days—encompassing the news announcement itself.[8]

Especially the Morning Call and Midday Call segments on CNBC-TV provide a unique opportunity to study the efficient markets hypothesis. Segments report analysts' current opinions on individual stocks that are broadcast when the market is open. Jeffrey A. Busse and T. Clifton Green have found that prices respond to reports within seconds of initial mention, "with positive reports fully incorporated within one minute. Trading intensity doubles in the first minute, with a significant increase in buyer (seller) initiated trades after positive (negative) reports. Traders who execute within 15 seconds of the initial mention make small but significant profits by trading on positive reports during the Midday Call."[9]

PROOF'S IN THE PUDDING

If you're not convinced yet, take a look at what happened to Emulex when an ill-informed intern spread a false news report to the masses.

Emulex was reportedly about to restate earnings and fire its CEO. Both reported "facts" proved to be false. What ensued was a massacre brought on by the dissemination of false news, driving the stock price south about 30 percent within the first hour of trading.

But when the news is good and you can get in early, look out! The profits can be shocking.

Take On2 Technologies (ONT:NYSE), for example. We tracked this play on news of a new licensing agreement that would add nicely to its bottom line. Having bought in at $1.05, we cashed out three times with profits of 138 percent, 270 percent, and 100 percent. Or how about Blue Square-Israel (BSI:NYSE)? On the announcement of a $1.18-per-share dividend and prospects of an improving Israeli economy, we bought in, walking away with 24 percent profits and $1.18 dividends to boot. Or think back to the mad cow disease scare that hit Canada in 2004. Exports of Canadian beef into the United States were suspended, and there was a frantic search for any cattle that might have been exposed, including some in America. The $80 billion U.S. cattle industry was under threat, while Canadian beef producers were losing $20 million per day. In this panicky atmosphere, Genesis Bioventures (GBI:NYSE) announced a quick, easy test for mad cow disease.

Or how about the lethality and legal issues that sent shares of Taser International to multiyear lows? As Taser shares were just beginning to tumble, we bought puts, cashing out twice in only four days for 41 percent and 253 percent gains. Or the 39 percent and 88 percent gains pocketed when Taser's competitor, Law Enforcement Associates, began flying on rumors that its stun gun was the safe alternative to Taser's products? Or even the one-day 41 percent gains taken from Martha Stewart Living Omnimedia (MSO) puts after the stock market herd pushed the underlying stock to a five-year high of $36? Believing the momentum had topped out and news of a new television series was dying down, we recommended buying the March 30 puts. Less than a day later, we were out when MSO shares tumbled $1.20.

Still not convinced that extreme volatility generated by news events can put the spring back into your step and the bounce back into your bungee? Consider our American Standard Companies' position taken on February 2, 2005, just hours before President Bush's State of the Union address. In the days after Bush addressed asbestos litigation reform, the stock soared, taking our American Standard Companies calls from $0.90 to $1.40—a 56 percent gain in less than two days.

The same thing happened to USG Corporation, W. R. Grace, and Georgia-Pacific stocks in June 2003. As soon as the Senate Judiciary Committee approved a trust-bill fund, shares in companies facing asbestos lawsuits moved north fast from the Senate's mouth to the stock market's ears to shareholders' pockets.

The point to be made in all of these examples is the same: This kind of trading success is based on *timing*, and that is not a matter of simple luck. We trade by identifying and anticipating extreme volatility and its underlying causes. Anyone can predict what a stock is going to do *after* something important has been announced. But sometimes the market is slow to react even when news is already public. For whatever reason, investors do not always immediately comprehend the possible ramifications of news. In 2002, for example, when we first put our working hypothesis on extreme volatility to the test, we had this enlightening experience:

Whenever large numbers of people start getting the flu aboard cruise ships, you might figure that prices of Carnival Cruise Lines or Royal Caribbean stock would plunge. But these stocks hardly moved on the day the story broke. Most investors didn't understand what the news would mean. It didn't register. We spotted the opportunity, bought Royal Caribbean puts, and earned a 120 percent profit in only seven days.

The beauty of the News Evaluative Matrix is that news does spread gradually, from the few to the many. There are a lot of time lags you can exploit if you know how to spot them. At the start, one or two people might know a story—the people directly involved. If it's a business story, only the top managers might know at first. When it's good news, maybe they'll put out a press release or casually mention it to an analyst. Conversely, they may not tell a soul, but just quietly start buying up their company's stock. Eventually, the story finds its way to a news service like Bloomberg or Reuters. Then it's on the cable news networks like CNBC.

By that night, you might hear the story on the nightly news summaries. Then it's in next morning's newspapers. And way down the line, the story will be in the weekly newsmagazines like *Time*, *Newsweek*, *BusinessWeek*, or *Forbes*. Unfortunately, that's way too late to do you any good financially.

BE A PART OF THE FIRST 1 PERCENT TO HEAR BREAKING NEWS

You don't have to be at the tail end of the news dissemination process. In fact, you can be in the first percentile.

But how do you do that? How can you position yourself between the source of a news feed and 99 percent of the rest of the world? It's easy, at least in theory. And, although in practice it takes a lot of work, I can assure you that it's all perfectly legal. There is no illegal insider trading here because the sources of information we use in our extreme volatility trading research not only are open to the public, most are found online.

You just have to know where to look. This information is public. You can probably guess some of our sources. The FDA has a web site. So does the FCC, the Federal Trade Commission (FTC), the Centers for Disease Control (CDC), the Department of Homeland Security, and on and on.

These are only a few of the great sources that can put you on the ground floor of big moves. In November 2004, for example, the FDA's web site revealed that the agency had approved an easy, oral HIV (AIDS) test that gives results in 20 minutes. The maker is Ora-Sure Technologies. We identified the opportunity, bought, and sold it in just three days with 15 percent gained.

Here's where our extreme volatility traders spend most of their days looking for news on the Web:

For health-related stocks, check out the web sites for the CDC (www.cdc.gov), FTC (www.ftc.gov), and the FDA (www.fda.gov).

For telecoms, we look at the web site of the FCC—the same

folks who are always trying to get Howard Stern to clean up his act: www.fcc.gov.

Often the earliest availability of important breaking news stories is on Matt Drudge's site, the Drudge Report: www.drudge report.com.

We spend a good part of our time looking at a number of investment-related web sites, including Yahoo! and Yahoo! Finance, MarketWatch, Reuters, MSN Money, Zacks Investment Research, TheStreet.com, CNN Money, and PR Newswire:

www.yahoo.com
http://finance.yahoo.com
www.marketwatch.com
www.reuters.com
www.msnmoney.com
www.zacks.com
www.thestreet.com
www.money.com
www.prnewswire.com
www.streetinsider.com
www.bloomberg.com
www.smartmoney.com
www.dhs.gov/dhspublic

On television, we watch "Squawk Box" and "Bullseye" on CNBC, Fox Morning News, and Bloomberg. We also listen to the talk on Internet message boards. A single message means nothing, but when there is a spike in volume concerning a company, product, contract, story, or rumor, then it's time to take a closer look. Our favorite message boards can be found on Yahoo! (www.yahoo.com) and Raging Bull (www.ragingbull.com).

You may be asking, "Can I really profit from news driving stock prices without having proprietary research?" The answer is yes. An ordinary person *does* have access to all this—but most don't have time, patience, or insight enough to sift through all the information.

This edge is attained by buying shares of companies whose stock price is likely to rise based on positive news that will soon become widespread—but right now has only been noticed and read by a limited number of people.

THE THREE TIERS OF EXTREME VOLATILITY TRADES

Sometimes, extreme volatility trades can fly so high, it really is like having a license to print money. You see, when you buy on breaking news, you often get two or more price run-ups as the news percolates from a few thousand people to a few hundred thousand to millions and millions.

First Tier. By constantly monitoring the early-phase information sources, most of which are online, we learn the important news first and can make a buy for the morning open.

Second Tier. As more investors learn the news, the price and volume soar—and *that* becomes news.

Third Tier. Then there's a reaction to the reaction. The huge jump in price or the amazing volume makes the nightly news summaries. And the next morning, even more investors jump in.

Think of all the times you've heard a broadcaster say, "Stock XYZ had the third highest volume today." Or "Widget Company was among today's top movers on the Nasdaq, with a 40 percent gain."

The first day's run-up is the reaction to the news. The next day the stock jumps again as investors react to the reaction.

We have seen this pattern over and over again in our extreme volatility trades:

- On2 Technologies jumped 28 percent the first few hours, and was up 224 percent in 15 days.
- Geron jumped 71 percent in four days on news of its cancer vaccine. Then it was up 91 percent in 15 days.
- Genesis Bioventures jumped 17 percent the first day and 40 percent in five days.
- SureBeam soared 119 percent in the first week on news of the anthrax scare.
- Lynch Corporation gained 24 percent in one day on news of insider buying. Then it gained another 11 percent a couple of weeks later.
- Ipix Corp. (IPIX) jumped 107 percent in three days, 246 percent in seven days, and another 144 percent in 12 days.
- Arotech Corp. (ARTX) shot up 26 percent in five days.

- Our Energy Select Sector SPDR (XLE) puts jumped more than 150 percent in only two weeks.
- Altair (ALTI) was up 79 percent and 29 percent in less than two months.

We typically see a gain in the first few hours or the first day. Then we see our profits go up again and again as the news spreads in exactly the way Ian mapped out in his groundbreaking News Evaluative Matrix studies.

WHEN TO PLACE YOUR TRADE

The toughest part of extreme volatility trading is knowing when there is enough valid information to go long or short on a stock—or buy puts or calls—on the strength of the news you are reading.

Unfortunately, there is no quantitative indicator—at least none that we have discovered yet—that tells you authoritatively the exact point in the News Evaluative Matrix when it's time to buy or sell. If you can get in early—that is, place a trade with confidence based on the first piece of advance information you get from one of your news sources—you can rake in profits from Tier 1, Tier 2, *and* Tier 3. As you gain in experience in the practice of trading extreme volatility, this is how most of your trades will eventually play out.

However, if you wait you can be safer and more confident and lower your risk of having a loser. You will miss out on Tier 1 profits, but can still make money on Tier 2 or Tier 3.

As I hope I have shown you in this chapter, most of the information on which extreme volatility trading is based is public knowledge, freely available on the Internet. Therefore you don't have a lot of time to make up your mind about whether you want to bet on the stock.

We recommend you place all of

Useful Information

Ian Cooper supplies the subscribers of his service Extreme Volatility Speculator with news-driven profit opportunities at www.vixtrader.com.

He also contributes to the RedZone Group's daily e-letter, *American Capitalist*, which you can subscribe to free of charge at www.dynamicmarket report.com/american capitalist.

your extreme volatility trades with a 25 percent stop-loss order to limit your downside risk.

A single blip on the "information radar screen" may not be a strong enough indicator that a stock is about to move. As a rule of thumb, and especially when you first start out, significant spikes in volume, price, news, and attention are the strongest signals that it's time to buy, often confirming that first, single blip. Knowing how to interpret the news, when to buy and when to sell, is based on subjective judgment that you can only fine-tune with experience.

ADDITIONAL EXAMPLES

Gigamedia, bought June 5, sold July 8, plus 40 percent
The story: Something looked to be taking shape in the Gigamedia camp. Volume jumped to six times the average on June 5, on news that management was attempting to negotiate with the company's directors to take it private. While the company decided to reject the management buyout offer, we walked away with a cool $4,000 profit on every $10,000 risked.

Rediff.com, bought July 2, sold July 8, plus 18 percent
The story: With the Asian stock rally just heating up, we had the opportunity to jump on the tail end of the run-up and walk away with a cool 18 percent gain in less than six days.

Lynch Corporation, bought July 2, sold July 8, plus 11 percent (on top of a *24 percent gain* in one day, June 23 to June 24)
The story: Insiders were tripping over one another to pick up shares and the company had just got three multimillion-dollar orders for capital equipment. We played this one twice in two weeks for profits of 24 percent and 11 percent.

CPI Aerostructures, bought June 27, sold July 8, plus 20 percent
The story: With insiders laying down $73,000 for 10,000 shares of their own company, the Extreme Volatility Speculator editors knew something had to be brewing. You simply do not put that kind of money on the table if you think your company is down for the count. Sure enough, the company released news that it had received $19.4 million in contracts during the first half of the year, up 46 percent from the past year's numbers, giving us the opportunity to walk away with a cool 20 percent gain in less than two weeks.

CHAPTER 11

TRADING SECRET NUMBER FIVE: STONE-COLD PROFIT PREDATOR

The Doji Master

The investor who takes the amount of time and effort needed to master candlesticks can reap handsome profits.

— Stephen W. Bigalow, *Profitable Candlestick Trading: Pinpointing Market Opportunities to Maximize Profits* (2002)

Thus far, we have been looking at patterns created by human greed. The downside to greed, of course, is the other dominant human emotion: fear. Fear and greed—the chickens and pigs of the market—are driving forces and, like other natural phenomena, they leave traceable and quantifiable imprints in the daily data flows. If you're comfortable stepping away from the emotion of the herd and using a logical system to rack up stunning gains, read on. Our team has created a system we call the Doji Master that could hand you hefty double-digit gains on a regular basis. In fact, during Doji's Master's brief existence since October 2004, the system has nabbed quick gains like 155 percent in one

157

day on DST Systems (DST), 100 percent in five days with National City Corp. (NCC) calls, 166 percent in one day with Northrop Grumman calls (NOC), and a whopping 558 percent in less than one month with MBNA calls (KRB).

Doji Master profits from fear. We look for situations where most investors are scared, and that's when we move in to seize quick profits. A hard-edged approach? Maybe. But it works. Even billionaire investor Warren Buffett agrees on this take-no-prisoners approach. His advice to investors hungry for profits: "Be brave when others are afraid."

Believe me, nothing spawns fear like a falling stock. When a stock falls for a few days, watch out! People start to panic. This is when Doji Master's mouth starts to water, because the more a stock price drops, the more people sell. Bottom line: Fear sends investors into a tailspin. Their emotions start raging and they think with their hearts instead of their heads. This creates a stunning profit opportunity for those thinking clearly and logically.

Doji Master uses logic: While other investors are running around like frightened children, we prepare to strike. Eventually, fear gets so out of control that selling goes beyond a sustainable level. The stock is then oversold.

This is the point where investor fear is at its highest. And this is where Doji Master steps in for big, fast profits. Let me show you how we do it.

TURNING PANIC INTO PROFITS

We use a technical indicator called the put/call ratio (PCR), also known as a put/call premium ratio.

As you may know, when people are afraid that a stock will go down, they buy put options. When people believe the stock will go up, they buy calls. If the PCR is going up, it means more people are buying puts. They are afraid the stock will continue to drop.

When a stock's PCR climbs over 1, this indicates that the stock is oversold; a PCR of 2 or 3 means panic is setting in and a reversal is pending.

Doji Master calmly waits, looking for a PCR of 4 or higher. This happens only when fear has grown to the point that it is virtually unsustainable. When you find a stock that has a PCR of 4, you can be darn sure a turnaround is coming.

But when? When will the stock stop falling and bolt upward? Rushing in too early could be very costly, like trying to catch a falling knife.

So how do you know when the stock is at its bottom and a turnaround is ready to happen? This is the beauty of Doji Master! The system employs a special technique allowing us to determine exactly when the stock is ready to rocket upward.

Ancient Japanese Profit Signal

Back in the fifteenth century, a Japanese family—the Honshu family—was looking for a way to dominate the rice trading industry. Rice trading was very competitive, so the family searched for a competitive advantage. They developed what is now called the Japanese candlestick chart.

The chart gave them a huge edge, and the family grew very wealthy exploiting this advantage. In fact, the family's wealth became legendary. Songs were sung about their wealth. The Honshu family became the financial powerhouse of all Japan.

Doji Master uses the same technique that made the Honshu family rich.

Japanese candlestick charts help us determine when a falling stock has reached its bottom. It gives us a signal that a stock is done falling and is ready for a reversal. Do candlestick charts work for stock investing?

So says Stephen W. Bigalow of *Technical Analysis of Stocks & Commodities* magazine: "The investor who takes the amount of time and effort needed to master candlesticks can reap handsome profits."[1]

Doji Master has perfected the use of candlestick charts. Let me show you how candlestick charts help us seize big profits.

Candlestick charts show a stock's open, close, high, and low. (See Figure 11.1.)

History has shown that different candlestick patterns mean different things. To determine if a stock has hit its bottom, we look for a doji, a formation that occurs when the open price is the same as the close price so that it looks like a cross. (See chart of doji variations later in this chapter.)

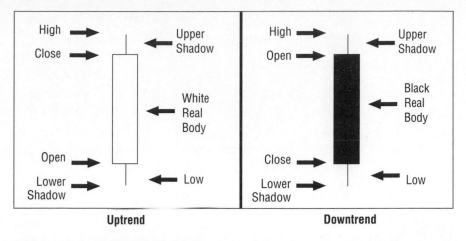

Figure 11.1 Candlestick Charts

A doji indicates a pull between buyers and sellers. And when a doji occurs after a stock has fallen, it indicates that the stock is near bottom and a reversal is imminent.

That's when we step in and seize profits. (Dojis are also referred to as profit stars.) For example, Figure 11.2 is a chart for BJ Services (BJS:NYSE). As you can see, BJS was in a downtrend until November 4, 2004.

Notice that the formation at the bottom of the downtrend is similar to a doji. This signals that a reversal is on the way. When we spotted this, we told our readers to buy BJS calls. Just one day later, the reversal occurred. Our Doji Master readers pulled in quick gains of 44 percent on BJS calls in about 24 hours.

On October 20, 2004, Doji Master noticed that DST Systems (DST:NYSE) had a high put/call ratio of 12.5. This stock was ready for a bounce . . . but when? We pulled up the candlestick chart and discovered a doji had formed. This was a surefire sign that a reversal was imminent. (See Figure 11.3.)

We immediately issued a buy on DST calls at $0.45. Just in time! The next day, the underlying stock made a strong recovery, and we issued a sell on our DST calls for $1.15.

That's a 156 percent gain in one day! Amazing? Yep. But listen: the Doji Master system is cranking out gains like this on a regular basis. Let me give you another example.

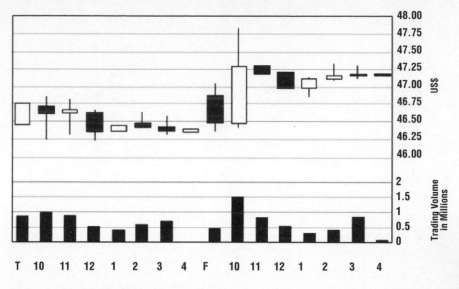

Figure 11.2 BJ Services Hourly

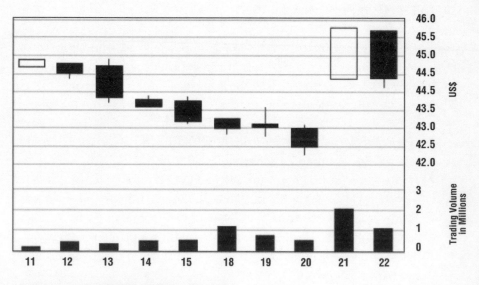

Figure 11.3 DST Systems Hourly

On October 22, 2004, we found that AKS Steel had a put/call ratio of over 10. A reversal was almost guaranteed. The only question was when it would happen. We looked at the candlestick chart of AKS and noticed that a type of doji called a hammer formation had formed at the end of the recent downward trend.

That's *exactly* what we wanted to see. We issued a buy on AKS calls at $0.50. Just four days later, the AKS stock took off and we issued a sell for $0.85, a 70 percent gain in four days.

Let's take another peek at Doji Master. The gains keep on coming. October 22, 2004, was also the day we recommended a trade on National City Corp. (NCC). We discovered NCC had a put/call ratio of 120. No doubt a big turnaround was on the way.

We looked at the candlestick chart and got the go-ahead we needed. We issued a buy on NCC calls at $0.15, and then waited.

You can probably guess what happened next. The underlying stock bolted upward, and the calls jumped to $0.30 in five days.

WHAT THE HECK IS A DOJI?

Dojis are commanding reversal signals and the bread and butter of Doji Master. They are formed when the candlestick opens and closes at the same level, implying bull/bear indecision in the stock price. They can be subdivided into categories, depicted in Figure 11.4.

1. *Doji.* Dojis are most significant when found after an extended set of long-bodied candlesticks
2. *Long-legged doji.* These are formed when the stock opens at a given level and trades in a broad range, only to close at the same level. They are most powerful when preceded by smaller candlesticks, as a sudden burst of volatility coupled with a volume spike, implying that insiders have leaked information and a change is coming.
3. *Dragonfly doji.* These open at the high end of a session, sell off a considerable amount, then rally to end the day at the same level as the open. These are usually seen after a decline and are reversal indicators. If they form in conjunction with an upward-sloping moving average, it's a buy signal.

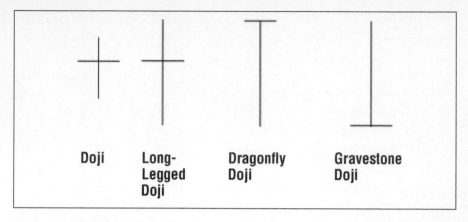

| Doji | Long-Legged Doji | Dragonfly Doji | Gravestone Doji |

Figure 11.4 Dojis

4. *Gravestone doji.* This is the reverse of the dragonfly doji and is a top reversal indicator when confirmed with a bearish engulfing candlestick. This is a long, black candlestick. The bigger it is, the more bearish the reversal. As the name implies, gravestone dojis look like gravestones and could signal the death of the stock.

OTHER INDICATORS TO LOOK FOR

Hammers are short-body candles with little or no upper shadow, and a lower shadow at least twice as long as the candle body, that are formed after declines or downtrends. (See Figure 11.5.)

When confirmed, the hammer becomes a powerful reversal signal. The ubiquitous Wall Street expression "hammers out a bottom" refers to a day when the downtrend in a stock runs into a point when enough buying interest is generated to bring prices close to where they open.

Confirmation comes from a bullish engulfing candlestick, signaling to the Doji Master that the uptrend is established. The color of the hammer is unimportant, but some consider white hammers more potent reversal signals.

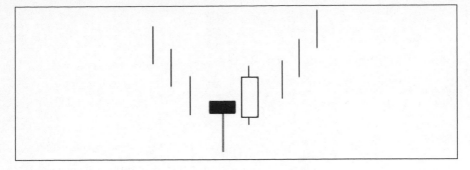

Figure 11.5 Hammer with Bullish Engulfing Candlestick

Hanging man candlesticks are short-body candles with little or no upper shadow and a lower shadow at least twice as long as the candle body that are formed after advances or uptrends. (See Figure 11.6.)

When confirmed, the hanging man is a powerful reversal signal. In fact, this signal has saved me on more than one occasion. I distinctly remember the America Online (AOL) sell signal given at the top of the Internet bubble of 2000.

Confirmation comes from a bearish engulfing candlestick, signaling to the Doji Master that the uptrend is finished. The color of the hanging man is unimportant, but some consider that the solid-color hanging man indicates a more potent reversal signal. The wise trader respects the power of the hanging man.

You may also know the shadow of death by its popular candlestick moniker, the dark cloud cover. (See Figure 11.7.) While the initial setup may look bullish, once the second-day candle closes below the midpoint of the first-day candle, the bulls begin to question their position and start pulling out.

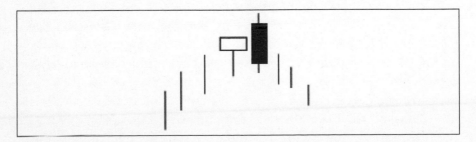

Figure 11.6 Hanging Man with Bearish Engulfing Candlestick

Figure 11.7 Dark Cloud Cover

A typical shadow of death scenario plays out like this. A long white candlestick is formed on the first day, followed by a gap up on the second day. While encouraging to the bulls, watch the chart very closely on the second day for any intraday crossover of the first day's midpoint.

Since this candlestick is not the strongest reversal indicator, use the bearish momentum divergence option to confirm a coming downtrend. Momentum divergence is a method to compare how strong a stock's price action is in comparison to the stock's underlying momentum. Traditionally, to find this divergence, an analyst will draw trend lines along significantly low points and significantly high points on the stock chart. This is compared to the slopes found on a momentum indicator chart such as the moving average convergence/divergence (MACD) chart.[2] The best way to play the dark cloud cover scenario is to short it or buy puts.

NARROWING YOUR SEARCH EVEN FURTHER

Most people simply don't have the time or inclination to sift through tens of thousands of stocks looking for doji formations. There's a much easier and efficient way to search through all those stocks to find the perfect doji candidates: the put/call ratio.

Doji Master preys on fear simply by using the PCR. When fear-motivated investors get scared, they run away like frightened schoolgirls, and once you know this you can simply move in and pick up the profits they miss. Nothing spawns fear like a falling stock. And when a stock falls for days on end, watch out. People start panicking and selling. That's when our mouths start to water.

While many traders are educated in the flexibility that options trading offers, most are not aware that options can also be used as predictive tools. You see, one of the most reliable types of indicators of market and equity direction is the sentiment indicator, especially when the indicators are contrarian, or going against the favored grain. The put/call ratio is exceptionally reliable in gauging the overall fear or confidence levels among traders.

Too many put buyers signals a near-term bottom, while too many call buyers indicates a near-term top. When the market gets overly bullish or bearish, market conditions are ripe for reversals. Unfortunately, most of the nervous herd is too caught up in the feeding frenzy to notice.

Bottom line: *Fear of losses sends your average investor into a tailspin.* When that happens, those same investors start trading solely on emotion, not logic, creating a profit opportunity. In fact, according to Zeal Intelligence, "The thundering herd is always wrong, as most people are blinded and enslaved by their own emotions." Eventually that fear subsides. At the point where fear is at its pinnacle, the stock is oversold. That's where dojis are found hiding at the bottom of trends, waving that it's time for a reversal.

Still, how do you know when the stock is at rock bottom and a turnaround is likely? When you find a stock with a PCR above 1, pull up a three- to six-month candlestick chart. If any of the doji candlestick formations are sitting at the bottom of a recent downtrend, buy.

THE SYSTEM IN A NUTSHELL

While this system is based on complex technical indicators, it boils down to a simple three-step process.

1. First, we look for a stock with a high PCR—the higher the better. This indicates that the stock is oversold and a reversal is imminent.
2. Second, we check to see if the falling stock has a doji. The doji indicates that the stock has hit bottom and is poised for a breakout.
3. Third, buy the stock, or calls on the stock, and then wait for the herd to rush in on oversold conditions and buy, buy, buy.

When that happens, the stock moves up, handing us quick, fat profits. We usually take profits in one to two weeks' time.

As a system for identifying short-term opportunities, nothing—not even our PCR trading secret—is perfect. But it does improve your odds and your advantage. And in the market, that is usually enough.

Useful Information

For recent applications of the Doji Master system, check www.dojimaster .com.

CHAPTER 12

TRADING SECRET NUMBER SIX: ACTIONPOINT TRADING

Investing in IPOs

Economists can no longer assert that a particular event is a bubble; instead, we must provide empirical evidence that the event conforms to a strict, standard definition of a bubble.

—Robert P. Flood and Peter M. Graber,
"Market Fundamentals versus Price-Level Bubbles:
The First Tests," in *Speculative Bubbles,*
***Speculative Attacks, and Policy Switching* (1997)**

Unless you lived on Mars for the past few years of the late and lamented Internet bubble market, you know that some of the biggest gainers in the market were made in initial public offerings (IPOs).

Back then, in the late 1990s, it was quite common for hot IPOs to see 100 percent plus gains on their first trading day. You may recall that these big gains always made the headlines in the *Wall Street Journal* and other financial publications.

Of course, the bear market that started during the presidential campaign of 2000 took some luster off IPOs. Not only did venture capital dry up as the autocatalytic process of the technology bubble ran out of its main catalyst—cash. The unappetizing and corrupt collusion among underwriters, investment bankers, and other financial institutions turned IPOs from a booming subsection of the markets into a veritable graveyard: Too many small investors had bought the hype and tried to pile in the early trading days of a new issue, and got burned when the buzz subsided and cut prices down.

These days, however, it looks like IPOs are coming back into their own. And with them an old idea returns as well: If you could look into a crystal ball and know which of today's IPO stocks were going to be tomorrow's Netscape and Microsoft stocks, you would be set for life.

Unfortunately, even if you knew which new IPO stocks were going to be hot on their first day of trading, the average investor will have problems purchasing the stock at the offer: Unless you are a big investor, you probably will only manage to buy very little, if any, of those companies' stocks at the initial offering price. And the worst mistake you can make in the IPO market is to buy these stocks on the first day after the feeding frenzy has already started (i.e., after the stock begins to trade and sees furious first-day price increases).

AVOIDING THE SUCKER BET

But how does the average investor get in on the fantastic profits that hot IPOs can offer? By knowing not only which IPOs are going to be big winners on their first day of trading (which is a pretty good trick all by itself) but also which IPOs will continue their winning ways and the time to buy in (and you need to remember this term) the aftermarket.

The aftermarket is the general market where an IPO trades following the initial offer. Any investor can buy these hot IPO stocks through their broker in the aftermarket. Of course, when over 600 new IPOs traded each year in the late 1990s (the vast majority of them big losers) with information on upcoming IPOs being about as scarce as ice water in Hades, the odds were (and still are) heavily weighted against the average investor being anything but chum for the predators in the market.

As you may have guessed, there's always a way. There are several extremely effective indicators that you can use to help weed out the weak IPO stocks from the strong, viable ones.

Our staff analysts use these very factors as part of their daily analysis of each and every newly filed small-cap IPO stock. Our chief IPO specialist, Siu-Yee Ng, created the following evaluative grid to separate the wheat from the chaff.

OUR OWN SECRET RECIPE

We like to zero in on a short list of key ingredients for success:

Management needs to be present that has extensive specific industry-related experience, preferably with successful large companies. Their tenure with the company is very important—you don't want management to serve only as hired guns or used for window dressing. Watch out for management teams consisting of investment bankers and professionals. They usually spell trouble.

The *board of directors* should be dominated by members not affiliated with the company in any other capacity, and who provide specific industry-related experience. This type of director can often set the course for a good company to become a great company. Again, be on the lookout to avoid a predominance of investment bankers and professionals with little industry experience.

Strategic niches should be well defined. It is best if the company fills a need that exists but is poorly served. A good candidate should have already proven through revenue growth that there is a demand in the area. Be on the lookout to avoid black-box technology that isn't patent-protected or explained in detail. Companies that rely heavily on proprietary formulas as their sole or primary rights and so have to prove the demand via sustained revenue growth are high risks.

Marketing channels are also essential. These are well-defined, proven revenue generators. Channels can take several forms such as direct sales, a system of independent sale representatives, and established contractual relationships with distributors. Even when a company has the best products or services ever, if it can't move them to market, then it can't pay the rent.

Proceeds use is also a key teller of tales. Traditionally, companies went public because they were growing. Today, they go public for all sorts of other reasons: paying down debt, cashing out major shareholders, being spun off from larger companies, and on and on. Although in certain circumstances any reason for going public may be justified, the best indicator of a possible winner is growth.

There are, of course, many, many other factors that we look for in each company we review. The only way to get to know any of these companies is to read all the filings; having a wealth of experience in the IPO market wouldn't hurt, either.

Driven by their primary emotion of greed, many herd-mentality investors have a tendency to scurry trying to get in on the next big deal, only to find out that the "next big deal" was the one they just got out of. But making consistent profits in the stock markets means being in on the right stocks at the right time and having the nerve to stick with an investment in a solidly fundamental company with a good market niche until it reaches its potential. Now, this may sound easy.

At the core, profitable IPO stocks are true growth stocks. They are value investments rather than quick in-and-out trades. The primary (but not always the only) reason companies begin to sell their stock to the public is because they are growing faster than their cash flow and credit facilities can handle. They turn to the public capital sector for help. After all, it is the cheapest source of capital available.

Historically, fundamentally sound IPO companies with strong management, that have expressed a clear operating plan from which they do not veer ultimately, return their initial investors 100 percent, 200 percent, 300 percent, and more over the first two to four years after they go public.

PICKING TOP IPOs OF THE COMING STOCK MARKET BOOM

The most important thing about IPOs is knowing when to take your profits by selling at the right time. There are certain signals you should watch for that tell you that it's time to take profits and look for the next big gainer. Following are several of the most significant signals that are peculiar to IPOs.

Round Trippers

I'm sure you have seen the headlines announcing 50 percent, 100 percent, and higher first-day gains on the hottest new IPO company. And you may have wondered why. It's quite simple. IPOs are unknown quantities. When public companies first begin trading, they often don't follow normal market rules. Hype about a specific market segment, or new technologies they have developed, often translate into quick and sharp increases in the initial prices of many IPO companies.

Unfortunately for average investors holding these companies, once the hype has died down and they have to start playing by the normal market rules, they normally can't sustain lofty price growth and they fall back to close to their original offering prices—hence the term *Round Trippers*. This is a very common occurrence, and you can spot these opportunities almost from day one. Buy on the way up, and when you spot the hype cooling take your profits. And don't forget, once the round trip is complete, you should consider buying back into these companies and letting them regain their prices as they grow, which is also another common occurrence.

Early Management Changes

One of the surest signs than an IPO company may be in trouble early on is a change in management. If the management team that made the company successful in the first place changes shortly after the company goes public—and this was not disclosed as a planned event in the company's prospectus—this usually marks danger. It tells us that there may be internal problems with the company that won't come to light until much later. In such cases we strongly suggest that it would be better to be safe than sorry. Exit and take profits while you can.

Sharp and Steady Changes in Cash Position with Slow Operating Results

This is a little tricky to monitor, but it can be a sure sign of coming problems with an IPO company. After you have taken into account the stated uses of proceeds from the prospectus (e.g., debt repayment, equipment purchases, etc.), watch to see how fast the company spends the remaining funds compared to its operating achievements.

This works well only when the majority of the remaining proceeds are used for working capital. A good rule of thumb is that proceeds should last the company about 24 months. If the company is spending in excess of 12.5 percent per month of the remaining proceeds raised, it may have to go back to the market sooner than expected. This usually results in decreased prices when the secondary offering is announced. You are better off exiting the stock early and waiting for the secondary offering to dilute the price. That's a good time to get back in.

Changes in Stated Goals

What we often see with IPOs that ultimately fail is an early change in the company's goals, without disclosure in advance in the prospectus. This signals a lack of direction and focus on the part of the management team and usually spells big trouble for investors. You usually have to look pretty closely at the press releases and quarterly reports to pick up these changes because they can be subtle. Favorite changes include the addition of an acquisition strategy that did not previously exist, entry into a new market segment that was not previously contemplated, or the abandonment of a particular part of the company's business.

Analyst Coverage

Most IPOs have only one or two analysts following their progress from the beginning, and at least one of these works for the lead underwriter of the offering. However, most *successful* IPOs will begin to pick up additional analysts within the first six to 12 months after going public. This is a great sign of wider interest in the stock, usually the result of rising stock prices. By the same token, the absence of additional analysts in this time frame may serve as a red flag. Without that added interest, the IPO may be running out of steam.

PROFIT ZONES

The IPO market offers the potential for both short- and long-term returns. But getting the shares at the cheapest price possible is a challenge, especially for the small investor. In the past, shares were allocated mostly to institutions and to the preferred investors. For the most part, this is still true, although changes may be on the horizon. The Google IPO broke that mold, indicating a trend toward the democratization of finance. This may signal the beginning of the end for a jealously guarded IPO market as well.

But change is slow, so you need to be patient. You can participate in the IPO market by finding the most convenient channels. First, select a broker who actively participates in the IPO market and who understands how it works. Your account has to be active. Some of the leading investment bankers involved in underwriting IPOs are Goldman Sachs, J.P. Morgan, Credit Suisse First Boston, Lehman Brothers, Merrill Lynch & Co., and Bear, Stearns & Co. These are the big players and, of course, all full-service brokerages, meaning you'll have to pay full retail commission.

Or you can choose to start an account with a regional underwriter like Jefferies Group, Inc., Kashner Davidson Securities Corp., Dain Rauscher Corp., Ferris Baker Watts, Inc., or William Blair.

Some investors have chosen to try using the online broker option. Charles Schwab, Fidelity, E*Trade, DLJ Direct, and Wit Capital are prominent in this group. But Internet brokerages in the past received preciously few shares to allocate, and then allocated these shares to investors with active accounts. If you shop for the cheapest online trading company, you will also find that they limit their activities to only the most plain-vanilla trading services. IPOs probably won't be among the trades offered by Ameritrade, Scottrade, and other low-cost discounters.

Keep in mind that sometimes even institutions do not receive all the shares requested. Accordingly, some institutions themselves will have to buy in the aftermarket. Indeed, 1999 was a record-breaking year for aftermarket gains. The average gain per issue for 1999 was 199 percent. So for those investors who missed out on the IPOs, the aftermarket offers another opportunity for huge profits.

Unknown to most investors, there are two profit zones in 78 percent of all IPOs. Play these profit zones correctly, and retail investors like you can reap huge gains.

There is a consistent pattern that new issues follow during the five years after their debut that we tracked during the heyday of the IPO market. We call this system ActionPoint Trader.

In the first six months of an IPO's life, insiders are restricted from dumping their shares. And during this time, hedge fund managers and brokers do all they can to pump up the stock price. This period is the profit zone when ActionPoint Traders can move in and out quickly and turn a quick profit.

A second profit zone is created by IPOs that debuted two to four years prior. They have undergone the typical new-issue hype-inspired appreciation as well as the inevitable drops created by the expiration of the lockup period and the corporate struggles to determine whether the new kid on the block is going to flourish or wither away. After two to four years, most of the flimsy, fly-by-night IPOs have been shaken out by the natural selection of market forces. Investment bankers are no longer interested. What remains are the companies with a real future and an additional margin of safety.

But no matter what stage these companies are in, timely information is key to the success of any investment. We look at the short-term six-month period after the IPO and the first five years of its public trading. We're interested in creating consistency in the methods used to beat the IPO averages. Going the traditional route is high-risk. So our ActionPoint system is not for the impatient (the pigs) or the thin-skinned (the chickens). But it does work well for the pragmatic investor who likes beating the odds, and who enjoys creating and then taking profits.

CHAPTER 13

TRADING SECRET NUMBER SEVEN: PROFITS FROM THE RED ZONES

Paying attention to the float, the hype, and when the insiders are going to be pumping or squeezing the share price, you can make a lot of money.

—Christian DeHaemer, IPO expert (1999)

Imagine, for just a moment, that there was a *hidden* stock market, a market within the market, where returns were two to five times greater than the gains you make on your average stock position. Now imagine that the shares in this hidden market could be traded by only a select group of large institutional money managers, plus maybe a handful of extremely wealthy individual investors, and that the brokers were deliberately selling all the shares of these fantastic high-profit stocks to their private clientele, making it nearly impossible for average investors like you and me to get in on these trades. Would you feel cheated? I sure do!

But if you think that this sounds far-fetched, like your run-of-the-mill conspiracy theory against the little guy, think again.

This is one of the vestiges of the old markets, those we knew prior to the democratization of the markets that started globally in the 1960s. For decades, only the wealthiest investors have had easy access to a certain profit-rich subsection of the total stock market, one that, as a general rule, performs two to five times better than the market as a whole. The major underwriters and their private clients winked, nodded, and smiled as shares of these high-profit stocks—many of which turned out to be the next Microsoft, Xerox, AT&T, or IBM— were funneled into the accounts of this exclusive group of investors at prices far below their real market value.

These companies—and the returns on investment their stocks generated—include: Microchip Technology, up 605 percent; Hollywood Entertainment, up 340 percent; Wholesome and Hearty, up 600 percent; Sitel, up 609 percent; Adtran, up 311 percent; American Power Conversion (if you have an uninterruptible power supply for your PC, chances are this company made it), up a whopping 7,300 percent; and dozens more.

What is the hidden market that so dramatically outperforms the stock market as a whole? Actually, we've already introduced you to the nuts and bolts of it in the preceding chapter: it's initial public offerings (IPOs). In this chapter, I am going to tell you about a little-known but advanced trading system that combines the pace of momentum trading with the almost academic phase analysis explained in Chapter 10 on extreme volatility. We call it the Red Zones.

With the Red Zones, you can earn double- and triple-digit profits in a relatively short time (from months to a year or two) by buying and selling shares of relatively new initial public offerings at specific intervals.

THE ABCs OF IPOs

You already know that in a primary market IPO, a company decides to go public. Usually, the company needs capital to fund operations, growth, and expansion. To raise money, the company sells shares.

If an IPO consists of 10 million shares for sale and they are all sold at the opening price of $10, the company has raised $100 million in new capital. It then has acquired market capitalization (market cap) of

$100 million. In other words, the market values this company at $100 million in equity.

The company whose shares are for sale is called the "issuer," and the stock is referred to as the "issue." The investment banking firm (or investment banking division of the brokerage house) that helps facilitate the IPO is called the "underwriter."

Top underwriters include well-known institutions like Goldman Sachs, Merrill Lynch, and Morgan Stanley. They are required to register all new IPOs with the Securities and Exchange Commission (SEC). Imagine how much money you could make if you knew which way share prices of a new issue were going to go—right out of the gate! For example, WebMethods moved up 506 percent in one day (our teams knew it, and we recommended it). And if you had known ahead of time that Valinux Systems, Inc. was going to drop like a spent booster rocket, you could have made 43 percent in less than four months by selling it short. Or imagine how much money you could have made if you had known ahead of time that short sellers were going to drive Vitria Technologies down from $100 to $22 a share, and that it was going to climb back to $70 a share right afterward. You could have made a very tidy 168 percent profit in less than four months by playing both sides of the move!

What if you could pick just the right time to buy a new issue? What if you knew just when the price was going to reach its lowest point, right before the stock went on a two-year rocket ride? You could easily make 24 times your money, or more. In other words, you could turn a $5,000 investment into $120,000 in about two years.

It's a given: the Wall Street insiders have some dirty little secrets. They use this inside information to manipulate stock prices. And what's more, these market manipulations and insider moves have nothing to do with the overall market or the economy. The insiders make money on their moves in any market and in any economic climate. A wise old card sharp once said that when you sit down to play poker, take a look around the table. If you don't know who the sucker is, then it's you. The same rule works on Wall Street. Here's how you can beat them at their own game.

NEVER PLAY CARDS WITH A MAN NAMED DOC

The market is a lot like a game of poker. But when you consider how this small piece works, it's as though you are sitting at a table after the other players already have all the aces in their hands. You see, when a new stock is issued, only a certain percentage of the company's stock is offered to the public for sale. This is what is known as the "float." The rest, often as much as 90 percent of shares, is held by underwriters, company officers, and other insiders. Furthermore, most of that other 10 percent that is issued to the public goes to favorites of the brokerage as a reward for their business.

John Q. Investor, hoping to get in on the action of new shares, is usually only getting a shot at a small percentage of the game. The rest is carefully controlled and manipulated for the best possible gains. Accordingly, there's a rush for shares by new investors at a certain point (news is released at certain strategic intervals); short sellers squeeze the prices at certain points (insiders sell their shares); and company management changes at certain points. All of these events influence share prices. And it often matters very little what the fundamentals of the company are. What matters more is when large amounts of insiders' shares are dumped, when news is announced, and so on. All these occurrences are controlled by the insiders, and in compliance with SEC rules. It's a sucker's game if you don't know how the deck is stacked. But if you do, you're in with the insiders— smack-dab in the middle!

Back in the late 1990s, RedZone Group publisher Christian DeHaemer created a service known as The Hammer that targeted the soft underbelly of Wall Street. It was during his research into what goes on behind the scenes on Wall Street that he began to put together the secrets of the Red Zones. He started to notice a pattern in the price moves of new issues. Many issues followed similar price patterns, and a few were different. He knew that if he could crack the secret of why some behaved differently from others, he'd be on the track of a real inside system for generating massive profits.

The thing he noticed was that average investors were getting in at all the wrong times. They seemed to be buying just when they should have been selling, and selling just when they should have been buying. You see, the insiders know that it's fairly easy to predict which way the prices are going to go, and they make their moves accordingly.

There are three Red Zones you need to know about to make a lot of money with our system.

RED ZONE I: THE WIDOWMAKER

The first period after a new issue comes out is usually characterized by massive price swings in the share price. We call these swings widowmaker momentum plays, because there are certain factors that cause the price to move either up or down—or one and then the other—very rapidly. This phase can make your fortune in an afternoon, or leave you bankrupt and crying in your beer. (I remember back in November 1998, when Theglob.com IPO'd. Shares debuted at $9 and ended up trading as high as $97 before closing at $63.50 on the first day of trading. But within a year, the stock had fallen to below its IPO price. Wealth moves very quickly, and you must possess iron discipline and be able to make snap decisions. And you also need to have superior information.)

The Widowmaker is the most speculative of the Red Zones. Its inherent price moves are determined by the number of shares issued and the demand level. Both these factors are controlled. The underwriters—along with the company insiders—determine the number of shares issued and the supply. And the Wall Street hype (delivered by the underwriters, media, analysts, and the company) determines the demand.

Understand this, and you can understand which way the price will move. For instance, take a look at what happened with Interwoven, Inc. We knew there was a huge demand for Interwoven and that the float was small compared to the expected demand. We knew what was going to happen, and locked in profits of 515 percent in a year. (It was really a no-brainer.) Now that's some serious money. In other cases the price can plunge just as quickly, and you can make money off the drop, too.

RED ZONE II: THE SHARE DUMP

The second phase in the Red Zones of profits is created by the law. This little secret behind the insiders' manipulations is called the lockup effect.

It's simple: When a company goes public, only a percentage of the company's stock is offered for sale. We know already that this is called the float. The rest, often up to 90 percent of all shares, is held and owned by underwriters, company officers, and other insiders. By contractual obligation, insiders and underwriters can't sell their stock for a period of time, usually between six months and a year from the date of the IPO. This is commonly referred to as the lockup period, and it's set up to ensure that insiders can't profit from the early trading frenzy generated by an IPO. It provides trading stability, because insiders cannot simply dump their shares.

But once the lockup period ends, anything goes. Insiders may have been standing on the sidelines watching people get filthy rich without them being able to turn a dime. To make up for lost time, insiders in many cases flood the market with shares in an attempt to cash in.

We've already seen how they manipulate prices by deciding when to withhold news and when to release it. The time before the lockup period expires is the next profit zone. And if you know what to look for, you'll see that certain things happen to the share price right on schedule.

First of all, in the Share Dump (or the Unlock Zone), the stock starts to drop in price about two months before the lockup period ends. What's happening is that short sellers are making their move to cash in on the inevitable price drop that occurs when insiders begin dumping their unlocked shares.

Poor John Q. Investor, though, doesn't know what's happening. He has bought this stock on the hype of the underwriters and the company's media blitz, and now his share prices are dropping like cement ducks in a pond. And he thought he was going to get rich on this one. If you know what's going on, though, you can cash in on this drop—because it has nothing to do with the company itself. What it boils down to is legal stock manipulation orchestrated by smart insiders playing the market. Simply by having that same information, you can join them in their victory lap and take a lot of money to the bank. It's a beautiful thing if you understand how it works.

We've dubbed this phenomenon The "Flying V" lockup effect because if you look at a new company's chart for the two months prior to the end of the lockup period and the two months afterward, the price line resembles a "V." If you know when the price will fall, you can short with the short sellers.

But insiders want to sell their shares for the best possible price. Therefore when they are allowed to sell, usually six months after the IPO, the underwriters start putting out "buy" recommendations. The company insiders feed positive press releases to the media. And because it's a new public company without a lot of history, the mainstream financial media generally gives it glowing reviews.

This will create demand. The market will absorb the dumped shares, and the price will rise again, so you can profit on the long side, too. It's like a license to print money. (We thought this was such an important indicator that we dedicate a separate chapter to it.) You can find specific company lockup dates at this web site: http://ipoportal.edgar-online.com/ipo/home.asp.

RED ZONE III: THE VALUE ZONE

Now we come to the point where all logical investors should want to get in.

Unfortunately, by this time most of them feel like they've been taken for a ride, and won't get back in until late in the game. You see, about 18 to 24 months after the new shares are listed, the stock begins its first real climb. It's now a true value play.

For one thing, the underwriters have sold off all their shares. And it takes time for the company to evolve. By this time, start-up management has usually been replaced by mature corporate officers. And over six to eight quarters the company has shown whether it can produce. In other words, by now we know if it's a stable, working company with a track record and whether it's at the best possible price for the long haul, or if it is dead in the water and waiting to be gobbled up by some other outfit. Now is the time to step in and buy for a holding period of anywhere from a year to two years or more. And the profits can be staggering.

To turn these phases into profits as IPOs regain most of their luster in the last phase of the big bubble market that is lying ahead, you need to keep your eye on the news—positive and negative— about each IPO as it travels through the various Red Zones. (See Table 13.1.) Which company will be the next Widowmaker, which

TABLE 13.1   INITIAL PUBLIC OFFERING AND RED ZONES

TIMING	ZONE	COMMENT
IPO launch date	Red Zone I: Widowmaker	Demand generated by hype. Supply of shares (float) controlled by issuer. Typically, only 10% of IPO shares are available to retail investors. Strong demand + limited supply = drives up price.
45 days after IPO	Red Zone I: Widowmaker	SEC permits release of mergers, acquisitions, and other positive news. Good news drives price higher.
4 months after IPO	Red Zone II: Pre–Share Dump hype	SEC forbids insiders from dumping shares for six months after IPO. Short sellers begin shorting stock at four months post-IPO in anticipation of share dump to occur at six months.
6 months after IPO	Red Zone II: Share Dump	SEC permits insiders to dump shares. Sell-off drives prices lower.
18–24 months after IPO	Red Zone III: Value Zone	Company has posted 6 to 12 consecutive quarters of earnings. Business proven to be viable. Becomes a value play.

company is about to become a medium-term value play, and which company appears to be set for shorting? What cyclical trends will be coming to bear on each market sector? Again, you'll be essentially playing the insiders' game: Remember, if you have no idea about the timing of these phases, then you're like the poor rube at the card table with Doc. But by paying attention to the float, the hype, and when the insiders are going to be pumping or squeezing the share price, you can make a lot of money.

Useful Information

The RedZone Group team, managed by Christian DeHaemer, Siu-Yee Ng, and Ian Cooper, publishes daily market analysis in their free daily e-letter *American Capitalist*, which you can order at www.dynamicmarketreport.com/american capitalist.

More information on the RedZone Group services can be found at www.redzoneprofits.com and at www.redzonevip.com.

CHAPTER 14

TRADING SECRET NUMBER EIGHT: PLAYING THE "FLYING V" LOCKUP INDICATOR

Competition never lets entrepreneurs rest on their laurels.
—**Thomas J. DiLorenzo,** *How Capitalism Saved America* **(2004)**

Of the three Red Zones, Phase II, the lockup phase, has the most potential for short-term traders. In most cases, the pattern allows you to profit on the upside *and* on the downside.

Not every company qualifies for such a trade, however. Every company we look at is measured and assigned a specific weighted score, based on a formula using nine different criteria to determine if a company is a prime candidate for the "Flying V" lockup effect.

These criteria consist of float, average daily volume, number of shares released, inherent value, revenue growth, insider selling, media buzz, stature of the underwriter, and chart (price point and support levels).

If a company scores more than 100 points (the minimum we've determined to make it an ideal candidate), that's a sign under our system to make a move. And if it scores between 150 and 200, well, let's just say that's when we get really excited because, based on past experiences, that company is going to make us a lot of money, perhaps 100 percent or better within a four-month trading window.

Without fail, companies that meet the "Flying V" criteria fall dramatically in price in the two months prior to the lockup expiration, and recover substantially in the two months that follow. When this happens the chart looks like a "V."

Here's the rub: To successfully short a stock, you must borrow shares of a company at a high price, and buy them later in the open market at a lower price. You then repay the borrowed shares and pocket the difference. The difference between what you paid for your shares, say $30, and the price they were when you borrowed them, say $90, is your profit—in this case 66 percent.

The risk inherent in shorting a stock is that the downside is unlimited and the upside can't be more than 100 percent.[1] If a trade goes against you, and the shares you borrowed at $90 go to $1,000, you still must buy that stock at market price, meaning you lose $910 per share. And since there is no mathematical limit to how high a share price can go, your potential loss is limitless.

On the flip side, your potential gain is only 100 percent. If a stock goes from $90 to $0—that is, it goes bankrupt—you've made 100 percent gains on your investment. Since a share price cannot drop below $0, that's the best possible gain on a short play.

The risks of short selling are manageable by adhering to stop-losses and paying attention to the supply and demand factors that make up the "Flying V." In fact, when done right, you'll have the added benefit of making money while the rest of the world is losing their shirts.

Eventually you need to return the shares, or cover your short position. If the stock drops, you can buy back the borrowed shares at a cheaper price, netting the difference in profit. But if, instead of falling, the stock actually climbs after you short it, you will eventually be forced to close out the position at a loss, or at least put some money into the account to satisfy the margin call and to keep your position going.

Let's say, for instance, that you short 500 shares of a stock at $10. Under current regulations, you have to put 50 percent of the market value of the stock and the proceeds of the short sale into a margin account to hold a short position. You get $5,000 for shorting the stock and are required to add $2,500, leaving you with $7,500 in equity. If the stock rallies to $15, the market value of the shorted stock climbs to $7,500, wiping out your entire account. At this point, you have to meet a margin call (demand for additional equity from your broker), or simply eat the loss.

Short selling is a little more complicated than buying or going long a stock. It requires more preparation, and a very precise use of limits. Short selling is an alien concept to most investors. Many have been brainwashed to believe that share prices can move in only one direction: up. They also believe that if stock prices come down, they will always go back up.

Even a brokerage firm that will gladly sell you shares of a company that it's touting will take advantage of Wall Street's dirty little secret. It will short sell many of the shares its customers are buying, knowing that the stock will quiet down at some point and it can buy them back at a lower price. Regardless of which company's shares you buy, the brokerage is sure that it'll be able to buy them back on the market for less—maybe even from you, as the price will eventually fall before recovering again. This can also be quite profitable for "Flying V" lockup traders.

While short selling remains a novelty for most investors, it is also one of the most profitable ways to invest. Not only is it a numbers game, it's a waiting game. When the buyers no longer match the sellers, the stock will go down. It is during this lull in the action that a short seller pounces on amazing opportunities and socks away some meaty profits. Short selling is not for everyone. Most would-be short sellers jump off the boat the minute they have placed the order and the stock ticks up. They can't take the heat or the mind-bending pressures of betting against a company, especially one that everyone else is touting.

Here are some keys for survival with "Flying V" scenarios. First, never try to short a stock on a shoestring budget. Let's say you have $10,000 to risk. You could short 133 shares at $75. Borrowing the shares from your broker, you need to put at least 50 percent of the $9,975 down to hold the short.

Now, if the stock goes up to $150, you'll be completely wiped out. Sound crazy? Plenty of investors tried to short Netscape at a high of $74 on the day of its IPO. The company had never earned a dime, was hyped by the mass media, and had an IPO price of $28—the perfect short-sell candidate. The problem came when Netscape skyrocketed to $175, wiping out all of the short sellers.

If the stock had fallen to $25 as they had expected, they would have made almost $50 per share, or $6,650—a 66 percent profit.

The aggressive types among the short sellers could have shorted 226 shares on a 50 percent margin. The shares borrowed initially had a market value of $19,950. If everything turned out as expected, the stock would fall to $25, and you'd be out buying a new hot tub. However, as the stock approached $112.50, you would get a margin call. Now, if the stock ran up to $150 before your broker liquidated the position, you would be liable for a $9,975 loss. And, if you couldn't come up with the cash, your broker could come and repossess your home, your car, your pet goldfish, and anything else not nailed down. Well, not really, but your broker can put a lien on your personal property. If you aren't well versed in the art of short selling a stock, things can get pretty ugly.

A more recent example is Google. This company went public in August 2004 at $96. Many people shorted this dot-com leftover stock with a price-to-earnings ratio over 100. The short sellers got burned as the stock doubled in the next few months. But there are ways to protect yourself.

"FLYING V" LIMITS THE SHORT RISK

There is no reward without a corresponding risk. But because of the nature of the insider lockup expiration, you have an edge that can beat the market. It's simple. As we stated before, when any company goes public, only a percentage of its stock goes on sale. This is called the float.

The rest of the shares, often up to 90 percent, are held by insiders. And, by law, insiders cannot sell their stock for six months to a year from the date of the IPO. This is called the lockup period. It ensures trading stability, because insiders can't simply dump their shares the day of the IPO.

About 60 days after the IPO the quiet period ends. When this happens, underwriters and PR flacks release three months of pent-up good news wrapped in hype that they've been saving up for the occasion. In a bullish market, this will send the share price up (remember, the float is thin; increased demand + limited supply = upward price movement).

It is after this rally that you want to short the company. About two months before the lockup period ends, the share price will start to drop as investors anticipate the coming oversupply of stock. No one wants to buy a stock that will increase in supply without a corresponding increase in demand (stable demand + increase in supply = falling price movement).

Short selling can be a dangerous game. If a normal stock (non-lockup) seems overvalued and ripe to be shorted, you should think twice before calling your broker. You don't want to get caught in a short squeeze. The traditional problem with shorting a stock that has a small float and a large number of shorts is that all of the shorts eventually have to be covered. In the case of a ridiculously overvalued stock, the total short position could come close to 50 percent of the entire float. That means that if the stock moves up on news or some other catalyst, the shorts might decide to cut their losses.

All of the shorts covering (buying back shares to repay the ones they borrowed) at the same time exaggerates the upward movement. Momentum traders see this happening and jump on board. This sends the stock even higher.

In other words, in a thin market, many people short naked, which means that you have to short without actually borrowing the stock certificate. The lenders can force the shorts to produce stock certificates. Once liquidity dries up, the professional traders step in and jack up the price. Since the shorts are margined, they will tend to panic and buy back the stock if it begins to skyrocket. The naked shorts are forced to pay high prices to buy back the stock. The momentum players see what's happening and buy into the volume spike; this pushes the share price even higher as more demand chases a limited number of shares.

After a time, the price climaxes and falls off. All of the shorts have covered, and there are no more momentum players willing to buy. When you know that the float is going to increase dramatically, this decreases the risk of a short squeeze and increases the chance that a short will be successful. This is one of the fundamental things we look for in candidates for a "Flying V" lockup trader.

In November 1999, Telecorp PCS (TLCP:Nasdaq) went public. It steadily rose from $33 per share on opening day to over $50 in the four months after its first day of trading. Insiders knew that 3.7 million shares (43 percent of the company's float) would be unlocked in May. So in early April, the short selling began. Two months later, the stock price fell to an all-time low of $26 per share. Now, had you shorted stock when the selling began, you would have made a 49 percent profit.

Not too shabby. Then, if you had gone long on the stock in the days and weeks following the lockup period, you could have sat back with a fat Cuban cigar and watched the price climb back up to $40 within 60 days, for another gain of 60 percent. Or, put another way, you made $5,450 on $5,000 risked—$2,450 on your short position and $3,000 on your long position.

The lesson learned? Always look for an opportunity to make a nice profit playing the IPO companies four to eight months down the road.

Take the Internet marketing company NetCreations Inc. (NTCR:Nasdaq), which launched its IPO in November 1999 and was sailing along at $60 per share. Without the "Flying V" approach, the average investor in NetCreations didn't know that 17.7 million shares were set to be unlocked on May 10, 2000, six months to the day from its IPO, thereby increasing the company's stock float by a mind-blowing 354 percent. (See Figure 14.1.)

We, as well as the insiders, knew that this situation would occur. The investors knew that flooding the market with that many shares in such a short period of time would have a devastating effect on the price. They did what you would have done had you known in advance that the stock price was about to fall. They began shorting the stock in early March. NetCreations' stock price fell from $62 per share to $1.81 on May 10, 2000—the day the lockup period expired—and finally settled at a low of $22. Once the market was able to absorb the flood of shares, NetCreations' stock price started to rise again, peaking in late June at $60. Had you known what insiders knew about this stock, you could have shorted NetCreations along-

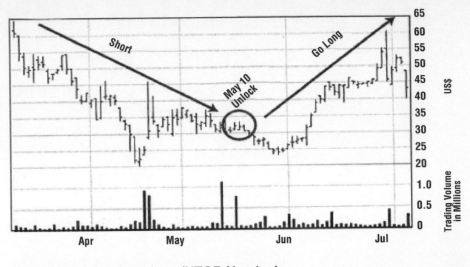

Figure 14.1 NetCreations (NTCR:Nasdaq)

side them two months before the lockup period ended and made a quick 61 percent gain. Then, you could have bought the stock in the days following the end of the lockup period and made another 78.8 percent profit on a long position.

In other words, you make money watching the stock plummet, and more money as it rises again. You could have taken a $5,000 short position and made more than $3,000 in profits in just 60 days. Then you could have taken a $5,000 long position and made another $3,590 in a little over a month. To look at this another way, that's a profit of $6,590 in less than five months on just $5,000 risked.

What happened to NetCreations was not a rare event. Not by a long shot. During the last IPO boom, there were months when over 1.8 billion shares from more than 45 different companies were being unlocked.

Figure 14.2 shows what happened with a company called Symyx Technologies (SMMX:Nasdaq). In the four-month period after the company's IPO, the stock price began climbing from $22 to $73 per share. Then, like clockwork, insiders went to work two months before the lockup was set to end. Symyx's stock tumbled from $73 back down to $22, which would have given you a 70 percent gain on a short position.

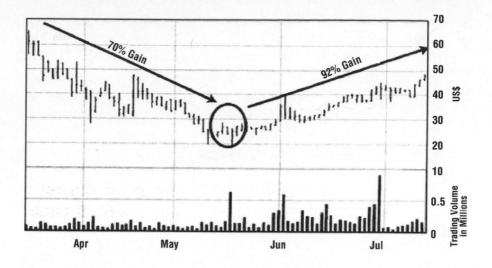

Figure 14.2 Symyx Technologies (SMMX:Nasdaq)

Then, right on schedule, the shares bounced back after the lockup period ended to a high of $51. Assuming you bought when the stock started its comeback and sold two months after the lockup period ended, your profits on the long side would have been 92 percent. In other words, on $5,000 risked, you could have enjoyed a $8,100 total trade profit.

ANOTHER 337 PERCENT PROFIT

Take a look at Quintus Corporation (QNTS:Nasdaq). (See Figure 14.3.) This company was flying high out of the IPO gates, trading as high as $54 per share, until two months before its lockup period was to expire. In that time frame, the company's stock took a nosedive to below $10. A short position would have netted you a nice 77 percent gain.

Sure enough, within two months the stock popped back up to $26 per share. Had you bought following the lockup expiration period, you would have scored a 260 percent profit on the long play.

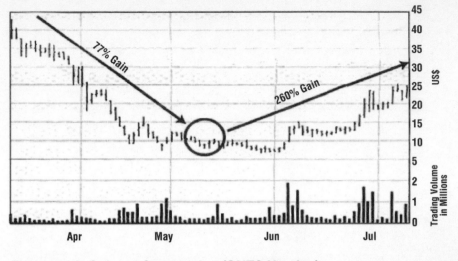

Figure 14.3 Quintus Corporation (QNTS:Nasdaq)

Your profit on this trade, with $5,000 risked on each play, would have netted you $3,850 on the short and $13,000 on the long—a total of $16,580.

Another example: Sage Inc. (SAGI:Nasdaq) went from $26.75 two months prior to lockup expiration to $13.88, and then ran back up to $17.13 a short time later. Total profits in four months on $5,000 risked—a 361 percent gain.

A few days after the insiders are allowed to sell, many do. In general, these are people who have been investing time, money, and tears to get a new company off the ground. Many will see this as their opportunity to cash in. Even if the stock is now trading below the IPO price, the insiders didn't pay anything for it—it's all free money to them.

What everything boils down to is legal stock manipulation orchestrated by insiders playing their cards right on Wall Street. Because we now have an insider's view, we'll be there to cash in on some impressive profits.

There are four fundamental rules for "Flying V" lockup trades:

1. *Never chase a stock.* If you chase a stock above our buy limit, you're betraying yourself and other traders.

2. *Cut your losses.* Always use stop-losses. If you have a system for cutting losses, you'll win over time even if not every trade is profitable. We pick stops that are as close as possible to the market, but under levels that will attract buyers. Our standard stop-loss is –25 percent.
3. *Never add to a losing position.* If a stock goes against you, there's no point in being a hero. You can lose your hard-earned gains and come away with nothing. That's the worst mistake a "Flying V" trader can make. You should get in, pick a stop-loss and profit margin, and then kick back and let the profits roll in.
4. *If you miss out on a trade, wait for the next one.* A thinly traded stock might spike over our buy limit. Don't worry about getting into a stock if you miss it. There will be plenty of other opportunities.

The IPO market—like the market in general—runs in cycles. The last big IPO bull years were in the late 1990s and died with the market in March 2000. When the tech bubble deflated, many IPOs, like Google, were pulled and set on the shelf. There was simply no market demand in 2001 and 2002.

After that period, the IPO market began heating up again. Many of the new crop of IPOs proved to be better values than those of five years before. The SEC investigations into Wall Street corruption have momentarily cooled the hyperbole. Stocks were priced at more reasonable levels and the companies were five years more mature. Many held real value.

A total of 233 companies went public on the major U.S. stock exchanges in 2004, a 195 percent increase in the number of IPOs over 2003. In the fourth quarter of 2004, 80 new IPOs were listed.

The biggest winners as of 2005 were Gurunet, up 264 percent; New River Pharma, up 229 percent; and Shanda Entertainment, up 168 percent. You can find information regarding new IPOs at Edgars: www.hoovers.com/global/ipoc/index.xhtml.

The bottom line is not complicated: There is money to be made but you have to know how to game the players, or play the gamers.

CHAPTER 15

TRADING SECRET NUMBER NINE: THE TRI-DIRECTIONAL INDICATOR

The reason the mainstream is thought of as a stream is because it's so shallow.

—George Carlin

The core concept behind the Tri-Directional Indicator (TDI) is the moving average, one of the oldest technical indicators around.

Now, the moving average is just the average price of a stock at particular moments in time. Over a period of time, you can chart the direction of a stock price. Because it's so easy to comprehend and follow, numerous analysts use it to make projections about a stock.

Moving averages tell you the trend. I don't know about you, but I like my systems so easy to comprehend a five-year-old can figure them out.

The secret to the TDI is twofold:

1. Know the difference between up and down.
2. Up is good, down is bad.

If you can figure that out, you're ahead of 90 percent of the ex-jock brokers on Wall Street.

The problem comes when you don't know the direction of a stock. This is where the Tri-Directional Indicator comes in. But first let me tell you about moving averages. There are two types.

A weighted moving average simply gives more weight to recent data and less weight to previous data. A simple moving average gives equal weight to the entire period. So if you have a 20-day moving average, it takes the closing prices from each of the last 20 days, divides them by 20, and adds that number to today's line.

Since I'm simple, and my goal is simple—to know the difference between up and down—I use the simple moving average. No muss, no fuss, less chance of an error.

In the next step, we run three separate moving averages, using periods of 20 days, 35 days, and 50 days. I use those numbers for two reasons. First, they aren't the default numbers found in off-the-shelf software, which means that computerized buy and sell orders aren't interfering with my trades, and second, I've found through experience that they work best for me.

BEATING THE ODDS

To apply the data to produce consistent profits, a very strict set of five rules has to be used that tell you exactly what to do according to the action of each of the averages. When you apply these rules to the data that has been generated so far, they reveal:

- When to buy.
- When to sell half.
- When to sell your other half.
- How—on the rare occasions that a trade goes against you—you can sell at one particular point to recoup most of the loss.
- When to go short on a stock.

You want to buy a stock when the three moving averages that make up TDI are sloping upward, equidistant, and parallel. Note the following examples.

You sell half of your position when the lines move from being parallel and start closing together. In other words, the fast line (20-day moving average) will start to flatten.

You sell you entire portion when the stock price drops through the 20- and 35-day moving averages.

If the stock gets hit by bad news and drops below all three moving averages before you get a chance to sell, wait three days for a bounce with the idea you sell at 10:30 the morning of the third day. If you don't get a bounce, sell on the third day anyway.

To short a stock you do the opposite. You enter your trade when you find a stock that has the TDI sloping down, equidistant, and parallel.

And since it is always good to have a secondary signal with a momentum indicator, you have to know when the markets will turn—when up becomes down, and down becomes up.

This last piece of information comes from the volatility index (the VIX). It measures the put/call ratio—or in other words, what the professional traders are betting on the market.

Whenever the VIX spikes and plummets like a shark's tooth, you know there's going to be a turnaround in the market. Take a look at how clear this signal is.

TURNING $10,000 INTO $42,100 IN JUST ONE MONTH

In Figure 15.1 you can see that the volatility index formed a double top on October 7 and October 9, revealing that a move was about to be launched to the upside. On October 9 we recommended an option on the OEX and issued a sell on it two days later for a 127 percent profit.

But that was just for starters. We waited for the pullback and recommended QQQ options. This worked like a charm also: within three weeks we booked 194 percent profits.

All together we made 321 percent off the same move. A $10,000 investment turned into $42,100 with just two trades in one month.

The bigger and more dramatic the spike, the bigger and more dramatic the turnaround. Not only does this Tri-Directional Indicator tell us which way a stock is going to go, but we also layer that in with a knowledge of where the market is going to go.

The result is that we know exactly when to change from short to

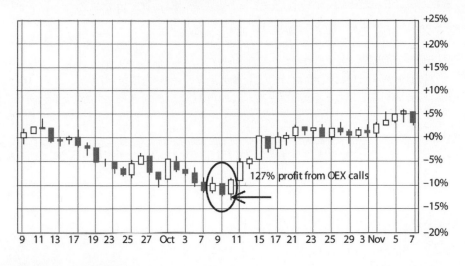

Figure 15.1 OEX Daily

long, like we did to catch the recent rally. The TDI also tells us when to stay long so we don't get faked out of further gains.

Let me give you a few examples to show just how powerful this system is and how quickly you can rack up large gains. You could have doubled your money in just six weeks with this one.

In May 2004, RedZone founder Christian DeHaemer, who developed the TDI for his RedZone VIP trading service, recommended a stock called Intertrust Technologies. Intertrust is a company that holds a number of patents that protect digital media (like CDs and DVDs) from piracy. It had just signed a $28 million deal with Sony.

Actually, Christian couldn't care less about all that. What he cared about was what the data were telling him. And when he saw the chart shown in Figure 15.2 (and applied the rules), he immediately sent out a fax and e-mail telling RedZone VIP members to buy.

As you can see by this chart, the stock price doubled from our entry price of $1.65 on May 24 up to $3.31 on July 9. Not bad, especially while the market was dropping like a stone in a pond. And obviously, the outcome was delightful as well: 85 percent profit in less than two months.

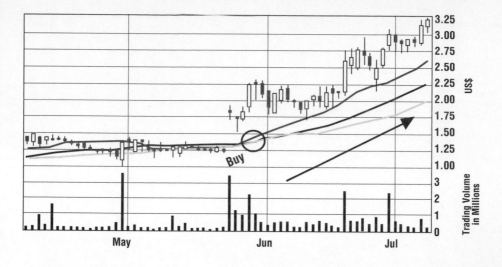

Figure 15.2 Intertrust Technologies (ITRU:Nasdaq)

Then there was Red Hat. You might remember Red Hat from the boom, boom, bubble days of 1999. Back then it could do no wrong in the Linux business. But that was then, this is now. Who could have known that you could double your money in this stock during one of the biggest tech sell-offs in history?

Our RedZone VIP trading service members knew. Figure 15.3 shows how it looked.

If you bought when the system said "buy" at $4.50 and sold when the system said "sell" at $8.34, you would have made 85 percent in less than two months. It was easy. And then there was Talk America. This one signaled a buy at $0.88 on April 22. (See Figure 15.4.)

When it hit $3.60 we saw a 309 percent gain in less than four months. That's how you accumulate real wealth. And it's simple with this system.

But the best thing about this system is that it, too, works in every market: In good times and bad, in blue chips and micro caps, and both long and short. It has even worked during the most brutal bear market since the Great Depression.

Just take a look at how the system read Freddie Mac, Wall Street's latest "can't-lose" stock.

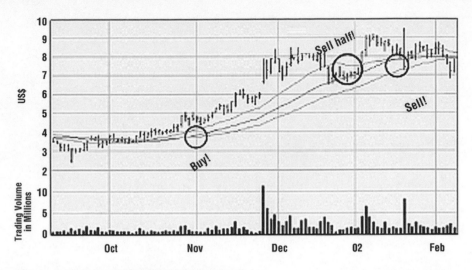

Figure 15.3 Red Hat (RHAT:Nasdaq)

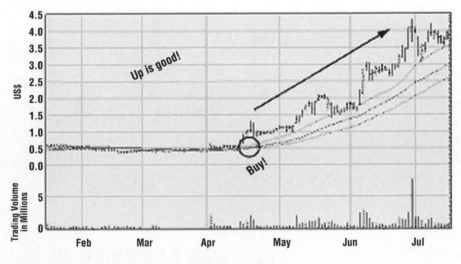

Figure 15.4 Talk America (TALK:Nasdaq)

THE MYTH BEHIND FREDDIE MAC AND FANNIE MAE

You see, the popular belief has always been that Freddie Mac and Fannie Mae are backed by the government and therefore can't go down. The theory goes: as long as mortgage rates are low, these companies will continue to make money for their shareholders.

Well, Figure 15.5 tells a different story.

As you can tell by this chart, Freddie Mac is in a clear downtrend. Starting on June 25, when the stock was trading for $62.50, the three moving averages were sloping down and running parallel. At this point you should have initiated a short or bought a put option. (This is where the fast-moving profit shot comes into play.)

Two Doubles in Two Days

As it happened, Christian waited until July 8, at which point he recommended two put options. The underlying stock was trading at $61.80.

The first option had an August expiration with a 55 strike price.

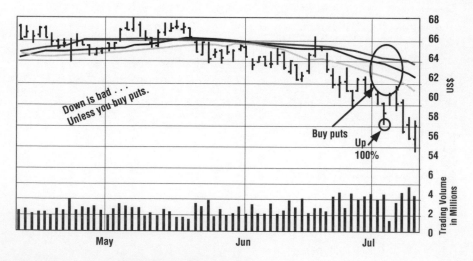

Figure 15.5 Freddie Mac (FRE:NYSE)

Two days later, the stock was selling for $56.80 and the put was up more than 110 percent. It worked like the clockwork in a Bentley.

The second put was the January 30. Two days later, that put was up 100 percent. And that's just at the start of the downtrend.

It turned out that these two mortgage companies had been accused of accounting irregularities and were forced to restate four years of earnings. The Securities and Exchange Commission (SEC) even accused Fannie Mae of serious accounting problems and earnings manipulation to meet Wall Street's quarterly targets. The company was ordered by the SEC to restate its earnings back to 2001, a correction estimated to reach an estimated $11 billion.

Freddie Mac's accounting debacle erupted in June 2003. It misstated earnings by $5 billion in the period from 2000 to 2003. The three top executives lost their jobs as a result.

No one but the insiders knew it at the time. But the chart knew. It was speaking loud and clear.

This system works with any chart, including the major indexes.

THE NASDAQ HANDS US 75 PERCENT PROFITS

The Triple Qs (QQQ:Nasdaq) is a Nasdaq tracking investment tool. Nasdaq was getting killed over the two years of 2003 and 2004. And the Red Zone VIP trading service told us exactly how to make money as it was falling. (See Figure 15.6.)

On June 14, we recommended buying a put option on the QQQs with a December 20 expiration. The option was trading at $0.85. We sold it on July 22 for at $1.35—a 59 percent increase. And that's in a brutal bear market.

LIMITING YOUR RISK

Not only does this system cut through the noise and produce results, but it also keeps your money in profitable stocks while avoiding the traps of down and sideways markets. Take a look at Figure 15.7, a two-year chart of Freddie Mac.

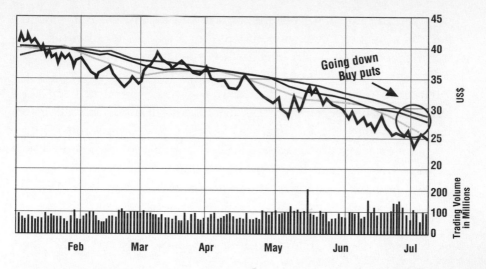

Figure 15.6 QQQ

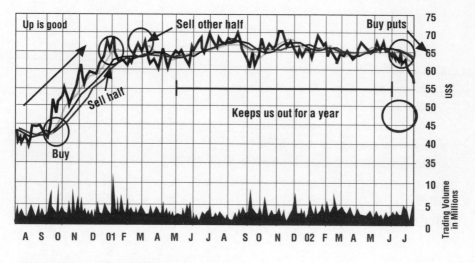

Figure 15.7 Freddie Mac Two-Year

As you can see by this chart, the Red Zone VIP trading service made 35 percent and 42 percent just for buying this stock at the start of the uptrend. There was a "buy" signal at $46.25 and a "sell half" signal at $62.75. Another "sell the bounce" signal came at $65.75.

But, equally important, the signal told those using it when to stay out of this stock, as it went nowhere for the next year and a half!

That means investment capital isn't tied up in a loser and could be used elsewhere—like Talk America, for instance.

That's how we've continued to make money all through this market.

MAKING 87.8 PERCENT AVERAGE GAINS FROM SEPTEMBER 5 TO NOVEMBER 4, 2002

During this period some of the biggest names on Wall Street posted devastating earnings. The fear of attacking Iraq, tension reaching a boiling point in the Middle East, and new fears of global terrorism drove the Nasdaq down 18 percent, the Dow down 19 percent, and the S&P 500 down more than 15 percent. But the Red Zone VIP team laughed in the face of all this bad news—and came out with an average gain of 87.8 percent at the same time.

Buy-and-hold works only half the time.

The average length of a boom or stagnation has historically been 16 to 20 years. The most recent bull market was the longest in history, lasting 18 years. But from 1905 to 1921 buy-and-hold investors lost money. From 1929 to 1950 they lost money again. From 1966 to 1982, they lost money. There have been 53 years of bear markets altogether.

As you can see, unless you are in a bull market, the buy-and-hold philosophy is nonsense. But that doesn't mean you can't make money. You can, quite a bit, even in a bear market.

Let's look at the two biggest bear markets this century, the 1929–1950 Dow and the 1990 to present Nikkei. As you can see by the Dow depression chart in Figure 15.8, the markets staged a huge 300 percent rally from 1932 to 1937.

The perma-bears will always point to the 1929–1932 area as their poster child for bad markets, but their charts always seem to

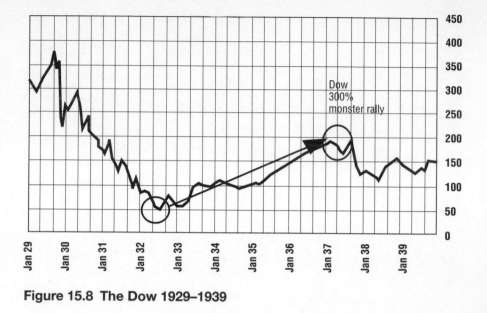

Figure 15.8 The Dow 1929–1939

end before this 300 percent five-year rally. The bear market wasn't over, though. It took until after World War II for the Dow to make a new high.

Look at the case of Japan. Two and a half years after the crash, the Nikkei staged a 33 percent one-year rally. Then in 1995 there was a 53 percent rally. And in 1999 the market jumped again, handing over another 45 percent rally. (See Figure 15.9.)

Now here's a Nasdaq multi-year chart in Figure 15.10. The time scale is different from the other two charts, but if you look at the dates, you can see that we are only two and a half to three years out in the stagnation period.

Chris wrote the above and dissected the chart in October of 2002. As you can tell by Figure 15.10, he wasn't right on the money.

In fact, his 2003 Red Zone VIP portfolio went up 3,488 percent. That number is not manipulated or cherry-picked, it was obtained simply by adding up the winners and subtracting the losers.

The bottom occurred in October 2002 and ran until January

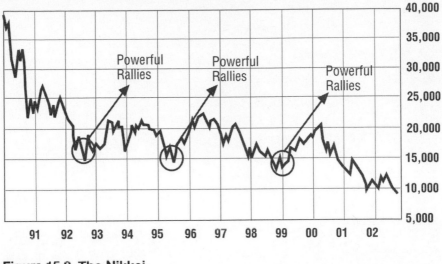

Figure 15.9 The Nikkei

2004. By the beginning of 2005, we were in a sideways market and the Tri-Directional Indicator pointed to the wisdom of staying on the sidelines.

That said, the one thing I know about the market is that it is constantly changing; with the Tri-Directional Indicator, you will be on the right side of the market at the right time.

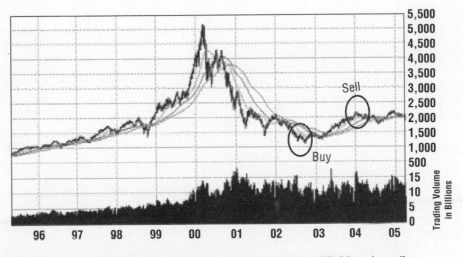

Figure 15.10 "3,488% Total Gains for Red Zone VIP Members"

CHAPTER 16

TRADING SECRET NUMBER TEN: TRADING THE MONEY-FLOW MATRIX

Capitalism does not operate on the principle of altruism or "benevolence." . . . Capitalism succeeds precisely because free exchange is mutually advantageous.

—**Thomas J. DiLorenzo,** *How Capitalism Saved America* **(2004)**

On October 9, 2002, my colleague Briton Ryle, chief analyst of the Money-Flow Matrix trading service, called a bottom for the Dow Jones Industrial Average. He told his subscribers to buy IBM and Dow Jones Industrials 1/100 Index (DJX) calls. Those who followed his advice made a total net profit of nearly 700 percent in the next eight days.

Lucky timing? Gut feeling? Not by a long shot! Those positions were the result of a market timing system Brit spent the last eight years developing. Before I let you in on the nuts and bolts of his trading method, there are a few things we need to cover. First, in advance of implementing any trading system, you need to ensure that you know how important it is to stay open—that is, open to whatever happens after you get into the trade. In other words, understand the risks and accept the risks.

Why? In trading you get it all. Sometimes you'll knock down huge triple-digit gains. Sometimes, you'll find yourself chiseling only 15 percent and 20 percent gains. Other times you'll end up taking a loss. Recognizing—and accepting—what the market offers is crucial.

FEAR OF SUCCESS

Oddly enough, the biggest problem a novice trader faces is accepting really huge gains. Taking 50 percent and 75 percent after a couple of days is never a problem.

Brit writes:

> I have to be honest and acknowledge that even on such "small" trades, my anxiety level would start rising from the moment I pushed the buy button. I remember the trade where that changed. I bought put options on Vivendi (V:NYSE) in May of 2002. I bought the puts based on my system. It wasn't until after I was in the trade that I started digging into what was going on at Vivendi. I won't go into the details here, but my research convinced me that this should be much bigger than typical three-day, 60 percent trades I was used to.
>
> The final take on that position was around 480 percent. And let me tell you, it wasn't easy watching your position hit 150 percent, and then 200 percent, and still not selling. I would review my research almost every day just to calm my nerves. People were telling me I was crazy to pass up 250 percent. So you know what I did? I bought more puts. That's right. I was already up nearly 300 percent when I bought more. Talk about your sleepless nights. But when you're right, you've got to maximize the opportunity. My system and my research were dead on and in addition to the 480 percent on the first position, the second netted around 200 percent. Huge, huge gain, both for my account and my psyche. I went on to hit Vivendi one more time for a double. But the point is, I now had the faith in my system and my own analysis to hang on for the really big score.

THAT'S A BOTTOM!

On October 9, 2002, Brit wasn't looking for a major turn in the market. As always, he was simply trading his system. In fact, he was holding puts on the morning of October 9. Needless to say, holding puts had been the trade of choice for two years. And his readers had done very well with puts. For instance, they rode the semiconductors for some huge gains during the summer of 2002. Brit had even started calling KLA-Tencor, Novellus, QLogic, and Linear Tech "the Four Horsemen of the Semiconductor Apocalypse" in his daily advisories.

You can imagine that Brit was a little leery when his system started flashing buy signals in early October 2002. For one thing, October is traditionally not a good time for stocks. And two, a basic trading maxim is that "the trend is your friend." With the Dow and Nasdaq making new lows nearly every day, that downtrend had made his readers quite a nice profit. Brit certainly didn't want to turn his back on such a profitable friendship.

Going against the Grain

But when the Money-Flow Matrix system started flashing the buy signs on October 9, 2002, Brit was thinking bear market bounce, not trend change. As with his Vivendi trade, it wasn't until he had been in the IBM and DJX calls for a few days that Brit started to think that perhaps there was more going on than a simple bear market bounce. In retrospect, it may have been a mistake to sell the DJX calls for just 80 percent gains. But Brit made up for it by buying more IBM calls.

This brings me to the second point: A good trading system should work in any and all market climates. Brit's system does. It works on the 15-minute chart for futures trading, it works on the intraday chart for day trading, it works in the one-to-five-day-period short-term trend, it works on the multiweek trend, and, as I've shown you, it actually can identify major turns in the market.

Define Your Terms

To succeed as a trader, you need to work within a system with clearly defined objectives, rules, and trading methods. And you have to have the discipline to follow those rules. Trading a system can be a beautiful thing: You become the conductor of a symphony. Every note, every crescendo and break is right there on the page in front of you. All you have to do is orchestrate the action.

In a symphony, the notes written on the page allow the musicians to harness random sounds and tones and refine them into a coherent, recognizable, and repeatable form. Listeners may have no understanding of what the notes on the page mean. The sheet music may look like a bunch of indecipherable lines and squiggles that mean absolutely nothing. But listerners still can appreciate and enjoy the music that is produced. What those listeners may never understand is that the sheet music is a language that can be learned and understood. There's no magic at all. And with just a little study, even the most nonmusical person can begin to understand what the sheet music is saying.

THE MARKET SYMPHONY

To the casual observer, the financial markets may look very chaotic. And even to the trained eye, stocks, bonds, and currencies often act as though they have a mind of their own. But with just a little study, you can start to see the underlying symmetry and form of these financial markets.

There are many different ways to read the market's "music." Analysts specialize in selecting substrata in the seemingly random imprint of information, searching for recurring patterns, for unique constellations of catalysts that mark impending moves of single stocks or entire markets—the subtle cadence and harmony of the market.

Brit Ryle has identified one of these unique constellations of catalysts and built a trading system around it. He calls it the Money-Flow Matrix. The name of the system is programmatic. To Brit, it serves as a daily reminder of why he is in the markets: money. The financial markets are all about money. Money moves stocks, options, futures, and bonds. And money is smarter than most individual investors and analysts.

You'd be surprised at the number of investors who don't understand this very basic truth. And that's exactly why so many of them continue to lose money in the financial markets. They think that the markets are about economic reports, new technology, a cure for cancer or AIDS, interest rates, demand from China, or any of the other supposed catalysts that the financial media bombard us with day after day.

Unfortunately, not a single one of those things qualifies as a catalyst. They are signs, auspices, like the flight patterns of birds that Roman augurs used for foretelling the future. But if you want to make money in the markets, you don't pay attention to birds.

Let's visualize what is going on in the markets. The markets are simply all about how and where money flows. Trillions of dollars change hands every day. And all that money leaves a trail. Follow that trail and you can find more profit opportunities than you ever thought possible, because *prices react to money*.

Think of cash flow like the ocean's tide—it's either coming in or going out. When cash is flowing into the stock markets, prices rise. When it flows out, prices drop.

Cash flow works the same way as the tide. At any given moment of the day, billions of dollars are simultaneously moving in and out of stocks. But over time—whether it's days, weeks, or months—cash is either entering or leaving, which means stock prices are either rising or falling.

The Money-Flow Matrix is really nothing but a highly sensitive cash flow meter. It gives us the early read on which way the money is flowing. So by the time everyone else figures out what's happening, Money-Flow Matrix traders are often counting their profits.

DAYS, WEEKS, OR MONTHS: THE MONEY-FLOW MATRIX CHURNS OUT WINNERS

As you may have experienced yourself, markets can turn on a dime, creating incredible short-term opportunities to make money, or pitfalls in which to lose. But markets also grind out advances or declines that can take weeks. That's why the Money-Flow Matrix operates in distinct time frames.

Long-term trends in cash flows are determined in part by tracking institutional and mutual fund money, examining put/call ratios, and volume studies. Short-term opportunities are pinpointed using a variety of tools including momentum indicators, price oscillators, and chart patterns.

Brit spent years developing the Money-Flow Matrix because early on he boiled down trading theory to the simple fact that *money moves the market.* He also knew that if he could find a way to track the flow into and out of equities, he could make substantial amounts of money.

Here is the six-step method he follows:

The Matrix

1. First, Brit studies on-balance volume (OBV). This is a broad market indicator that was pioneered all the way back in 1963 by the great trader Joe Granville. It's like watching swells in the sea before a storm. Instantly, it shows you the how the institutional investors can force big surges in trading volume.

2. After OBV, Brit applies the advance-decline line (A/D line). The A/D line is one of the most watched market indicators, and it's also one of the best ways to foresee broad market reversals. The A/D line simply shows the number of shares going up in price compared to the number of shares going down. Historically, almost every turn in the A/D line is soon followed by a turn in the market index it's tracking.

3. The Money-Flow Matrix also tracks the price-to-time ratio using stochastics.[1] This means just what it sounds like: a measurement of the time it takes for a specific company's shares to rise or fall in price.

4. The Money-Flow Matrix also zeros in on the volume-and-price ratio using the momentum indicator. Momentum isn't just about the speed of a change in a share price, but about the underlying *force* behind that change. Think about it. If you saw a grand piano rolling down a hill, would you step in front of it to stop it? Of course not.

5. Money flow itself is the driving force. The measurement of money flow means that we watch, via careful calculation, how *much* money is rushing into or out of a specific investment at any given time. This is as close as you're going to get to taking the pulse of company insiders. No other indicator is better or

more underreported when it comes to knowing what the smart money wants to do next.

6. And finally, there's volume. Brit watches both daily and intra-day volume on stocks and indexes. Volume studies show where support and resistance trading levels are found, especially on the intraday charts.

THE TRADING SCREEN

After applying the analytical tools, Brit uses a number of trading screens every day. He normally uses a real-time charting system that costs around $2,000 a year. But you can generate your own screens at no or almost no cost using services such as www.bigcharts.com. The resulting chart may look somewhat like the one shown in Figure 16.1.

I use this IBM chart because it demonstrates several important aspects of the Money-Flow Matrix. First, at the bottom of the chart,

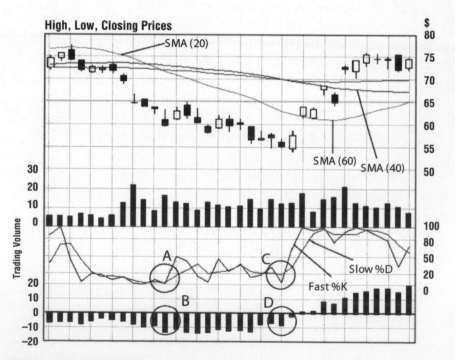

Figure 16.1 IBM Daily

you'll find the indicators discussed earlier. I want to take you through the setup for the trade this chart generated and show you exactly how each indicator was working.

But first, let me remind you of the market climate. Summer and early fall of 2002 were devastating for stock prices. It seemed like every day the Dow was dropping 100 or 200 points. Our traders had been making a killing on put option trades.

Brit wasn't looking for an upside trade in this environment. In fact, he was holding puts right up until the day he recommended his subscribers buy IBM calls and cleaned up as IBM exploded to the upside. And in all honesty, we'd have missed this huge trade if it weren't for the Money-Flow Matrix.

You probably do not remember the summer and fall of 2002 fondly. The Dow and the Nasdaq were falling apart. It got so bad that market commentators invented a new term, the "red waterfall," to describe the plunging stock prices. As it turns out, the market was putting in a very important bottom in early October 2002. But fear of corporate accounting problems, declining earnings, and massive layoffs had most people convinced that stocks would continue to drop forever.

This fear caused most investors to miss one of the most eye-popping profit opportunities to come down the pike in the past few years. I'm going to show you exactly how you could have seen the turn in the markets coming, and how you could have pulled down 80 percent, 112 percent, and 480 percent in less than 10 days like some of our Money-Flow Matrix traders did.

I've included a chart so you can follow the action. In the days and weeks leading up to the October 9, 2002, market bottom, Money-Flow Matrix traders had been cleaning up on put options on some of the Nasdaq's stars—companies like Novellus, QLogic, and KLA-Tencor. We were bagging 25 to 50 percent gains regularly.

But as the Dow and Nasdaq began hitting lows not seen in five years, the Money-Flow Matrix began flashing buy signals. Let me show you exactly how these events translated into a massive windfall of cash: You'll notice that as the stock fell to $60 a share, all of Brit's indicators were hitting very extreme readings. Daily stochastics were floored, momentum was picking up steam, and volume was increasing. It looked nasty.

A week later, when prices started dropping again, talk of another Black Monday was rampant. IBM continued to drop, hitting a low of $55. Funny thing, though, the charts were saying something completely different: The daily stochastics failed to hit the extremes they had only two weeks earlier, even as prices continued to fall. And the daily momentum had actually started to move higher, despite the dropping prices.

Brit alerted his traders that a divergent situation was developing between his technical indicators and stock prices. On October 8, 2002, he wrote:

> It's been clear that the market is at an important juncture. Yet most of my indicators have been giving very contradictory signals. . . . My volume and money flow studies have not been showing the extreme reading you expect from a market bottom (I swear, the discrepancies have been keeping me up nights).

On October 9, 2002, the setup was perfect. Brit's recommended play had already bought the Dow index calls when he told his traders:

> I want to raise our exposure to this potential bounce. The place to look is blue-chip tech. And as it happens, IBM has dropped from $70 to $55 in the last three weeks. My indicators suggest a strong bounce for IBM is likely.

I'm sure a lot of traders thought Brit had gone off his rocker. The very next day, when the Dow opened down 100 points and IBM dropped another dollar, he told his traders:

> This morning's extreme move to Dow 7200 is just the extreme move the markets can bounce back from.

By the end of the day, IBM had rallied to $57.50. And Money-Flow Matrix traders were sitting on some very nice gains. But there was more to come. A lot more. Because not only had prices moved higher as Brit expected, but the turnaround was confirmed as the money-flow line turned higher. That meant that big money had now recognized the turn, and all we had to do was sit back and wait.

And that might have been enough for most traders. But we had the advantage and weren't going to let up. On October 15, Brit provided more details:

> Let's go ahead and get some limit orders lined up. Buy the November 65 IBM call option, symbol IBMKM, at 4. If this buy order gets filled, put your stops in at 2.

That buy order was filled the very next day. And on October 17, Money-Flow Matrix took profits. We pulled down 480 percent on the first IBM calls, 112 percent on the second round, and we sold the Dow Industrials Index calls for 80 percent. All in nine trading days.

THE NUTS AND BOLTS

The first thing to notice about the IBM chart is that stochastics bottomed two weeks before the stock did (point A). Despite the fact that IBM dropped another $5, stochastics clearly showed that there was buying going on.

Now look at point B on the momentum indicator. This indicator also reached maximum readings well before the stock price actually bottomed.

If we fast-forward a few days to when the stock price actually bottomed, you'll notice that both stochastics (point C) and momentum (point D) did not move to extremes. At first glance, you might think the failure of these indicators to hit extremes was forecasting more lows for the stock price.

But if that were the case, one of the indicators would have been weakening. And as you can see, both indicators were actually getting stronger. This is a *divergent* situation and is one of the strongest indicators that a reversal is coming. The subsequent reversal and rally was confirmed by the double bottom on the money-flow indicator.

Based on this analysis, Brit recommended IBM calls on October 9, 2002. His readers made a 481 percent gain in nine days. Some even did much better.

These are just a few of the indicators that make up the Money-Flow Matrix. But if you make these indicators a part of how you look at the stock market in general and stocks specifically, you'll get a much clearer picture of what's going on at the moment and what's about to happen next.

Now I'm going to show you a few more charts that are exceptional examples of the Money-Flow Matrix in action. Remember that each trade is slightly different.

Figure 16.2 shows a trade entered on 11/15/04, exited 11/24/04 for 345 percent gains. A second trade entered on 11/22/04 and sold 12/2/04 for a 46 percent gain.

Figure 16.3 shows a trade entered on 10/05/04, exited 10/15/04 for 175 percent gains.

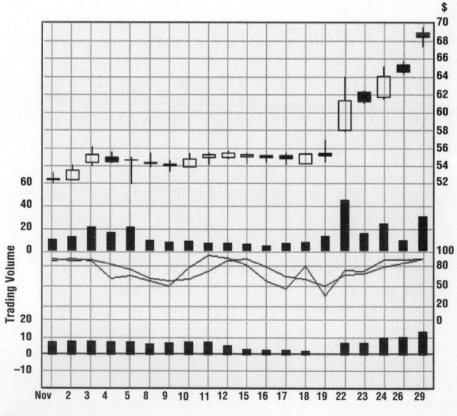

Figure 16.2 AAPL Daily

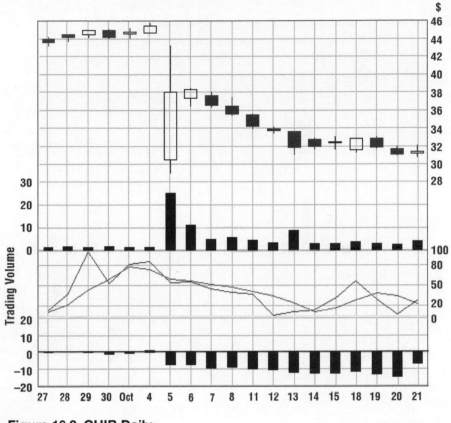

Figure 16.3 CHIR Daily

Figure 16.4 shows a trade entered on 11/1/04, exited 11/03/04 for a 90 percent gain. Note the dramatic improvement in momentum.

WHAT TO TRADE

Knowing which way stocks are headed is only half the battle. Of equal, if not more importance, is finding the right sectors and the right stocks to trade. The Money-Flow Matrix is designed to zero in on the sectors and stocks that have the highest probability of giving you the highest returns on your capital. It does this through a series of top-down screens.

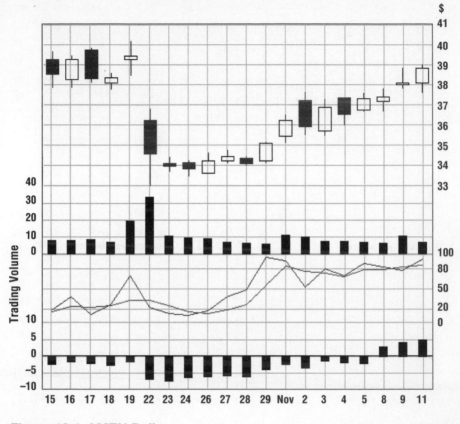

Figure 16.4 AMZN Daily

Think of it like a satellite camera zeroing in on a specific location of the earth. The first shot is of a whole hemisphere of the earth. You see a couple of continents and an ocean or two from way out in space. In the next frame you see just a continent. Then you get closer and you can make out physical features of a country like rivers, mountains, and cities. In the next frame, you're looking at an urban sprawl. Then you zero in on a section of the city, then a neighborhood, and finally a house.

That's how the Money-Flow Matrix screening process works. Every day, it starts with an overview of the stock market—the S&P 500 and the Nasdaq. Then each index is broken down into its component sectors, like biotech, retail, energy, financial, software, and so on.

All it takes is a glance at the Money-Flow Matrix selection screen to see which sectors are the high-beta sectors of the day. Then we apply the selection screen to the stocks within the sector to find a few attractive trading candidates.

Once the best trading vehicles have been selected, then it's time to narrow the field once again. This is done with a combination of technical and fundamental analysis of the stocks as well as an analysis of the puts and calls.

THE BETA TEST

The key component that the Money-Flow Matrix uses to select a trading vehicle is called beta.

Here's a quick definition of beta from InvestmentFAQ.com:

> Beta is the sensitivity of a stock's returns to the returns on some market index (like the S&P 500 or the Nasdaq). . . . A stock with high beta responds strongly to variations in the market, and a stock with low beta is relatively insensitive to variations in the market.

Clearly, a stock that moves more than the major indexes is exactly what you want in a trading stock. But here's the problem with beta: If you simply ran a screen for high-beta stocks, you'd get a list of issues that have historically outperformed the major indexes. A simple beta screen will not tell you what the stock is doing right now. Nor will it tell you what the stock is likely to do over the next few days.

And that's where the Money-Flow Matrix distinguishes itself. It tracks the highest-beta stocks in the highest-beta sectors in real time. We can find the best trading stocks in about two minutes at any point during the trading day.

And what's more, Brit has pioneered a new use for beta by applying it to a stock's volume. Often, volume will start to pick up on a stock before the price starts to move. Brit uses 10 percent increments of volume above the average daily volume to calculate the volume beta on the mid-cap and large-cap stocks he tracks.

In addition to being a good indicator of a price move to come, a rising volume beta also shows accumulation and distribution patterns.

This information is critical for precise timing of exit points that maximize gains.

OPTION SELECTION

There's one more aspect of the Money-Flow Matrix perfect trade that I haven't covered. Many investors might think that if you find the right stock in the right sector you can trade any option on it and do just as well. But selecting the right option is critical to maximizing your potential gains. So after Brit has run the Money-Flow Matrix selection screen, he usually lets the options screen decide which of the three of four high-beta stocks will be the appropriate trading vehicle.

Brit applies five evaluation criteria for choosing the proper option contract to trade. They are: premium, daily volume, outstanding interest, the underlying price relative to the strike price, and the expiration-to-premium ratio.

Now, let me just say that as a general rule, we don't believe in any hard-and-fast rules for selecting an option to trade. Some traders will tell you never to buy out-of-the-money options. Others will say never buy the front month's contract. Still others will warn you away from options that have too much premium in the price.

It's been our experience that trading requires flexibility, and so you should feel free to be creative in choosing the right option to fit the objectives of your trade. However, we've found that the best-performing options share certain characteristics. And we have made these characteristics part of the option selection process.

Volume and Outstanding Interest

The first thing to look at when selecting an option to trade is volume. And by volume I mean both the daily average volume and the outstanding interest, or the total number of this particular option that is in circulation.

Since recommendations can result in hundreds of contracts changing hands, we like to see at least 2,500 contracts outstanding and daily trading of at least 300 contracts. Also, on popular trading stocks, we try to avoid the strike price with the highest outstanding volume. It's usually a good idea to get between the current price of the underlying asset and the option strike with the highest outstanding volume.

Strike Price

If you've traded options before, you've seen strike prices that come every $5 (i.e., $5, $10, $15, $20) and ones that come every $2.50 (i.e., $2.50, $5, $7.50, $10). It probably goes without saying that options with strike prices denominated in $2.50 increments are better for trading purposes.

For one, this lets you be more selective when it comes to pricing. Second, the $2.50 increment can make it easier to trade the out-of-the-money contracts. And third, they let you be more precise in setting your stop-loss.

Premium (Price)

The price of an option contract, and the way the price moves in relation to the underlying asset, is the most complicated and misunderstood aspect of options trading. That being said, I'm not going to get into a long discussion of the variables that dictate how an option price moves.

For one, it's overly complicated and I don't have room here to explain the variables thoroughly. And two, there are some simple rules that you can follow that will help you buy the option with the most upside, without running a complex and time-consuming options price calculator.

The first rule is: don't trade options that are at-the-money (an option where the strike is the same as the price of the underlying asset). The premium is usually highest on these options. Plus, it's too easy for the option to go against you and become out-of-the-money. And that could cause you to suffer more of a loss than you should.

The second rule is: don't buy a front month option that is more than 5 percent out-of-the-money. We've all seen stocks run 8 percent or 10 percent after an earnings announcement or an important news release. In fact, if you scan the prices during the day, you'll see a bunch of stocks moving that much or more.

But what are the odds that the stock you're trading options on will jump 10 percent? Well, considering there are literally thousands of stocks that you can trade options on, your chances are pretty slim. So if you limit the percentage gain you need in order to get in-the-money, you increase your chances of making money.

There are two aspects to an option's value: intrinsic value and time value or premium. Only in-the-money options have intrinsic value. And that's because if you exercise the option, you're buying the stock at a discount to the current market value.

But unless you go deep in-the-money, in-the-money options usually have some time value built into the price. We don't ever trade in-the-money options that are more than 50 percent premium. And even that percentage is a little high unless you're in a strongly trending market.

An out-of-the-money option is all premium. There is no intrinsic value. And that means you need to be especially careful how much you pay for it. As a rule of thumb, for an option that's 5 percent out-of-the-money, we add $0.25 per week until expiration to find a reasonable price. In other words, you shouldn't pay more than $1 for an option that's 5 percent out-of-the-money four weeks before expiration.

PUTTING IT ALL TOGETHER

Now you've seen how the Money-Flow Matrix works. I've shown you how to use the Money-Flow Matrix indicators to get a read on where the market is headed—how to quickly find the stocks that are outperforming the market and will give you the best shot at maximizing your gains. And I've given you some general rules for selecting the proper option for trading.

Everything I've shown you here is designed to give clear signals that will allow you to make the right decision quickly. And that's a key element for the successful trader. You have to be patient when waiting for your entry signals. But once you get them, you have to be able to act decisively.

The Money-Flow Matrix is a great trading system. It's easy to understand and easy to use.

RISK MANAGEMENT

Risk management is the most important aspect of successful trading. If you don't manage your risk position sizing and exit strategies, you will lose most or even all of your money.

I've seen studies that prove you can use a completely random entry point for a trade, have a less than 50 percent success rate, and still make money if you practice proper risk management.

There are several simple strategies to managing your risk. I like stop-losses.

If you believe that it's impossible to be right 100 percent of the time, then you have to establish, before you enter a trade, the point at which your position is no longer valid. That point is a stop-loss. It's the point where you admit you're wrong, sell the losing position, and move on to the next trade.

I prefer mental stops to actual stops. Mental stops are specific price levels that will force you to sell. You may find some difficulty in entering stop-losses for options trades. That's another reason why using mental stops is a good idea.

POSITION SIZING

Despite many instances of short-term gains, please keep in mind that trading is a long-term activity. If you're looking to make a quick buck so you can retire early or finance a vacation, you should try something else. Trading will disappoint you. But if you want to build your wealth over the years, trading is a great way to do it.

Stop-losses are one aspect of managing risk. But position sizing is equally important. The best way to size your positions is to put only a certain percentage of your total trading capital on each trade. Over time, as your total trading capital grows, the dollar amount of your trades grows as well.

As I said, trading is for the long term. And that means you have to be able to stay in the game if you want to win. Using good position sizing techniques is the best way to guarantee that you'll stay in the game.

The options trading aspect of this system may be complex, but most people can master the complexities of long positions in options without too much trouble. The real benefit of this knowledge comes not from simply trading options, but from having the ability to overlay options transactions in the Money-Flow Matrix.

Useful Information

Brit Ryle has incorporated his Money-Flow Matrix into a high-carat trading service called the Money-Flow Matrix Trader, which you can read up on at www.moneyflowmatrix .com.

He also publishes a free daily e-letter called *Daily Digest*. Find out more at www.dynamicmarket report.com/dailydigest.

TRADING SECRET NUMBER ELEVEN: PROFITING WITH THE WAVESTRENGTH OPTIONS TRADING SYSTEM

The most complex patterns and cycles in nature actually evolve from very simple formulas or patterns that repeat and evolve over long periods of time.

—Harry S. Dent Jr., *The Next Great Bubble Boom* (2004)

Up to now, I have focused on analytical strategies allowing you to determine the optimal entry and exit points for single stocks. Our trading strategies make good use of the micro-climates that cause stocks to soar upward or to plummet. But how about marketwide trends, like the Dow Jones Industrial Average, the Nasdaq, or any of a dozen other market, sector, or currency indexes?

When you become involved with indexes beyond individual stocks, it requires more thinking. Remember, the markets move according to natural behavioral patterns, which are the very basis of technical analysis. The obvious problem: The conclusion of a given wave and the beginning of a new one are perceived retrospectively: You can be 100 percent sure only if you're looking back over your time series. But yesterday is no good for traders who make their decisions today on what they expect tomorrow to bring.

Over the years, our editors Adam Lass, Brit Ryle, and Bryan Bottarelli have been tinkering with an analytical tool that would allow them to determine the *probability* of each move with a reasonable degree of success. They've called it the WaveStrength method of analysis.

The WaveStrength system uses a proprietary technical analysis system to see beyond the apparent chaos of index movements. Its predictive method is able to forecast future market moves with as much as 73 percent accuracy.

WaveStrength analysis is based on the premise that neither underlying value nor news events provide the genuine catalysts for market movements. Rather, short-term price changes are psychological in nature, the predictable result of large numbers of buyers' and sellers' predispositions toward value and news events. WaveStrength translates predictions made on this premise into options positions on the respective index in question.

The system is comparatively complex. When Adam explained it to the FBI agent who was following up on just how and why he made such an uncannily accurate prediction on September 10, 2001, I saw her eyes glaze over. But mastering it doesn't take much time at all. In the summer of 2003, for example, Bill Bonner, the president of Agora, Inc., which owns the Taipan Group LLC, asked me if I had space in my organization for a young man from our Paris office, who had been bounced from department to department. Diplomatically, I said, "Of course, Bill," even though I knew the Frenchman couldn't tell a stock from a sock. I put him on Adam's system, with a view on adapting it to the FTSE100, the DAX, and the French CAC40. What he lacked in social skills, he made up in chutzpah and ambition: Not only did he show up uninvited to the rehearsal dinner and nuptials of a colleague, but after six weeks and about $2,000 in books he charged on my corporate credit card, he played these indexes like a virtuoso. Had his record keeping been better, he'd still be working for me. As it is, he was hired to manage a European hedge fund within four months of learning the system.

But make no mistake about it: Technical analysis and options pricing are extremely sensitive. Mandelbrot compares the valuation of options as a "high-roller game, but the rules are all messed up."[1] Change one variable and you create radically different outcomes. Accordingly, the WaveStrength charting system encompasses and improves on several techniques to determine future market moves, including:

- Traditional Western indicators such as rising or falling tops and bottoms, head-and-shoulders formations, and expanding/contracting pennant structures.
- Japanese candlestick charts—a 500-year-old method of interpretive technical analysis that underlies the Doji Master method.
- Fibonacci sequence-driven retracement grids revealing hidden support and resistance points.
- Waveform theories that use years of historical data to account for minute-by-minute market moves.

When applied to the markets, these analyses yield a series of probable scenarios that we use to develop options plays. From this we are able to calculate the most likely outcomes. WaveStrength editors Adam Lass and Bryan Bottarelli chart these moves each and every day to produce profitable options trades based on the WaveStrength predictive system.

- Bryan Bottarelli is the "Trading Tactician" of the WaveStrength team. After paying his dues on the trading floor of the Chicago Board Options Exchange (CBOE), Bryan left the ruthless and chaotic option pits for the wonders of WaveStrength's predictive system.
- Adam T. Lass is the publisher and "Charting Guru" of the WaveStrength team. Adam's deep insights into the consciousness of the herd give him unique foresight that has enabled him to reliably guide his readers around the minefields of today's incredibly volatile market.

Now, I could sit here and ramble on endlessly about technical analysis and how WaveStrength theories and methods produce winning trades. But I suspect after a few minutes of reading all the arcane, jargon-filled details, you'd be bored to tears and slumped in your chair! So instead, before we get into the nuts and bolts of the system, let's take a step back and first look at the vehicles we will be using to trade the system.

OPTIONS: A CRASH COURSE

An option is an intangible financial instrument that gives you the right to buy or sell a specific underlying security at a specific price, and within a set time period.

Let me break down every piece of that definition for you:

Intangible financial instrument means it has no physical value; it is a contract, a right, and a way to leverage capital. But it's also an investment—that is, it can be bought and sold. Once you buy an option, you can resell it to another investor for a profit or loss, but only until expiration. After expiration, the option is worthless. Options are flexible. Notice that options give the buyer a *right*, not an obligation. That is, you choose whether you want to exercise that right. It's up to you whether you want to exercise the option, sell it, or let it expire.

Within a set time period means the option has a limited life. When you buy a stock, you can hold it indefinitely, but with options, you don't have the same ability. It could be a matter of weeks, months, or, in certain options called LEAPS (which we'll discuss in greater detail later), up to three years. If you don't exercise your right in that given time, the option expires worthless. Securities options always expire on the Saturday following the third Friday of a specific expiration month. Since the market is closed on Saturday, if you want to exercise your option (buy or sell the underlying optioned stock), you must do so by the third Friday of the month. Or if you want to sell it, you have to place your order in time for its execution before the same deadline.

Options have been around for a long time. In the old days, merchants would pay out a small amount of capital for the rights to future crops or ocean-bound cargo. When the crops were harvested or the cargo arrived, the merchant had the first opportunity to buy the goods. The Greek sage Aristotle tells of a philosopher in ancient Greece who wanted to demonstrate the usefulness of his craft in "real life." He studied the stars and determined that the constellations anticipated a good olive harvest. Accordingly, he bought "futures" on the use of the olive presses in the region. When the harvest came in better than usual, he made out like a bandit on his olive press futures.

Futures trading led to futures options, and for our purposes here, suffice it to say that both of these instruments—futures and options—share some of the same characteristics. Both are transacted for the purpose of fixing the price of a commodity, precious metal, currency, or stock so that if and when the buyer decides to exercise, a purchase can be made at the fixed price, even when current market value is different. And as companies began to issue stocks, it was only natural that options would evolve on stocks as well. Formal options trading came to the United States in 1900. But the use of options and related instruments got out of hand in the 1920s, exacerbating some people's losses when the market crashed. In the 1930s, Congress stepped in to try to regulate the options market.

Options went mainstream again in 1973 when the Chicago Board Options Exchange opened, with member market makers ready to serve investors with a two-way options market. Risk takers who wanted to buy or sell options could now be rapidly accommodated.

The difference between over-the-counter options and CBOE options was astounding. Contracts were standardized, with terms making options more accessible to the average investor. The popularity of options soared. They became so popular that in 1977 the Securities and Exchange Commission halted any further expansion of the industry and spent years reviewing it. But try as they might, the folks at the SEC found nothing wrong, and more options exchanges were soon opened. With that, more investments were optioned, including futures on the commodities exchanges. Options had evolved.

These days, you can buy options on the American Stock Exchange, the New York Stock Exchange, the Pacific Stock Exchange, and the Philadelphia Stock Exchange. You can also find index options on the Chicago Board Options Exchange and the Chicago Board of Trade.

The options world is very big, but it is also regulated to keep everyone honest. This close monitoring helps limit your risks, giving you some fraud protection and recourse. (I wish stocks on Wall Street were this closely monitored!) You can rest assured that options trading is as safe as—perhaps even safer than—owning stocks, if you know what you're doing.

One of the options we like to use to translate our WaveStrength predictions into options plays is derived from the Nasdaq-100 Trust (QQQ:AMEX). The Triple-Qs, as they are known, is a basket of the top 100 companies on the Nasdaq lumped together into one instrument that trades like a stock. In our opinion, the QQQ is the safest and cheapest way to play the trends of the overall market.

That's why we watch it, and trade it often. Buyers can make large profits from price moves while risking only a relatively small amount of capital (I'll explain all that in more detail in just a bit). When you buy a QQQ option, you are buying the right to buy or sell 100 shares of the QQQ at a set price within a set period of time.

A QQQ option gives you "the right to buy or sell" the QQQ. When you buy the option, you must choose whether you expect to profit from a rise or a fall in the price of the underlying instrument.

- If you expect the QQQ to rise, you buy a call.
- If you expect the QQQ to fall, you buy a put.

This brings us to another important aspect of the options market: the two option types. A *call* gives the buyer the right (but not the obligation) to *buy* the underlying security. A *put* gives the buyer the right (but not the obligation) to *sell* the underlying security. Options on stocks or indexes usually refer to 100 shares. So one option contract gives the option holder these rights over 100 shares of a specified security. (As one of the standardized terms, every option is related to one security, and cannot be transferred.) You are not required—as an option holder—to buy or sell the underlying security. You can also sell the option itself for a profit or at a loss.

How to Use a QQQ Option

Every QQQ option gives you the right to buy or sell 100 shares of the QQQ. Let's assume our system has determined that at a certain point in time, the Nasdaq is undervalued. The probabilities are in favor of a turnaround. The QQQ currently trades for $38 per share—a good price, but you're pretty sure the QQQ will be at $50 by the end of the year. But "pretty sure" isn't good enough for you to risk your money. After all, the market could collapse again.

How do you make sure you get the stock at a good price without the risk? QQQ call options solve this problem. (See Figure 17.1.) Now, there are many trades you could make, because there are many options to choose from. They come with a variety of strike prices and monthly expirations. And each option carries a different price—and therefore offers different profit opportunities.

Say WaveStrength recommends a QQQ January $40 call option for $300 (or $3 a share, since each option represents 100 shares) and you decide to buy it. This means that the option fixes the price of QQQ you would pay at $40 per share and if you decide to exercise the call, that is what you will pay. For example, even if QQQ's value goes up to $50, $60, or $100, the call fixes *your* exercise price at $40 per share—at any time between now and January.

Let's take a look at the option's components:

The price you pay for the option—in this example, $300—is called a premium.

The premium level changes with time and movement in the underlying security, and depends on a wide range of factors, the most important being the actual price of the stock (other factors play a role, and I'll discuss them at greater length later on).

This call gives you the right to buy 100 shares of the QQQ for $40 per share. In buying a call, it means that you think the QQQ is going higher in value, so you're making an educated guess in acquiring the right to buy 100 shares of QQQ stock for $40 a share anytime before the third Saturday in January, no matter what the market price of the QQQ is at the time.

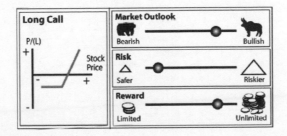

Figure 17.1 Long Call

ANATOMY OF AN OPTION

1. QQQ   2. January   3. $40   4. Call @   5. 3

1. Underlying instrument
2. Expiration month
3. Strike price
4. Type (call or put)
5. Price premium (3 represents $300)

If the QQQ rallies to $45 a share, your call option could be worth as much as $800, netting you a 266 percent return. (QQQ January YO call: $3. QQQ rallies up to $45 per share. $5 worth of premium is added to January YO calls [could differ given time and volatility]. New value: $800.)

If the QQQ does not go in the desired direction, your maximum loss is the $300 you paid for the call option.

January is the expiration month for the option. In some cases, it may be next January or (for longer-term LEAPS options) a January two or even three years out.

The $40 amount represents the strike price, the amount you will pay per share if you decide to exercise the option. (Options are offered at various strike prices, known as a series.)

Now, let's take the opposite approach. A month or two later, the QQQ is trading for $43, and you think it has gotten into overvalued territory. Rather than go through the expensive hassle of selling short, you decide to buy QQQ puts instead. (See Figure 17.2.)

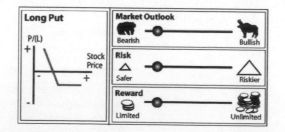

Figure 17.2 Long Put

Like calls, puts are available at a variety of terms—strike prices and expiration months—but in this example, let's say you buy a January $45 put for 5 ($500). Anytime between now and January, you have the right to sell 100 shares of QQQ for $45 per share.

If the QQQ falls in your predicted direction to, say, $40 a share, your put will be worth approximately $800, netting you another nice gain. QQQ January US put: $5 QQQ falls down to $40 per share. $3 worth of premium is added to January US puts [could change given time and volatility]. New value: $800.) *Congratulations!* While most investors have lost money on this down move, your put option enabled you to sell 100 shares of the QQQ for $45 even though it currently trades for $40.

If the QQQ does not fall, your loss will be limited to the $500 you paid for the put. As you can see, calls and puts give you limited risk with unlimited profit potential.

Some people buy options as insurance. They either take a wait-and-see approach to a stock they are interested in by using call options or they hedge against loss by buying put options.

But big profits in options can also be made by buying and re-selling the options themselves. The problem is, about three-fourths of all options expire worthless, so it is no easy task to consistently make a net profit in options. You need an edge.

The key to making this strategy a winner is getting an accurate market forecast and finding the right QQQ option at the right price. And that's the essence of the WaveStrength forecasting system.

So just where do option premiums come from?

The premium of any option depends partly on its relation to the underlying security. This is signified by the option's strike price in relation to the market price of the security at the time you purchase the option. If the option's strike price is equal to the current market price, the option is at-the-money.

For example, with QQQ stock trading at $36 per share, a QQQ 36 call and QQQ 36 put would both be at-the-money.

A call with a strike price above the market price or a put with a strike price below the market price is out-of-the-money. That simply means it would be worthless if it expired today.

With the QQQ stock trading at $36 per share, a QQQ 40 call and a QQQ 32 put will be out-of-the-money.

You would be likely to buy an out-of-the-money option because you believe that, given the volatility of the shares, they will move beyond the strike price before the option expires—putting them in-the-money (that's when the call's strike price is below the current market price or the put's strike price is above the market price). The option now has intrinsic value—a calculable worth.

Obviously, in-the-money options will command a higher premium than out-of-the-money options. In fact, for every dollar an option is in-the-money, it will acquire a dollar of premium value to reflect that condition. (Options often exceed the intrinsic value equal to the number of points in-the-money; more on this phenomenon later.)

Out-of-the-money options move far more rapidly in favor of the buyer than in-the-money options when the underlying price moves your way. (More on this in Bryan Bottarelli's "Six Trading Rules" section in Chapter 19.) Depending on the time until expiration, they also deteriorate more slowly than in-the-money options if the underlying stock moves adversely—as a general rule.

A BRIEF REVIEW

An option's premium—the price you pay for it—is determined by several factors: at-the-money, in-the-money, or out-of-the-money.

Calls:

When the current market value of the security = strike price, the call is at-the-money.

When the current market value of the security > strike price, the call is in-the-money.

When the current market value of the security < strike price, the call is out-of-the-money.

Puts:

When the current market value of the security = strike price, the put is at-the-money.

When the current market value of the security < strike price, the put is in-the-money.

When the current market value of the security > strike price, the put is out-of-the-money.

THE MISUNDERSTOOD VALUE OF OPTIONS: TIME VALUE

The price you pay for an option is made up of two variables: *intrinsic value* and *time value*. (Time value is also called extrinsic value.)

- Intrinsic value is easy to understand. It's based on the underlying stock price, which is pretty much set in stone. Intrinsic value is equal to the number of points an option is in-the-money. For example, when a call's strike price is $45 and a current market value is $47 per share, there are two points of intrinsic value ($47 and $45). The opposite direction applies for puts. For example, if the put's strike price is $45 and current market value is $47, there is no intrinsic value. However, if market price falls to $44 per share, the put gains one point of intrinsic value.
- Time value is the remaining premium after calculating intrinsic value. In cases where there is no intrinsic value, the entire option premium consists of time value. We may further define time value as a perception of value caused and affected by the option and underlying security's volatility and time until expiration. The value of an option can be pushed up or down significantly due to the psychological and risk factors reflected in time value premium.

If options' prices were based on their intrinsic value alone, there would be no reason to buy options other than for insurance or hedging purposes. An option's premium would be fixed, moving up or down exactly in the same degree as the price value of the underlying security. But beyond an option's intrinsic value, it is time value that makes options so interesting—and which creates profit opportunities for you.

Options are described as *wasting assets*. They have a fixed term of life and die a little every day until they reach their expiration date. Unlike stock investors, options investors may not have time to recoup losses in a sudden turnaround. That risk can be reflected in the premium.

For example, say it is January and you're looking to buy more QQQ options. Currently the stock is at $40, and you think it will go up to at least $45, but you're not sure when. Well, to show how time value affects premium, consider what would happen if you were to buy a March 45 call or a December 45 call.

Both are calls on the same stock at the same strike price, but the premiums could still be miles apart. Why?

With the QQQ stock trading for $40, the QQQ 45 call option must go up five points before it would be at-the-money. The question is, would you rather have two months (March) for the stock to go up five points, or 11 months (December)?

Most people would pick 11 months and would buy the December 45 call. With more time, there is less chance of losing the entire investment. But of course, there is a price for that extra time. You will discover that the longer the time until expiration, the greater the time value premium—even when current market value and strike price are identical.

Options are speculative investments, and their value is as much a slave to supply and demand as anything else. As a general rule, the more risk someone is willing to accept, the more they're going to want to get paid for it (just as insurance companies expect more money from lousy drivers than from safer drivers).

The longer the time until expiration, the more time the option has to meet your profit target. That reduces your risk, but it also means you would have to pay a higher premium for the extra months.

The question is, should you bet money that the QQQ stock will rise five points in only two months? Answering that question is the key to making money with options.

Making Big Money from QQQ Options

Here is the WaveStrength secret you need to remember: *Buy an option when nobody wants it, and then resell it when everybody does.*

In other words, try to find a cheap option that you think is in for a big move, and then buy it. When the move happens, the price of your option will move, too. Your option will be in demand, and investors will be willing to pay you for your option. If you sell, you have instant profits.

That's the essence of our WaveStrength trading system, as you'll soon come to learn.

HOW WAVESTRENGTH FINDS THE WINNERS

Finding the right option takes work. Unfortunately, there is no easy way to teach you how to find these kinds of options on your own. You can learn to trade online yourself. But if you insist on using a broker, choose wisely. You may already have a broker you trust. If so, excellent; but make sure your broker has experience buying and selling options. And above all, don't forget to ask about commission rates. Option traders tend to be more sophisticated than the average broker client, so paying full retail for trades makes no sense. But there are four important caveats to remember.

Trading Costs

Whenever you buy an option, there's a commission. Whenever you sell that option back into the marketplace, there's a commission. Obviously, the more commissions you pay, the less money you keep in your account. If you go with a full-service broker, expect to pay higher commissions.

On the plus side, you can also expect a wider range of services and greater personal attention from a full-service broker. Discount and online brokers often charge lower commissions, but for the most part you are on your own. You may also discover that you are not free to engage in all forms of option trading, especially the more exotic (or higher-risk) forms of trading. Some online services limit what you can do with options, and don't allow uncovered call writing, spreads, or straddles, the higher-level option strategies. If you determine that you need the flexibility to use these strategies, you may also need to pay higher commissions to get a broader range of services.

While our examples are limited to single-option trades, you should also be aware that the trading costs on a per-trade basis are going to be lower as well. The difference in trading costs for a single contract and for 10 contracts is negligible.

Level of Service

Another consideration is the level of service. At first glance, you may think it's wise to do your options buying with a discount or online broker. But if your service broker at the discount house cannot execute your orders quickly or keep track of your positions, this might end up costing you thousands of dollars. If you want to stay with your broker, see if you can negotiate a reduced rate on the trades you will be doing.

Special Rules and Restrictions

pattern day trader

A third point to remember concerns your level of transactions. Under SEC rules, if you execute four or more trades within five consecutive days on a single security or its options, you are classified as a "pattern day trader," and you'll be required to have at least $25,000 on deposit with your broker on each day you execute those trades.

Investor Suitability

You also need to meet suitability rules before you will be allowed to trade options. Whoever your broker is, you cannot buy options unless you complete the paperwork and the broker determines that you understand the risks and are qualified to trade options. Make sure you read the literature your broker is required to give you, fill out the forms completely, and set up a cash account with enough money to pay in full for the options you want to buy. Also, understand that getting an options account sometimes takes up to two weeks' time. This should not discourage you from trading options. Going through the motions required by your brokerage to get an options account is well worth the wait.

Keeping It Simple, but Profitable

For most investors, we recommend keeping it simple. You may begin with buying calls and puts and not getting into more advanced strategies, at least not just yet. This guarantees that you cannot lose anything more than your initial investment. Let your broker know this when registering your options trading account and you shouldn't have a problem. This level of activity is called Level 1 trading in options.

"BUYING TO OPEN" OPTIONS

When you're ready to purchase an option, your instruction is "buy to open."

This means you are taking a new, fully paid options position that, when executed, will be entered into the exchange computer. You can tell your broker to buy the option immediately and to pay whatever the going rate is. This is called a *market order*.

Or you can set a *limit price*, meaning that your order will not be executed until the option hits a certain price. Of course, there is no better order to place. If the market is moving quickly, it could be best to use a market order to ensure you're in on the trade. In other cases, using a limit order guarantees that if you get filled, you'll get the exact price you want. (I prefer limit orders in most market conditions.) Your order may not get filled for a while, but your risk is limited, and there are always other opportunities in options.

For example, if you tell your broker to put in a market order to buy a "DJX March 80 call," you will pay whatever the price of the option currently is. If the option's price is moving fast, your order could be executed for far more than you're willing to pay.

However, if you tell your broker to put in a limit order to buy a "DJX March 80 call" for a premium of "5 to open," your trade will not be executed unless the price is at or below $500. Your risk is kept firmly in check, since you know exactly how much you will be paying for the option. This also means there is a chance your options order will never be executed if the premium never falls to $500 or below.

"Buy to open" is an important specification. For those who engage in short options, the initial transaction would be "sell to open" and it would be closed with an order, "buy to close." You want to be absolutely certain that your intention is made clear when you place your order.

"SELLING TO CLOSE" OPTIONS

When it's time to sell your option, tell your broker to "sell to close" the position.

You sell your option to the market, receiving money in exchange for giving up your rights to it. You could sell it for a profit or for a loss, depending on what the market is willing to pay. But either way, you're out of the game. Make sure you get the phrasing right.

You can also give your broker a *stop-loss order*. This is an instruction to your broker to sell your holding if the price falls to a certain level—to prevent further losses. This helps limit your risk and lock in gains.

For instance, if you bought your option at 5 ($500) and it goes to 10 ($1,000), you might want to tell your broker to put in a stop-loss at 7.50. This means if the price hits $750, your broker will automatically execute a sell order, thus locking in gains. But keep in mind that calling in a stop-loss only tells your broker to start executing the order when it hits your sell price. If the option is dropping rapidly, by the time your order hits the trading floor the price could be below the 7.50 level.

In general, you should make sure your broker understands that you want a stop-loss order and not a sell order; otherwise the order

---

A BRIEF REVIEW OF EXECUTING TRADES

When you're ready to purchase, for example, a QQQ option, your instruction is "buy to open." This means you are taking a new, fully paid-for option position.

- If you tell your broker to buy the option immediately, this is called a *market order*.
- If you tell your broker to buy the option for a designated price, this is called a *limit order*.

Although market orders are a good idea when the market is moving quickly, I prefer using limit orders to specify the exact price you want to pay. Your order may not get filled, but your risk is limited. For example:

- If you tell your broker to put in a market order to buy a March 40 QQQ call, you will pay the current price, whatever the level. If the option's price is moving fast, your order could be executed for far more than you're really willing to pay.
- If you tell your broker to put in a limit order to buy a March 40 call at 5 to open, your trade will not be executed unless the price is at or below 5 ($500).

When it's time to sell your option, tell your broker to "sell to close" the position.

might be executed immediately, and you could end up reselling an option worth 10 for 7.50. Simple mistakes like this illustrate why it is essential to find a broker you can trust and, more to the point, one who has the experience to understand the nuances and definitions of different types of option trades.

Worst-case scenario: If the market moves in the wrong direction relative to the option you picked and you are unable to sell it (also known as "bid goes to zero"), then it will expire worthless. In this case, there's nothing you or your broker can do unless you step in and enter a different order. But, again, just like any stock, your loss is always limited to the amount you originally paid for the option.

FOUR-STEP STRATEGY

In finding the best option opportunities, the WaveStrength strategy involves a four-step process:

Profit step 1: Establish a trend line.
Profit step 2: Monitor market fluctuations.
Profit step 3: Isolate an opportunity.
Profit step 4: Trade.

Here is one example of how these alerts work using our trade on Family Dollar Stores (FDO) from February 22, 2005.

Profit Step # 1: Establish a Trend Line

The trend line combines various indicators—Japanese candlestick charts, head-and-shoulders formations, and Fibonacci grids. It then charts out a trend line showing where the market has been and, more importantly, where it is likely to go. (See Figure 17.3.)

For this trade, WaveStrength indicated that Family Dollar Stores (FDO) broke out of its recent downtrend on October 22. This was an early indication that FDO stock was headed higher— but before making a trade, more analysis had to be done in Step 2.

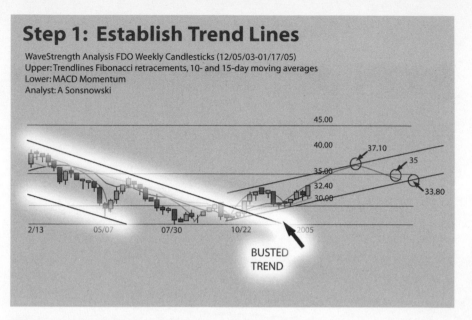

Step 1: Establish Trend Lines

WaveStrength Analysis FDO Weekly Candlesticks (12/05/03-01/17/05)
Upper: Trendlines Fibonacci retracements, 10- and 15-day moving averages
Lower: MACD Momentum
Analyst: A Sonsnowski

Figure 17.3 Family Dollar Stores: Profit Step 1

Profit Step 2: Monitor Market Fluctuations

Once a trend line is established, WaveStrength begins to monitor
market activity. (See Figure 17.4.)

WaveStrength not only watches daily price action, but also adds
information as the trading day unfolds.

In early 2005, FDO stock confirmed its new uptrend when it established support at the bottom of its new trend line. This support
meant that it was time to forecast the next up-move in FDO, which
leads to step 3.

Profit Step 3: Isolate an Opportunity

This is where things heat up. When WaveStrength spots a confirmed
up-trend at the bottom of its trend line, you know there's a very good
chance that the stock will rise to the top of that trend line.

As you can see from the chart in Figure 17.5, WaveStrength forecasted that FDO stock would go from $32.40 to $35 within two

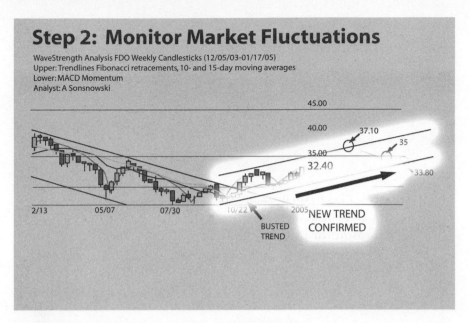

Figure 17.4 Family Dollar Stores: Profit Step 2

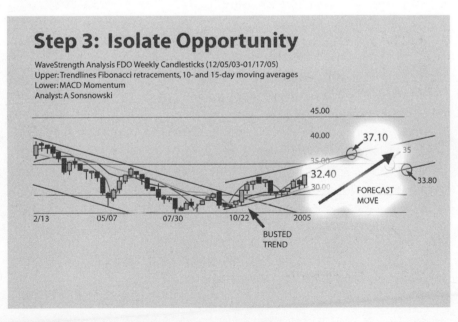

Figure 17.5 Family Dollar Stores: Profit Step 3

weeks—and it could even get as high as $37.10 over the next month. Once a forecast like that is made, then it's time for step 4.

Profit Step 4: Trade

Once you have a forecast in place, this is where you determine exactly what to do.

- On January 18 at 11:30 a.m., we told WaveStrength Traders to "buy the FDO April 32.5 calls (FDO DZ) between $1.85 and $2.10 per contract."
- As a measure of protection, we also told them to "place a protective stop-loss at US$1.00 per contract."
- By February 2, FDO stock had gone up $2.50—exactly as we predicted. Our April 32.5 calls were showing a 61 percent gain, so we immediately told WaveStrength traders to "sell FDO April 32.5 calls (FDO DZ) at or above $3.30."

To sum up the Family Dollar Stores trade:

- The strategy indicated a buy on FDO April 32.5 calls on 1/18/05 for $2.05.
- The strategy was entered with a protective stop at $1.00 to minimize potential losses.
- The strategy indicated a sell on FDO April 32.5 calls on 2/2/05 for $3.30.
- *Total gains: 61 percent in 14 days.*

To prove just how easy making money with WaveStrength options trading can be, here's another (recent) trade, on Office Depot (ODP), from March 18, 2005:

Profit Step 1: Establish a Trend Line

As explained earlier, everything starts by WaveStrength establishing a trend line. (See Figure 17.6.)

In this trade, WaveStrength identified a very strong uptrend in

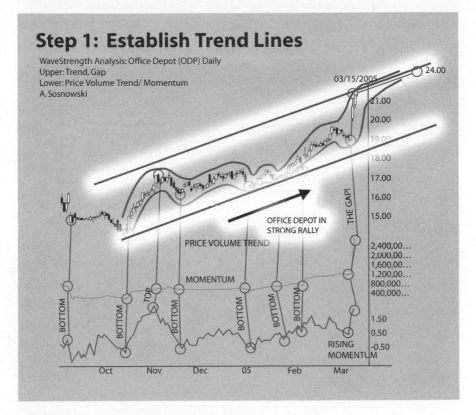

Figure 17.6 Office Depot: Profit Step 1

Office Depot going back to 2004—and forecasted the upward move would continue. But to be sure, we continued to step 2.

Profit Step 2: Monitor Market Fluctuations

When Office Depot made a big price jump in early March, we knew that WaveStrength's forecast was coming true. (See Figure 17.7.)

With the uptrend confirmed, prices were poised to move higher in the next 7 to 10 trading days.

Profit Step 3: Isolate an Opportunity

Momentum in Office Depot continued to rise, which gave us a fore-casted up-move from the current price of $21.50 to a high of at least $24 over the next 7 to 10 days. (See Figure 17.8.)

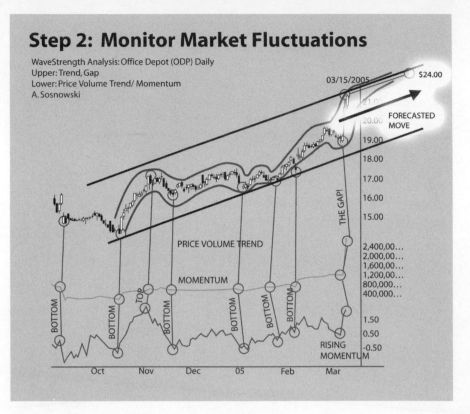

Figure 17.7 Office Depot: Profit Step 2

It was time to make a trade.

Profit Step 4: Trade

Once we had a forecast in place, we knew exactly what to do.

- On March 15 at 3:10 P.M., we told WaveStrength Traders to "buy the Office Depot July 20 calls (ODP GD) under $2.40, good for the day."
- As a measure of protection, we also told them to "place a protective stop-loss at $1.80."
- By March 18 at 10:00 A.M., ODP stock had gone up another $1.30, exactly as predicted. The July 20 calls were showing a 66

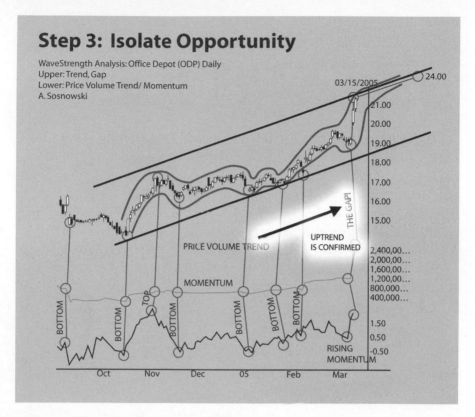

Step 3: Isolate Opportunity

WaveStrength Analysis: Office Depot (ODP) Daily
Upper: Trend, Gap
Lower: Price Volume Trend/ Momentum
A. Sosnowski

Figure 17.8 Office Depot: Profit Step 3

percent gain, so we immediately told WaveStrength Traders to "sell the Office Depot July 20 calls (ODP GD) at or above $3.00, good for the day."

To sum up the Office Depot trade:

- The strategy indicated a buy on Office Depot July 20 calls on 3/15/05 for $2.40.
- The strategy was entered with a protective stop at $1.80 to minimize potential losses.
- The strategy indicated a sell of Office Depot July 20 calls on 3/18/05 for $3.95.
- *Total gains: 66 percent in three days.*

TRADE FREQUENCY

Some of your option trades will be longer-term—perhaps as long as four months—and some will be short-term, one day to a week. We have found that for our subscribers, each trade lasts 7 to 10 days on average.

Remember, you pay for time when trading options. That's why we try to play the cheapest options to profit off a quick market move. Sometimes that involves playing "front month" contracts. Other times that involves playing a contract that is two to three months out. It all depends on which is the best tool for capitalizing on the mood of the market and making the most amount of money. And if our move takes longer than expected, we know that we can always roll our option into the next month.

Of course, the biggest question is, "When is the best time to sell?" Exposing yourself to the market for an extended period of time simply increases the odds of something going wrong. For that reason, our team likes to take profits at the drop of a hat.

Chicago Board Options Exchange (CBOE) trading rule: Ten base hits are three times better than two home runs!

- In baseball, if you hit two solo home runs, your team scores two runs.
- If you get 10 straight base hits, your team scores seven runs.

It's obvious which approach is better. Professional options traders know it's better to hit a string of consecutive singles than to hit one home run but then strike out three times. WaveStrength traders adopt this approach in their trading. They take their profits and run!

The minute one of our positions hits 25 to 30 percent gains, my finger starts to twitch. That tells us it's time to start thinking about locking in our profits. At that time, we talk with Adam. If he tells us we have more gains to make, we wait it out (as nerve-racking as that can be). Once Adam and Bryan agree our gains have been maximized, we know it is time to sell. The time between alerts can be anything between four hours and one month.

FIVE PROFIT-YIELDING OPTIONS SECRETS

The following five secrets were designed to help you to make the most of trading options in today's market.

Secret #1: Value Investing Is Becoming Extinct

Traditionally speaking, a value investor is someone who invests in stocks based on the fundamentals. The intense study of a stock's perceived value versus what a stock trades for has made investors like Warren Buffett seriously wealthy. Finding market inefficiency based on pure financial analysis reveals when a stock is undervalued compared to its peers.

For the past 50 years (or perhaps even longer) this thesis has been one of the main investing moneymakers for many people. But in today's market, value investors are getting hit hard for one reason: they are utterly dependent on reported "facts."

And, as we've come to know, accountants lie. CEOs lie. Brokers lie.

If you can't trust the financials, then how can anyone possibly make any traditional value assumptions? They can't! I'm sure you've heard more than enough about Enron, but let me give you an example that you probably haven't heard about yet.

A UBS PaineWebber broker named Chung Wu wanted to tell his customers to sell Enron stock. On August 21, 2001, he e-mailed 73 clients advising them that Enron was in financial trouble and despite UBS PaineWebber's "strong buy" rating, he recommended selling.

Once Enron's accountants and other officials got wind of Wu's e-mail, they took action. They wrote to Wu's superiors that "this is very disturbing" and to "handle this situation." By the end of the day, Chung Wu was unemployed.

When questioned, Enron officials and UBS PaineWebber had no comment. As it turned out, UBS PaineWebber's Houston office handled the accounts of Kenneth Lay.

We all know what happened to Enron's stock.

The sad truth is, there are probably hundreds of other Enrons out there shielding debt, fudging balance sheets, and putting a rosy spin on a bleak situation. In the end, the ones who get hurt are the individual value investors.

Today, you just can't trust numbers. But there is a way to get rock-solid data without having to question its validity for one second—data that's never changed, but still reveals all you need to know about making financial decisions.

That's why QQQ traders don't care when accountants lie. There are only four numbers we need to understand.

Secret #2: Four Numbers That Are Nothing but the Rock-Solid Truth

The only four numbers you can bet your life on are the ones that drive our WaveStrength Trading System. Unlike traditional long-term value investing (or any other sort of investing based on financial reports), index options trading is based on pure facts.

There are indeed four numbers that you can take to the bank each and every trading day. And these are the only numbers that pit traders focus on. They are the heart of our WaveStrength trading system.

The four numbers, simply enough, are open, high, low, and close. WaveStrength analysis charts the Nasdaq-100, QQQ, and an array of other indexes using the opening price, the high price of the day, the low price of the day, and the price at the market's close.

This is called candlestick charting, and it's one of the only trustworthy analytical systems out there today. Candlestick charting uses numbers that are indisputable facts. They cannot be changed by accountants or destroyed by paper shredders.

Making market forecasts using these numbers is the essence of WaveStrength. It allows us to be unaffected by the news. It allows us to remain unemotional about the markets. And we are never forced to question the validity of our figures.

Bottom line: The only numbers you can really trust are the very numbers we use to arrive at our market forecasts. Everything else has the potential to become smoke and mirrors.

Secret #3: The Secret of Delta

Options are purposely written in a language very few so-called Wall Street experts understand, and it's not every day professional QQQ traders will sit down with you and explain how they trade. They prefer to keep that to themselves, because the more people who understand it, the less money they will make. As a result, options trading typically means getting thrown in with the sharks—you either swim for your life or become the chum.

Well, here's a little tip that will help you swim with the sharks.

To understand how your QQQ option will move in relation to the QQQ stock, you must understand an option's *delta*.

You can access an option's delta using any higher-end tracking service. (We prefer the IVolatility.com web site (www.ivolatility.com).

An option's delta will always range between 100 and −100. Calls have positive delta. Puts have negative delta. Quite simply, the delta represents the change in dollar value of your option as the QQQ stock moves up or down $1.00.

For example, if the QQQ stock goes up $1.00, a QQQ call with a 50 delta goes up $0.50. If the QQQ stock goes down $1.00, a QQQ call with a 50 delta goes down $0.50.

The reverse is true for QQQ puts. If the QQQ stock goes down $1.00, a QQQ put with a −30 delta goes up $0.30. If the QQQ stock goes up $1.00, a QQQ put with a −30 delta goes down $0.30.

Get it? Okay, try this example:

QQQ stock trades for $30. You buy a QQQ call for 2.50 with a delta of 50. QQQ stock goes up $0.50. How much does your QQQ call go up? If you said $0.25, you're right.

Remember, the delta is based on a $1.00 stock movement. Since the QQQ increased only $0.50, the delta of 50 is cut in half.

Try another:

QQQ stock trades for $30. You buy a QQQ put for 3 with a delta of −30. QQQ stock goes down $2.00. How much does your QQQ put go up? If you said $0.60, you're right. A $2.00 down move with a −30 delta put means a 0.60 increase in your option premium.

Delta is a calculation that is drilled into the head of every professional QQQ pit trader. It is a valuable tool for calculating your option's value (and one that very few investors understand).

Secret #4: How to Turn Time Decay into a Benefit

If you've ever visited a trading floor, you've seen the pit traders screaming buy or sell orders at the top of their lungs. The reason there's such a mad rush to buy and sell options is time decay.

In other words, if you're holding an options position, time is constantly working against you. An option is like a new car. Once you drive that car off the lot, it starts to depreciate in value. Since every option has an expiration date, the clock starts ticking the moment you buy it.

Professional traders know this, so as soon as they have the opportunity to buy or sell a position to lock in gains, they scratch and claw to make it so. They take gains—no matter how large or small—at the drop of a hat, and never look back.

At the end of the day, their series of base hits has piled up into a nice stash of money. And that's where the majority of options investors go wrong. Instead of quickly locking in gains, many investors try to milk every nickel out of the trade.

Most likely, they end up holding too long, and their option expires worthless. Or they try hitting a home run every trade. Of course, they'll connect once in a while. But they'll also have a lot of strikeouts.

Here's a tip: It's nearly impossible to make the perfect trade (in other words, buying at the exact low and selling at the exact high). Trying to make the perfect trade every time will cost you more money than you make. (More on this in Bryan's Six Trading Rules in Chapter 19.)

This is why WaveStrength adopts the mentality of the professional options trader: quickly take your gains off the table and never look back. Not many advisory services offer this type of quick-hitting profit mentality. And that's why we consider it a secret.

Secret #5: Own the Entire Market for $150

There are two final points I'd like to make about QQQ trading secrets. They are:

1. When traded correctly, options are safer than stocks.
2. When traded correctly, options offer more explosive profits than stocks.

QQQ options allow you to own interests in the top 100 companies on the Nasdaq for about $150. This is a powerful statement.

Quite honestly, QQQ options are cheap. For a very small up-front cost, they allow you to control a large amount of stock. Instead of spending $1,000 on Cisco, eBay, Dell, and Microsoft, you can own interests in them all via a QQQ option for $150.

Plus, the risk is not as great. Say you think tech stocks are due for a pop, so you spend $1,000 on a leading tech company. Then, news hits that its accounting figures are being questioned, and the stock drops 15 percent. You've put all your trust in that stock, and as a result, you lose $150 right there.

But if you buy a QQQ option instead, your loss could be minimal—because the troubled company is just one out of 100 companies that make up the QQQ. So, even though one stock is going down, your hunch that tech stocks are in for a boost could be correct.

Playing the QQQ is safer than putting all your trust in a handful of stocks. It spreads the risk around. QQQ options also give you more bang for your buck. Say the QQQ stock goes from $40 to $42 a share. That's a 5 percent increase. A QQQ at-the-money call usually starts off trading for 1.50 ($150).

A $2 up-move in the QQQ equates to a one-point increase in the option price, or $100, which turns your 1.50 QQQ option into a 2.50 option. That's a 66 percent move.

Comparing a 5 percent move in the stock to a 66 percent move in the corresponding option, you can see that QQQ options offer more explosive profit-making power than stocks. Overall, QQQ options help you minimize losses and maximize gains. Now that's what I call power!

Useful Information

The WaveStrength team publishes a daily e-letter called *Market Report,* which you can find at www.dynamicmarket report.com/ws-market report.

For more current information on the system, check out www.dynamic marketreport.com/wave strength.

CHAPTER 18

TRADING SECRET NUMBER TWELVE: THE SECRET STRATEGIES OF CBOE FLOOR TRADERS

By Bryan Bottarelli

The following six secrets were taken directly off the floor of the Chicago Board Options Exchange. When I walked away from the CBOE pits, I took these secrets with me.[1] Today, I use these very same strategies to take the advantage *away* from the CBOE floor trader and give it back to the individual investor who follows my WaveStrength trading system.

Bryan Bottarelli was trained as a pit trader at the Chicago Board of Options Exchange (CBOE). He is the Chief Trading Strategist for the WaveStrength options trading systems.

CBOE FLOOR SECRET #1: YOU CAN USE THE SPREAD TO MAXIMIZE YOUR GAINS

If you want to trade options profitably, you have to look at exactly how professional options traders make their money and learn from it. But don't worry; it's a simple lesson to learn. Essentially, the game is rigged in their favor. And it's legal.

Options traders simply play what is known as a *spread.* Take, for example, the options string shown in Table 18.1 on the Nasdaq-100 (NDX). When you look at an options quote, you'll see a bid price and an ask price.

What this means is that at a given time—no matter what—options traders will buy the Nasdaq (NDX) 1,500 call for 8.90 and will sell the NDX 1,500 call for 9.70.

If you go down the line, you'll see that CBOE floor traders make their money from the difference in the bid price and the ask price. They buy 100 NDX 1,500 calls for 8.90 and sell 100 NDX 1,500 calls for 9.70—and pocket the 0.80 difference. (In dollar terms, that's $80 per contract. Do that 100 times, and a CBOE floor trader can make $8,000 off one trade.)

They play this spread all day, every day. All they do is match buyers

TABLE 18.1 OPTIONS STRING

STRIKE	SYMBOL	LAST	CHG	BID	ASK	VOL	OPEN INT
825.00	NDKDG.X	700.00	0.00	646.80	648.40	0	10
1,200.00	NDTDN.X	349.60	0.00	272.40	274.00	0	10
1,325.00	NDTDG.X	157.00	0.00	147.60	149.60	0	40
1,350.00	NDTDQ.X	132.70	0.00	123.00	125.00	0	100
1,400.00	NDTDR.X	80.50	3.50	75.10	76.90	3	243
1,425.00	NDTDI.X	61.50	5.20	53.00	54.80	60	303
1,450.00	NDTDS.X	34.00	2.40	34.00	35.00	184	293
1,475.00	NDTDT.X	19.50	0.50	18.90	19.80	352	834
1,500.00	NDVDJ.X	9.30	0.70	8.90	9.70	402	2,492
1,525.00	NDVDA.X	3.80	0.20	3.60	4.00	303	3,699
1,550.00	NDVDK.X	1.30	0.20	1.20	1.40	264	4,521

and sellers and keep the difference. So, naturally, traders need to buy and sell as many options as they can to make a profit.

The more they trade, the more money they make. If they don't trade, they don't profit. And if I know anything about working at the CBOE, it's that options traders are greedy as hell.

CBOE FLOOR SECRET #2: GREED IS THEIR BIGGEST WEAKNESS AND YOUR GREATEST ALLY

Options traders are fiercely competitive. They trade for their individual profits only—nothing else. That is why you'll see them fighting, scratching, and clawing for every contract they can get their hands on. But this is how the WaveStrength secret of the spread beats the options traders at their own game.

When Adam alerts me to a WaveStrength forecast, I milk the spread the traders play. In fact, not only do I milk it, I take it away outright. Here's how.

You can put in a lowball offer for certain options, and let the traders fight over who gets them. You then immediately sell them back to the *same* options traders when the market ticks in your direction. Using the earlier example, I'd have you put in a bid for the NDX 1,500 call. But instead of placing that bid at 9.70 (the price at which the pit traders would like to sell us that contract), you'll place your bid at 9.10—just above the 8.90 price where they'll buy that contract themselves.

Being the greedy crowd they are, it's almost inevitable that someone in the pit will bite and sell you the option. Then, as soon as the market ticks in your direction, you immediately turn around and sell the option back to the traders—*for a tidy profit.*

As you can see, you'll be using the options spread to *your* advantage. When using a limit order, always put it as close to the traders' bid price as possible. That takes away the floor trader's advantage, and gives you a great entry price on your options play. That's the secret of the spread.

CBOE FLOOR SECRET #3: THERE IS ONE TYPE OF PIT PLAY OPTIONS TRADERS FEAR MOST

Professional options traders fear *straddle* and *strangle* positions. Don't be put off by the options jargon; this secret is really quite simple.

Straddles and strangles are descriptive names for two types of options positions. They involve buying both a call and a put at the same time.

Hmm . . . since a call makes money as the market goes up, and a put makes money as the market goes down, isn't that a conflicting strategy? On the face of it, you might think so. But it's not. Not by a long shot. In a volatile market, these positions literally turn options traders' faces white.

I remember one instance when a big-time Merrill Lynch broker strolled in and wanted a quote for August 50 Apple Computer straddles. When asked his size (that's trader talk for "How many are you looking to buy?"), the broker replied, "300 by 300."

Remember the earlier example where a CBOE floor trader can make $8,000 hitting the bid and ask price. Well, this broker wanted 300 contracts. And he wanted both calls *and* puts!

In other words, this broker was saying to the options traders that, depending on the quote you give me, I'm willing to buy 300 calls *and* 300 puts. Now, this broker probably knew exactly which play he wanted more. He just asked for both prices to keep the pit traders guessing which side he was betting on.

Talk about bluffing! This kind of options trading is just like a game of poker. He wanted to keep the options traders guessing by acting like he was considering both up and down moves. Thus, he gets a good price on 300 contracts.

When the traders in my pit heard this, they all looked like they'd just seen a ghost. One new trader was so nervous, he literally bolted out of that pit! I kid you not.

These positions make options traders run for cover. And that's exactly why I trade them. Check out the graph in Figure 18.1 and you'll see why. It shows how a strangle position makes a profit.

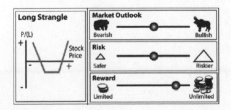

Figure 18.1 Long Strangle

As you can see, the downside is capped, while the upside is limitless. In this position, you profit if the market goes down, and you profit if it goes up. As long as the market doesn't trade flat (meaning go up 11 points one day, down 19 points the next, etc.), we profit. It's a beautiful thing. Now you see why I like these positions so much.

Trading like this makes the professional traders sweat. And that's the way you and I like it. The secret to trading strangles and straddles is in knowing that professional options traders hate having these positions eat away at their profits.

CBOE FLOOR SECRET #4: PROFESSIONAL OPTIONS TRADERS ARE THE WORST MARKET FORECASTERS YOU'LL EVER MEET

Given secret #2, it may seem unbelievable to you that this is true. But it is. Options traders are *not* market forecasters. In fact, most of these guys don't have the slightest clue where the market is going. And if you think about it, you'll understand why.

Options traders are trained to trade options. Nothing more. They are taught how to hedge, how to maximize their leverage, how to increase or decrease volatility, how to price their options, and how to play a spread to guarantee gains. None of that has a thing to do with market forecasting. As a result, the guys on the floor have no bias. Not one bit.

And that's by design. You see, the companies that give their options traders the money to trade with don't want them speculating. It's too costly for them to train traders how to speculate correctly. All they want them to do is trade the spread, limit the risk, and hedge against losses. That's it. No fancy stuff.

For example, it could be as clear as day to everyone that the market is set to fall. Nonetheless, options traders will sell you put after put. They'll do this because they have a spread to fall back on. But sometimes that spread is not good enough. And with a forecasting system like WaveStrength working against them, it's no good at all. To us, however, it's money in the bank.

In fact, our trades during February and March 2005 produced a total of 27 winning plays. So you'd better believe that some options traders out there are feeling the pinch from our system.

But if they want to play the game, they have to step up to the plate. So remember, just because floor traders know how to trade doesn't mean they have the slightest clue where the market is headed. That's why you and I have an advantage, and where they don't.

CBOE FLOOR SECRET #5: OPTIONS PRICES GET SOFT BETWEEN 11 A.M. AND 1 P.M.

This is a no-brainer for most floor traders. But an outsider would never have a clue. You'll understand what I mean when I tell you about a typical day at the CBOE.

The most intense action in the market happens right when it opens: futures trading. That typically forces the market to open either up or down. And this has the most profound effect on options prices.

Based on this initial burst, buyers and sellers scramble to open and close their positions. This is generally when you see floor traders screaming at the top of their lungs to get their options contracts filled. The adrenaline rush generally lasts until 10:00 or 10:30 A.M.

Then things calm down a bit. For the next hour, traders usually sit on their positions, waiting to see where they stand. Come 11:30, prices get soft. And when I say soft, I mean that volatility falls and prices lighten up.

This is when most of the traders take lunch. About half of them leave the pit. They just turn off their monitors and clear the floor. So they're not even in the pits. They leave their positions. Because nine times out of 10, nothing that would have a major effect on their options happens between 11 A.M. and 1 P.M.

And while they're not there to trade, you and I can go in and get some great options prices. Why? Well, once again, think back to the competitive nature of the options pits. Once all the big fish leave, the little fish can move in and grab some scraps of food. These little fish are the less established traders, those who get eaten alive when all the big boys are trading. But during lunch, they have the pits to themselves. So they finally get the opportunity to make some trades. And since these guys are hungry, you'd better believe they'll take anything they can get. That's our opportunity to clean up.

Often, if I'm sitting on a weeklong projection, I'll issue a tight buy range. And I'll expect it to get filled around noon, when the volatility is lower and prices loosen up. Keep that in mind when you're making your trading decisions. Some of the biggest bargains open up when the real traders are out of the pits.

CBOE FLOOR SECRET #6: VOLATILITY DICTATES PRICE . . . WHETHER TRADERS LIKE IT OR NOT

Unlike stock prices, which move based on supply and demand, options prices move based on a different model. Options prices move higher or lower at a greater rate than the underlying stock. Now, here's the secret.

Options traders are, in fact, able to move options prices of their own accord. They do this by tinkering with volatility. (I know, because I used to raise and lower options prices for Apple Computer using this very technique.)

But they can change prices only so far. Options traders cannot contradict the moves of the option pricing model, which is the all-encompassing determinant of options prices.

What that means is, no matter what options traders want to happen, if the market is moving against them, there is nothing they can do except take their lumps. For example, say an options trader has just bought 100 NDX calls. Then, the next day, the market plummets 76 points on the open.

The trader's calls are getting hammered, right? Yes, but as a floor trader, he also has the opportunity to push the price up a bit by using volatility to soften the blow. But only to a certain extent.

As much as you, the trader, would love to cover some of your losses, the more you move volatility, the more the automated options pricing system will sting you. Bottom line: If you buy the right options at the right time, you're golden, no matter what options traders try to do to your positions. So, as much power as options traders seem to have, in reality it's quite limited.

You don't need any complex calculations to capitalize on this, just an understanding of how the market works and how traders manipulate the numbers. As long as you know how to play the spread between bid and ask, you're a step ahead of the options traders (who depend on the usual rube who doesn't know how they operate). And as long as you remember the only model that really counts—that option values move more than their underlying stocks—you know how to master and profit from the secrets of this market.

CHAPTER 19

TRADING SECRET NUMBER THIRTEEN: BRYAN BOTTARELLI'S SIX TRADING RULES

By Bryan Bottarelli

Without question, trading for a living is a tough gig. To be successful, you need a system—and more importantly, you need the self-discipline to follow your system.

But in addition to a system, all traders have an internal set of rules that they follow each and every day. The following six trading rules govern my everyday trading.

I use these very same rules to make all trading decisions in my WaveStrength trading service. I'd like to share these six rules with you.

Bryan Bottarelli was trained as a pit trader at the Chicago Board of Options Exchange (CBOE). He is the Chief Trading Strategist for the WaveStrength options trading systems.

Rule #1: Before making a trade, set a price target, set a time line, estimate a gain, set a stop or a hedge—then trade.

Before I make a trade, I always calculate an upside or downside price target (most traders do). But what most traders *don't* do is calculate a time frame for the move to occur. Armed with a price target *and* a time frame, I can calculate which option will give me the best estimated gain while limiting potential loss. Then I'm ready to trade.

Rule #2: On short-term trades, open positions on Monday, and take profits on Friday.

I have a little bias toward taking profits on a Friday. When I have gains in hand (especially when dealing with options), I don't want to let a weekend event—or time decay—eat away at a position that was a winner on Friday. Therefore, if I have a 7 to 10-day trade that's showing a profit between 25 percent and 50 percent come Friday afternoon, I typically take the money off the table. (Come Monday, if the parameters of the play are still intact I can always reenter the trade—*often for a cheaper price than I sold it for on Friday!*)

Rule #3: There is **no** *perfect trade, so don't be afraid to sell half.*

The toughest aspect of trading is deciding when to sell. If the trade loses money, you question why you entered the trade. If the trade makes money, you question whether you are selling it too soon. Either way, this mentality can have you continually second-guessing yourself, which isn't healthy for successful trading.

The solution? Always be resigned to the fact that you will *never* make a perfect trade. In other words, you'll never buy at exactly the low, and you'll never sell at exactly the high. Once you have accepted this, your expectations about trading will vastly improve your mental moneymaking capabilities. (If I do find myself second-guessing a play, I sell half of the position at the first hint of profits, ignoring the desire to whine about commission fees, and hold the remainder to appease my what-if questions) *Typically, I find that selling the first half of the position was the right move.*

Rule #4: Make a conservative and a speculative play together.

There's a constant greed factor on every trade. That is, do I trade an option that's designed to make 25 percent to 50 percent if my forecasted move hits? Or do I trade an option that's designed to make 100 percent to 200 percent if my forecasted move hits? My answer, easily enough, is to trade both. For example, you're wise to allocate a portion of funds designated for this particular trade (maybe 70 percent) to play the conservative option (typically at-the-money) and use the remaining funds (maybe 30 percent) to buy a handful of more speculative out-of-the-money options. If you properly stack the percentage of conservative versus speculative trades, your overall losses will be almost the same had you simply owned 100 percent of the conservative play—*but your overall gains can be much, much higher with the combination of conservative/speculative plays.*

Rule #5: Own calls in the leaders, and own puts in the laggards.

I like to think that I do a fine job of timing the markets, but of course I'm not right 100 percent of the time. Nobody is. So in an effort to make money no matter what, I like to be long the leaders (via calls) and short the laggards (via puts) *at the same time.* I use an established trend line to determine which companies are strong and which companies are weak, often within the same industry (I've done this successfully with Home Depot/Lowe's and Office Depot/Office Max). *With a long/short position, you can profitably capitalize on up days and down days without being on the wrong side of a major market move.*

Rule #6: A slightly out-of-the-money option is often the best play in the book.

This rule applies to those who can't decide if they're conservative investors or speculative traders. If you find yourself in between these two designations, take note. When picking an option, I feel that the perfect balance between a conservative trader and a speculative trader is a *slightly* out-of-the-money option.

It all has to do with a balance between intrinsic value and time value. The value of an in-the-money option is comprised of these two price premium components: time value plus the amount by which each call or put is in-the-money (or, intrinsic value). Since an out-of-the-money option consists of nothing but time value, it has *no* intrinsic value. Quite simply, options traders make the most money when an option moves from out-of-the-money to in-the-money. That's when the option acquires intrinsic value premium *on a point-for-point basis* (one point of intrinsic value for each point away from strike price in the profitable direction). But there's more. The option continues to hold some of its time value premium—and that's where you clean up. The trick is picking an out-of-the-money option that you think will soon move toward strike price and surpass it. Buying a slightly out-of-the-money option before this move occurs gives you the best odds of making a handsome profit as your play moves from out to in.

The bigger the move, the bigger your profit. That's worth thinking about.

CONCLUSION

For an hour or more that evening I listened to his monotonous chirrup about bad money driving out good, the token value of silver, the depreciation of the rupee, and the true standards of exchange.

"Suppose," he cried, with feeble violence, "that all the debts in the world were called up simultaneously and immediate payment insisted upon. What, under our present conditions, would happen then?"

I gave the self-evident answer that I should be a ruined man, upon which he jumped from his chair, reproved me for my habitual levity, which made it impossible for him to discuss any reasonable subject in my presence, and bounced off out of the room to dress for a Masonic meeting.

—**Sir Arthur Conan Doyle**[1]

Since you've made it this far in our odyssey through market indicators and constellations of catalysts, I feel comfortable boring you with a sports analogy. After all—this is America!

The sport of fencing in the United States has undergone a curious evolution since the early 1990s. On the one hand, the United States Fencing Association, the regulating body of the sport in the States, has almost doubled its membership base. In the Olympic Games in Athens in 2004, two American women won medals: Mariel Zagunis even took the gold in the women's saber competition, a feat that would have been unimaginable a decade ago. In New York City, former American medalist Peter Westbrook has established a fencing school turning inner-city kids into high-carat fencers who give the corn-fed prodigies of France, Germany, Italy, and even Russia a run for their money in international competitions.

At the same time that U.S. fencing has become an international force to be reckoned with, a split has occurred in the member base. An increasing segment of fencers is dissatisfied with what they consider the "watering down" of the art of fencing by electric scoring apparatus, new techniques and weapons, pragmatic focus on winning, and rules that blatantly seem to ignore that, originally, fencing was about surviving a duel with sharp weapons rather than winning by scoring more points than one's opponent. A new movement has originated, a loose association of classical fencers who emphasize traditional form and technique over their modern competitive equivalents. Classical fencing, at the core, believes that the "hit and not be hit" philosophy that imprinted early fencing is more appropriate to the nature of the sport.

Oddly enough, you will not find many classical fencers among the top competitors. You'd think you would: after all, if you train to avoid an opponent's blade as if it were sharp, you would assume you'd be far better off than muscle-bound athletes who plow toward you without regard for their personal welfare.

Unfortunately, it doesn't work that way. In fencing, it matters most that you win in competitions against all comers. You may cloak your loss in the moral consciousness that you would have lived if only the blades had been sharp. But the bottom line is that you lost anyway.

It's the same with the stock markets: Markets are reflections of human emotion and as such are immune to moralistic directives of history. Classic perceptions of value, and hence of bubble theories, over the past two decades have developed a tendency to explain not how the market works, but how it ought to work.

This development is not new. Recent studies, such as *Famous First Bubbles* by Peter M. Garber,[2] are uncovering that much of what we believe to know about the Dutch "Tulipomania," for example, has been based on rather shaky assumptions that were fostered by moralist treatises whose general tenor we find in later key works such as Charles Mackay's *Extraordinary Popular Delusions and the Madness of Crowds*, and even in the 2003 *Financial Reckoning Day* of my dear friend Bill Bonner and fellow St. John's alumnus Addison Wiggin.

At the core of these deeply moralist treatises appears to be the basic ideal there is an "orderly market environment"—a market force of gravity that strives to converge prices toward historical averages.

We, however, take a pragmatic approach to the markets. As traders, we're not interested in historical averages but in the very forces that explosively and exponentially drive markets up and down. Without this dynamism, without the opportunity to buy low to sell high, or borrow high to repay low, the potential to make a profit is negligible indeed.

In our view, the markets are gearing up for their last bullish hurrah in 20 years. This upward pressure—a combustive mixture of demographic forces and technology maturation—might take the Dow Jones Industrial Average up to 40,000 by late 2009. But at the same time, forces are building that bode ill for the years after that. We believe that a major financial crisis, probably originating within China's banking and currency system, will rock the markets within 18 months after the conclusion of the 2008 Olympic Games in Beijing. This crisis will precipitate demographic and economic forces creating a bear market that will outlast at least two presidential cycles.

The good news is that you have a few years to get your financial house in order, optimize bull-market gains, get out of debt, and learn the tricks of trading outlined in this book that will help you survive and prosper in any market climate.

Of course, you need to be careful: No matter of how you allocate your wealth, you will incur a certain degree of risk. Those keeping cash under their mattresses run the danger of theft, fire, floods, and inflation. Those depending on gold bullion run the danger of falling through the floor by the sheer weight of the metal whenever they move their hoard, or watch gold prices plummet just like they did after 1980.

Trading has its own set of risks. You can gain a lot, and you can lose a lot. It's the nature of the game. Make sure you never lose more than you *think* you can afford to lose. Even better, never risk more than you *can* afford to lose. Once you've covered your liabilities, shelter, and basic income, set aside a fixed amount of money for trading. Paper trade first. Put your—and our!—ideas to the test. Focus on a strategy that fits your risk tolerance and overall lifestyle.

Most of all, don't look at the market as a divine tool whose task it is to validate your worldviews. It should be enough if they validate—and make possible—your market profits.

THE 55 RULES OF TRADING

By Christian DeHaemer

1. The market is always right.
2. Never buy a company run by a medical doctor. Doctors have a confidence that is great on the operating table but lousy in running a company. Buy companies run by salespeople.
3. When investing in Canadian resource companies, assume they are scams unless proven otherwise.
4. When a disaster occurs in an emerging market country, go to www.adr.com, find the company that has sold off the most, and buy it.
5. It is better not to make money than to lose it.
6. Always leave money on the table.
7. Never apologize for a profit.
8. After you sell a position, take the ticker off your screen.
9. If you make a certain type of trade and it works, make it again.
10. Do not hope, act.
11. Don't take sample opinions on a trade. You've done your research—live or die by it.

Christian DeHaemer joined the Taipan Group in 1997. He is founder, co-publisher, and editor-in-chief of the RedZone Profits group of trading advisories.

12. It is possible to make money going long a horrific company. I've successfully played dead cat bounces on Enron, Nortel, and Lucent.
13. Never catch a falling knife.
14. Have an investment goal. Work toward it.
15. Use stock screens.
16. A low P/E, high growth rate, insider buying, and no debt make any stock a buy.
17. Draw trend lines. If a stock is in a downtrend, don't go long, and vice versa.
18. If you learn only one candlestick pattern, learn doji at the top of a trend.
19. Never give a stock an even bet. If you don't have an advantage, you will lose.
20. The market is a ravenous beast. It wants to take your life savings, chew them up, and laugh at you as you squirm in the dirt.
21. Contrarians are correct at turning points in the market, but wrong the rest of the time.
22. There are four types of traders: momentum, technical, fundamental, and insider.
23. Insider trading is the most lucrative, though illegal.
24. Momentum traders are correct most of the time but wrong during turning points.
25. It is against self-interest for technical traders to reveal their buys and sells.
26. Fundamental traders want the world to know they bought and sold.
27. When you make a successful trade, take 10 percent of the profits and buy something tangible, like a new hat. Reinvest the other 90 percent.
28. When you hit 100 percent gains on any equity trade, take your original stake off the table and forget about the remainder. Look it up in 10 years.
29. Economists are wrong.
30. The stock market is a leading indicator of the economy, not the other way around.
31. There is no correlation between consumer confidence and the stock market.
32. Analysts from brokerage firms have bought and want you to buy.

33. Analysts from brokerage firms are selling and want you to buy.
34. Analysts from brokerage firms want you to sell so they can buy.
35. A Chinese firewall is as useful as a Chinese fire drill.
36. Watching CNBC has never made anyone any money.
37. The only sure way to become a millionaire in the markets is to start out a multimillionaire.
38. You are not Warren Buffett. You will never be Warren Buffett.
39. Successful options trading is like walking in front of a steamroller picking up dimes.
40. Eighty percent of options expire worthless. Or so they say.
41. Visiting companies and talking to CEOs makes me overly optimistic about those companies. The media is the same way.
42. Sometimes buying a ticker because it is a good ticker is a good idea.
43. I can be long a company while someone else is short, and we can both make money.
44. In the back pages of the *Economist* you will find the Big Mac index and GDP growth figures. Find the country with the most undervalued currency and the highest GDP growth. Buy it.
45. Monitoring insider buying is the best, easiest way to determine if a tech stock will go up in value.
46. Small-capitalization stocks always lead the way out of a bear market.
47. High volatility among small caps signals a top in the market.
48. Moves after a sideways market go up or down vertically as far as the sideways chart went horizontal.
49. Fifty-two-week highs are bullish.
50. High-volume up-days with no news are bullish.
51. The best times to buy and sell are at 10:30 A.M. and 3:45 P.M.
52. It always takes longer than you think for a reaction to occur.
53. Use 20 percent stop-losses on equities and 35 percent on options.
54. Trend lines work better than support and resistance.
55. The market is always right.

APPENDIX B

OPTIONS TRADING

Outside of your broker, there are many places where you can follow options.

NEWSPAPERS

Most newspapers have eliminated daily coverage of options, and if they do cover them, it's usually only the most actively traded ones. But there are still two sources I can recommend:

- The *Wall Street Journal* covers the most important aspects of the options world in understandable tables in its "Money & Investment" section. There's a box for the most active options, a detailed listing in alphabetical order of the previous day's activity, and a box for LEAPS.
- *Barron's* covers options in its weekly edition, available on newsstands every Saturday. It lists the premium ranges for the options it quotes each week, as well as the weekly ranges and volumes of the stocks listed for options trading.

INTERNET

There are many, many sites that offer options quotes. Most of them are paid services; the free ones usually provide only time-delayed quotes.

Use a Web search engine to find an options quoting service that matches your needs and desires. Some web sites to get you started:

- www.cboe.com—At the Chicago Board Options Exchange home page, you can get options quotes for free (delayed 20 minutes). You can also find what options are available for a particular stock, including LEAPS. If you want, real-time quotes are available for as little as $7 a month. Hint: Remember to put a space between the third and fourth letters in the options symbol (e.g. HET HH).
- www.moneycentral.msn.com—Once there, click "Investing," then bookmark the site. What you get is no-frills, free, 15-minute delayed options quotes. Hint: Remember to type a period before the symbol to get an options quote.

WAVESTRENGTH GUIDE TO CHOOSING A BROKER

For options trading, you should expect to pay between $7.50 and $21.50 per trade. Of course, the higher cost comes with a higher level of service, and vice versa on the cheaper side. You'd need to decide what level you're willing to pay for service.

NOTES

INTRODUCTION   *A Visit from the FBI*

1. That is, of course, what sets apart a scientific "theory" from a hypothesis, an assumption, a speculation, or an educated guess.

CHAPTER 1   *Markets Rise, Markets Fall—It Matters Not*

1. Nick and Anita Evangelista, *Country Living Is Risky Business*, Port Townsend, WA: Loompanics, 2000.
2. James Surowiecki, *The Wisdom of Crowds*, New York: Doubleday, 2004, p. 105.
3. Charles Mackay, *Extraordinary Popular Delusions and the Madness of Crowds*, New York: Harmony Books, 1980, p. 89.
4. Robert Menschel, *Markets, Mobs & Mayhem: A Modern Look at the Madness of Crowds*, Hoboken, NJ: Wiley, 2002.

CHAPTER 2   *What Exactly Is Value?*

1. In a way, this view of the markets is somewhat reminiscent of modern zoological gardens, where animals are kept in climate-controlled, seemingly natural habitats environments, which, however, effectively short-circuit the crucial natural predator-prey cycles for the sake of impressionable audiences.
2. Benoit B. Mandelbrot, *The (Mis)Behavior of Markets: A Fractal View of Risk, Ruin, and Reward*, New York: Basic Books, 2004, p. 226.
3. When encountering analysts who brandish P/E ratios like fetishes, I often feel compelled to think of things like the body mass index (BMI), the health profession's current touchstone for obesity. You see, at 6 feet 4 inches tall and weighing in at 206 pounds, converging to a BMI of 25, I qualify as "overweight" according to the guidelines. I'm actually in the best shape of my adult life. I can fence 10 15-point bouts against higher-

ranked épée fencers half my age without my legs quivering, run five miles and be able to do another two miles of wind sprints without previous conditioning, or knock out 100 push-ups without breaking a sweat. But according to the BMI, I'm overweight. So are 23-year-old varsity lacrosse players. Professional football and baseball players even qualify as obese. Then, in June of 2005, I had surgery. Within three days, I lost nearly 20 pounds. My BMI dropped to "normal." Unfortunately, all of the lost weight was muscle mass. It took me months to regain my weight—and my fitness level!

4. Mandelbrot, *(Mis)Behavior of Markets*, p. 250.
5. Robert R. Prechter, Jr., *The Wave Principle of Human Social Behavior and the New Science of Socionomics*, Gainesville, GA: New Classics Library, 2002, p. 23.
6. Elizabeth MacDonald, "Breaking Down the Numbers on Wall Street," June 6, 2002, www.forbes.com.
7. Laurence Kotlikoff and Scott Burns, *The Coming Generational Storm: What You Need to Know about America's Economic Future*, Cambridge, MA: MIT Press, 2004, p. 224.
8. William R. Bonner and Addison Wiggin, *Financial Reckoning Day: Surviving the Soft Depression of the 21st Century*, Hoboken, NJ: Wiley, 2003, p. 11.
9. The smart alecks among you may point out that stocks often slide, drop, plummet, or crash in intraday trading, frequently making it impossible to get out of a position exactly at a predetermined percentage stop-loss. I know. That's why we call it a general guideline.
10. Peter M. Garber, *Famous First Bubbles: The Fundamentals of Early Manias*, Cambridge, MA: MIT Press, 2001, p. 125.
11. Jared Diamond, *Collapse: How Societies Choose to Fail or Succeed*, New York: Viking, 2005, p. 186.
12. Ibid.
13. James Surowiecki, *The Wisdom of Crowds*, New York: Doubleday, 2004, p. xix.

CHAPTER 3   *A Story Is Just a Story . . . Until There's a Profit*

1. Greg Eckler and L. M. MacDonald, *Bull! 144 Stupid Statements from the Market's Fallen Prophets*, Kansas City: Andrews McMeel, 2003.
2. I meekly admit to suffering from the same syndrome whenever I visit a certain stretch of beach at the Patuxent River in southern Maryland, only my eyes are drawn toward the surf line, checking pebbles for fossilized shark teeth. It took me 10 years to find one, and I've missed out on some spectacular views.

3. Bill Bonner, *The Daily Reckoning*, March 24, 2004.

4. Interestingly, gold prices provided the backdrop for Ian Fleming's James Bond novel *Goldfinger*, whose titular villain took advantage of the price discrepancy created by the then officially fixed gold prices and export restrictions and the black-market prices paid for gold in India and Macao.

5. Our lawyers urge me to say that "past performance is no guarantee of future profits."

6. James Surowiecki, *The Wisdom of Crowds*, New York: Doubleday, 2004, p. 33.

7. Max Weber, *Die protestantische Ethik und der "Geist" des Kapitalismus* (1920).

8. A short squeeze is a source of constant buying pressure in the stock. If an institution wants to participate in a short squeeze, all it has to do is buy the stock. Or a brokerage house may put out an upgrade.

9. Gertrude Stein said, "Money is always there but the pockets change." (Quoted in *Time*, October 13, 1975.)

CHAPTER 4   *The Last Phase of the Bubble Market (2006–2009)*

1. The best book I've found on how to get a grasp of what reality you have to create to live happily ever after was written by my friend and mentor Michael Masterson. It is called *Automatic Wealth: Six Steps to Financial Independence* (Wiley, 2005). For some choice chapters, check out our resource page at www.dynamicmarketreport.com.

2. Laurence J. Kotlikoff and Scott Burns, *The Coming Generational Storm: What You Need to Know about America's Economic Future*, Cambridge, MA: MIT Press, 2004, p. 183. I firmly believe that this book should be required reading for anyone who takes their financial future seriously!

3. "Bet on a Personal Account or Stay in the System?" *Money*, April 2005, p. 158.

4. Kotlikoff and Burns, *Coming Generational Storm*, p. 35.

5. Harry S. Dent, *The Next Great Bubble Boom*, New York: Free Press, 2004. This is another book you should study to get a grasp on what our financial future may hold in store for us.

6. Ibid., p. 5.

7. Ibid., p. 21.

8. Ibid., p. 180.

9. Benoit B. Mandelbrot, *The (Mis)Behavior of Markets: A Fractual View of Risk, Ruin, and Reward*, New York: Basic Books, 2004, p. 245.

10. Robert R. Prechter, Jr., *Pioneering Studies in Socionomics*, Gainesville, GA: New Classics Library, 2003, p. 56.

CHAPTER 5   *Stagnation and Decline: The Inevitable Irrelevance of the*
                 European Union

1. There were some beautiful instances of how East Germany tapped into West Germany's nominally capitalist system to continue the stranglehold on its citizens. It bartered cleaning rags, potatoes, and paving stones for VW Golfs, and, through the dealings of the ultraconservative Bavarian governor Franz-Josef Strauss, obtained billion–deutschemark credits at rates that make current mortgage rates look like usury.
2. Kenneth R. Timmerman, *The French Betrayal of America*, New York: Crown Forum, 2004, p. 81.
3. I find it soothing to see that, despite all the ideological differences that have arisen between the United States and Germany over the past couple of years, we are still united by the very fact that, in both countries, the respective heads of the left-of-center political parties, the German Social Democrats and the Democratic party in the United States, are headed by loons!
4. Thomas L. Friedman, *The Lexus and the Olive Tree*, New York: Farrar, Straus & Giroux, 1999, p. 47.
5. Benoit B. Mandelbrot, *The (Mis)Behavior of Markets: A Fractal View of Risk, Ruin, and Reward*, New York: Basic Books, 2004, p. 231.
6. Hubertus Bardt and Michael Grömling, "*Sparen in Deutschland und den USA*," *W-Trends*, Issue 3 (2003).
7. Meinhard Miegel, *Die deformierte Gesellschaft: Wie die Deutschen ihre Wirklichkeit verdrängen*, 3rd ed., Berlin: Ullstein, 2004, p. 148.
8. www.eursoc.com, 2003.
9. "Germany's Demographic Time Bomb," Radio Netherlands, EuroQuest; broadcast #200507 on February 15, 2005; www.rnw.nl/cgi/?app=euroquest&page=index.
10. Kyle James, *Deconstructing Germany*, Deutsche Welle DW-World; www.dw-world.de/dw/article/0,1564,1316056,00.html.
11. Kyle James, *Shrinking Populations of German Cities*; Domino Immobilien Dienstleistungen GmbH; www.domino-dortmund.de/special/domino_konkret_2004_en.pdf.
12. "Shrinking Cities," www.archined.nl/archined/4385.html; November 8, 2004.
13. Kevin J. O'Brien. "Joblessness amid a Long-Term Bust: In Former East Germany Future Ghost Towns," May 28, 2004; www.iht.com/articles/522266.html.
14. "The New Demographics," *Economist*, November 1, 2001.
15. Ibid.

16. "Forever Young," *Economist,* March 25, 2004; www.economist.com/displaystory.cfm?story_id=2516900.
17. Pete Engardio and Carol Matlack, "Global Aging," *BusinessWeek,* January 31, 2005; www.businessweek.com/magazine/content/05_05/b3918011.htm.
18. Ibid.
19. Ibid.
20. "Europe's Population Implosion," *Economist,* July 17, 2003; www.economist.com/world/europe/displayStory.cfm?story_id=1923383.
21. Ibid.
22. Ibid.
23. Commissioner Markos Kyprianou, Member of the European Commission, responsible for Health and Consumer Protection; "The New European Healthcare Agenda," The European Voice Conference "Healthcare: Is Europe Getting Better?" Brussels, January 20, 2005.
24. "The Crumbling Pillars of Old Age," *Economist,* September 25, 2003.
25. Kyprianou, "New European Healthcare Agenda."
26. "Europe's Population Implosion."
27. David Fairlamb, "Europe's Pension Problem: Too Few Cradles, Too Few Graves," *BusinessWeek*, March 29, 2004.
28. "Europe's Population Implosion."
29. "Enough to Live On," *Economist,* March 25, 2004; www.economist.com/displaystory.cfm?story_id=2516863.
30. Ibid.
31. www.travelblog.org/World/us-econ.html.
32. Engardio and Matlack, *Op. Cit.*
33. Ibid.
34. "Europe's Population Implosion."
35. "Work Longer, Have More Babies," *Economist,* September 25, 2003.
36. Larry Elliott, *Guardian* (U.K.), March 28, 2005.
37. Ibid.
38. The Coal and Steel Community (EGKS).
39. Niall Ferguson, in an AEI Bradley Lecture published on March 1, 2004.
40. Peter Bofinger, *Wir sind besser als wir glauben: Wohlstand für alle,* München: Pearson Studium, 2005, p. 93.
41. Ibid., p. 233.

CHAPTER 6   *Dragon Out of Fire*

1. Jared Diamond, *Collapse: How Societies Choose to Fail or Succeed,* New York: Viking, 2004, p. 336.

2. Ibid., p. 337.
3. William Pesek, Jr. "China, India and Japan Duke It Out in Asia," Bloomberg.com, February 14, 2005.
4. This and the following quotes were compiled from subscription-only reports of the business intelligence service Stratfor in the spring of 2005. You can obtain far deeper and more recent levels of intelligence at the service's web site at www.stratfor.com. I've come to look at their reports as a kind of investor's CIA.
5. Ibid.
6. Ibid.
7. www.chinadaily.com.cn/english/doc/2005-03/19.
8. Dexter Roberts, "The Great Wail of China," *BusinessWeek*, January 31, 2005.
9. *China Daily*, March 27, 2005, at www.chinadaily.com.
10. "Lenovo Gets Green Light from Washington," March 9, 2005, at www.freerepublic.com.
11. www.stratfor.com.

CHAPTER 7   *Trading Secret Number One: How to Profit from Cyclicality*

1. Lorene Yue, "The Buy Cycle: A Guide to the Best Times of Year for Bargains from Wedding Gowns to Rugs to Beach Trips," *Baltimore Sun*, January 9, 2005, p. 3D.
2. John L. Momsen, *Superstar Seasonals: 18 Proven-Dependable Futures Trades for Profiting Year after Year*, Brightwater, NY: Windsor Books, 2004, p. 3.
3. Sy Harding, www.StreetSmartReport.com, July 16, 2004, as quoted in "The Driving Force Behind Seasonality," *Dick Davis Digest* (Fort Lauderdale, FL), August 9, 2004, p. 1ff.

CHAPTER 9   *Trading Secret Number Three: Follow the Money!*

1. Back in 1999, this service was still called Rogue Trader.
2. This is also the reason why it is absolutely necessary to limit the number of people we reveal our trades to: There is a strictly enforced limit to the number of subscribers Volume Spike Alert will take on at any given time. Right now that number is 1,000. It may be lowered if we see traders trading bigger dollar amounts and outinvesting the very insiders who are telegraphing these highly profitable moves. Below the 1,000-member cap, Volume Spike Alert subscribers have been getting into trades alongside the insiders without skewing the numbers. And as long as the profits keep rolling in without incident, we're happy, and our subscribers are happy.

CHAPTER 10   *Trading Secret Number Four: "Profits at the Speed of News"*

1. Gene D'Avolio, Efi Gildor, and Andrei Shleifer, "Technology, Information Production, and Market Efficiency," Harvard Institute of Economic Research Discussion Paper #1929, September 2001.
2. As usual, all our customer testimonials are archived for legal backup.
3. www.people.hbs.edu/ptufano/einfo/index.htm.
4. Benoit B. Mandelbrot, *The (Mis)Behavior of Markets: A Factal View of Risk, Ruin, and Reward*, New York: Basic Books, 2004, p. 237.
5. Mark Twain, *Following the Equator: A Journey Around the World* (Hartford, 1897), Mineola, NY: Dover, 1989; p. 141f.
6. Wesley S. Chan, "Stock Price Reaction to News and No-news: Drift and Reversal After Headlines," *Journal of Financial Economics*, 70(2), 2003, pp. 223–260; and http://ssrn.com/abstract=262452, April 24, 2001.
7. John H. Maheu, University of Alberta, and Thomas H. McCurdy, University of Toronto, "News Arrival, Jump Dynamics and Volatility Components for Individual Stock Returns," Cirano Centre Interuniversitaire de Recherché en Analyse des Organizations, 2003, at www.cirano.qc .ca/pdf/publication/2003s-38.pdf.
8. Andrew Jackson and Timothy Johnson, "Unifying Under-reaction Anomalies," www.journals.uchicago.edu/JB/papers.html.
9. Jeffrey A. Busse and T. Clifton Green, "Market Efficiency in Real-Time," Goizueta Business School, Emory University, May 2001; http://ssrn .com/abstract=270958.

CHAPTER 11   *Trading Secret Number Five: Stone-Cold Profit Predator*

1. Forgive me when I quote promotional literature here: http://store .traders.com/v20594wormon.html.
2. Moving average convergence divergence, a trading method developed by Gerald Appel. Three steps are involved: find the point spread difference between two exponential moving averages to find price velocity; plot a signal line; and subtract the signal line from price velocity to find price acceleration.

CHAPTER 14   *Trading Secret Number Eight: Playing the "Flying V" Lockup Indicator*

1. Of course, as in all trading, this is a matter of looking at the numbers: If you establish and keep a trailing stop, you can look at the maximum amount you're willing to risk as your investment and calculate your gains

based on that number. Say, you borrow a stock at $10 and are only willing to lose $2 at most. To lose this principal, the stock would have to rise to $12. But if it drops $4, to $6, you've made $4 a share, or 200 percent of the money you risked. It's window-dressing for sure, but I've met a couple of stock market gurus who've made a living following this scoring method.

CHAPTER 16   *Trading Secret Number Ten: Trading the Money-Flow Matrix*

1. This technical indicator, the "stochastics oscillator," compares a stock's close to its trading range over recent periods (hours, days, or weeks, for example). The theory is based on an observation that in uptrend markets, closing prices tend to be close to the high; in down markets, near the low.

CHAPTER 17   *Trading Secret Number Eleven: Profiting with the WaveStrength Options Trading System*

1. Benoit B. Mandelbrot, *The (Mis)Behavior of Markets: A Fractal View of Risk, Ruin, and Reward*, New York: Basic Books, 2004, p. 268.

CONCLUSION

1. Sir Arthur Conan Doyle, *The Lost World*, London, 1912; New York: Penguin, 2001, p. 9.
2. Peter M. Garber, *Famous First Bubbles: The Fundamentals of Early Manias*, Cambridge, MA: MIT Press, 2001.

GLOSSARY

AMEX   Stands for "American Stock Exchange." Founded in 1921, AMEX trades small- and medium-sized stocks. AMEX is located in Manhattan and trades more foreign stocks than any other U.S. stock exchange.

ask price   The offer price, or the going price at which a market maker offers to sell you shares of a company.

bear market   A period when the market steadily declines in value, or when stocks remain at depressed levels.

bid price   The price that a market maker is willing to pay for a set number of shares. There may be several market makers establishing bid and ask prices for a stock at any given time.

Big Board   Stocks that trade on the New York Stock Exchange (NYSE) or on the American Stock Exchange (AMEX).

book   A broker's book that contains the names and addresses of customers, notes, and trading records.

breakeven price   The price that an underlying instrument must reach in order to produce intrinsic value in the option equal to the buyer's cost of initiating the position. Calculating the breakeven price helps you make an intelligent decision about whether to buy the option.

bull market   A period when the market steadily rises in value, or when stocks remain at high levels.

call   The option to buy a share at a specified price within a given period of time.

cash account   Your securities account with a brokerage firm with which you pay for your purchases in full.

churning   Willful, excessive trading in a customer's account that results in continuous losses of the customer's funds and continuous commissions for the broker.

close   To exit the options market. When you sell an option, you are selling back to the market, telling your broker to resell it "to close."

commissions   Fees that brokers charge investors when buying and selling options and other investments. Many brokers have special deals on volume trades—if you can arrange them.

common shares   Securities that represent an ownership interest in a company.

covered call   A call where the writer already owns the stocks that he may find himself obligated to sell.

crossing   A form of trading in which stock is sold from one account to another without actually reaching the market.

dividend   A portion of the earnings to be paid out to the holders of each share of stock. The amount is determined by the company's Board of Directors and is usually paid out quarterly.

EPS   Stands for "earnings per share." The earnings that are available to common stockholders divided by the number of common shares outstanding.

exercise   The act of buying or selling the underlying optioned material. You would not exercise an option unless it is a winning position.

expiration date   The last day an option can be exercised or offset. Make sure you know the exact expiration date of any option you purchase. Once an option has expired, it no longer conveys any rights and, in effect, ceases to exist.

extrinsic value   The worth of the premium represented by time and volatility, as opposed to the option's real or intrinsic value.

fixed costs   Costs that remain constant regardless of the volume of operations.

front   Buying or selling a security before a promoter begins to push the stock.

gross   The total commission that is earned by a broker.

hedge   Any maneuver to protect capital or profits, either by buying or selling the underlying item or by using an option or derivative.

hold   In WaveStrength, this just means to continue to hold what you have with whatever stops have been noted in our most recent alert. Do not sell off the position or add to it.

insider trading   Illegal trading of securities based on trading information that is unavailable to the general public.

in-the-money option   An option with intrinsic value. An in-the-money call option has a strike price below the current price of the underlying instrument. An in-the-money put option has a strike price above the price of the underlying instrument.

intrinsic value   The portion of the premium representing real value. An option has intrinsic value if the difference between the market and strike prices would make the option profitable if exercised.

IPO   Stands for "initial public offering." A corporation's first offering of stock to the public.

IPO shares   The number of shares that are available on the IPO date.

issue   To authorize the sale of shares of stock.

juice/bone   The potential commission a broker sets in a buy or sell transaction.

LEAPS   Stands for "Long-Term Equity Anticipation Securities." It is an acronym for options that can run up to three years in time. They are traded on various options exchanges and include stocks, stock indexes, and other instruments traded on those exchanges. In effect, a LEAPS call is a substitute for the actual shares of stock during its life—if it is in-the-money. If it is out-of-the-money, a LEAPS call may be considered a cautious way to control the price of a rising stock with limited risk over a very long time.

limit order   A buy order to purchase an option at or below a specified price, or a sell order to sell an option at or above a certain price. Use limit orders to minimize risk, but be aware there is no guarantee your option can be bought at the desired price.

liquidity   The ability of the market to absorb a reasonable amount of buying or selling in a particular security at reasonable price changes.

lock in   Protecting gains. This can be accomplished with a trailing stop, or by buying a protective, out-of-the-money option to act as a hedge and keep the door open to further profits if the trend continues.

lockup shares of total shares   The percentage of lockup shares versus the total number of shares outstanding.

long position   Long means buy. If you hold a long position in CPST shares, you just bought Capstone.

margin   The amount paid by a customer when using a broker's credit to buy or sell a security.

margin accounts   Good-faith deposits investors make to their broker when borrowing from the broker to buy securities and futures. Buying on margin exposes you to unlimited risk. Margin risk may differ depending on the WaveStrength service.

market maker   A member of an options trading exchange who stands ready to sell or buy back options, giving liquidity to the system.

market order   An order to buy or sell an option at the market price, synonymous with telling your broker to "do his best" as quickly as possible. Using a market order means you have no control over your entrance or exit price, making your risk uncertain.

market price   The last reported price at which the stock or bond sold.

naked call   The opposite of a covered call; a call where the writer does not own the shares he may become obligated to sell. Instead, he writes the call against a cash deposit in a margin account.

Nasdaq   Stands for "National Association of Securities Dealers Automated Quotation System."

NYSE   Stands for "New York Stock Exchange." The oldest (1792) and largest organized securities market in the United States.

offer price   The price asked for a share of stock; the going price at which a market marker is offering to sell you shares of a company.

offset   Closing out a position in a previously purchased option by selling it in an offsetting transaction prior to expiration. This is done by exercising an option and immediately putting the just-acquired security back on the market, either by selling stocks gained from exercising a call or by buying stocks sold in a put. This immediately captures the option's intrinsic value and locks in profits.

option   A financial instrument giving an investor the right, but not the obligation, to buy or sell a specific investment at a set price for a predetermined time.

OTC   Stands for "over-the-counter." A market for securities made up of securities dealers who may or may not be members of a security exchange. It is the primary market for bonds of all types.

out-of-the-money option   An option with no intrinsic value. That is, if you exercised the option you would lose money on the difference between the market and strike prices.

overvalued   The description of a stock whose current price is not justified by the earnings outlook or the P/E ratio.

paper trade   Tracking options daily on paper, without actually investing any money in them. This is a good way to learn about premium movements as they relate to the underlying stock or future without risking any capital. Once you've paper traded for a while, you'll be ready to start investing in QQQ options.

premium   The price you pay to open a put or a call. The premium is the sum of an option's intrinsic value and time value. Premiums are arrived at in the open competition of buyers and sellers.

price-earnings ratio   The price of a stock divided by the earnings per share of the company. A stock selling at $45 a share with earnings of $3 per share would have a price-earnings ratio of 15.

prospectus date   The date at which a security is offered for sale to the public (IPO).

put   An option giving the buyer the right, but not the obligation, to sell 100 shares of stock or a futures contract at or by a specified date at a set price (the strike price). Often used as insurance against falling stock prices, a put buyer is looking to profit from a decrease in the price of the underlying instrument.

quote   The highest bid to buy and the lowest offer to sell a security in a given market at a given time.

ramping up   The point at which a firm decides to concentrate on buying a stock with the intent of pushing up the price.

resell   The act of selling an already-bought option back into the marketplace, thus closing the position. Use the term "resell" so brokers will not make the mistake of selling (writing) an option in the subscriber's open instead of closed account.

SEC   Stands for "Securities and Exchange Commission." The SEC is a federal agency created by the Securities Exchange Act of 1934 to administer that Act and the Securities Act of 1933, duties formerly carried out by the Federal Communications Commission (FCC).

series   The range of strike prices available for an option.

Series 7   A standardized test that a broker must pass before he or she can sell securities.

shares   The number of shares a company has authorized to be sold but that have not yet been issued; shares of a company that have been issued for outstanding shares.

short   Selling a security to profit from an anticipated fall in its price.

short position   (1) Stocks sold short and not covered as of a particular date. (2) The total amount of stock an investor has sold short and has covered.

short squeeze   Occurs when investors who have sold borrowed shares in anticipation of replacing them at lower prices are forced to cover those borrowed shares by buying shares, even at a higher price.

stop-loss   An order placed with a broker to liquidate once a specific price level has been reached. A technique used to limit losses.

strike price   With calls, the specific price at which the buyer of a call option has the right, but not the obligation, to buy the underlying instrument; with puts, the specific price at which the buyer of a put option has the right, but not the obligation, to sell the underlying instrument.

superleverage   The art of using other people's money to try to profit while maintaining limited risk at all times. The purchase of put and call options is one form of superleverage.

tight float   The float is the total number of shares (other than those held by institutions, insiders, and the firm) estimated to be trading. A tight float refers to the lack of shares trading in the marketplace and is an indication of the volatility of the issue.

trailing stops   A stop-loss order that automatically goes higher as an option moves up in price. This can lock in greater profits if the market reverses, but be aware that sometimes profitable trades may reverse, triggering the trailing stop, and then resume their upward move.

underlying instrument   The investment instrument an option gives you the right, but not the obligation, to buy or sell. While WaveStrength primarily deals with stock options (security options), options are available on a wide variety of investments. The current price of the underlying instrument directly relates to the cost of the option (premium).

underwriters   A group of investment bankers who assist in selling IPO shares at the offering price. Their primary purpose is to assist in the distribution of the new stock and spread the risk associated with the offering.

volatility The fluctuation in market price of the underlying security. Volatility can be a key factor in an option's premium.

writer An individual who sells calls and puts. The writer has an obligation to sell the stock (in the case of a call) or buy it (in the case of a put) if the option buyer decides to exercise the option. All the money an options writer will make is known at the time the option is written: it consists of the premium received from the buyer, less the commission the writer pays his broker.

SELECTED
BIBLIOGRAPHY

While WaveStrength is a unique, groundbreaking system in itself, it is rooted in the concepts of technical analysis. So if you'd like to read more on the underpinnings of the system, as well as basic information on options, we highly recommend the following books:

Bittman, James B. *Trading Index Options*. New York: McGraw-Hill, 1998.

Bulkowski, Thomas N. *Encyclopedia of Chart Patterns*. New York: John Wiley & Sons, 2000.

Fischer, Robert. *Fibonacci Applications & Strategies for Traders*. New York: John Wiley & Sons, 1993.

Natenberg, Sheldon. *Option Volatility and Pricing*. New York: McGraw-Hill, 1994.

Nison, Steve. *Beyond Candlesticks*. New York: John Wiley & Sons, 1994.

Nison, Steve. *Japanese Candlestick Charting Techniques*. New York: New York Institute of Finance, 1991.

Options Institute Education Division of the Chicago Board Options Exchange. *Options: Essential Concepts & Trading Strategies*. New York: McGraw-Hill, 1999.

Pardo, Robert. *Design, Testing and Optimization of Trading Systems*. New York: John Wiley & Sons, 1992.

Pring, Martin J. *Technical Analysis Explained*. New York: McGraw-Hill, 1991.

Schwager, Jack D. *Schwager on Futures: Technical Analysis*. New York: John Wiley & Sons, 1996.

Tufte, Edward R. *The Visual Display of Information*. 2nd ed. Cheshire, CT: Graphics Press, 2001.

Wilder, J. Welles, Jr. *New Concepts in Technical Trading*. Greensboro, NC: Trend Research Systems, 1978.

For more information on the WaveStrength tiered trading system, visit our web site: www.wavestrength.com.

RECOMMENDED READINGS

If one or more systems I introduced to you in these pages has made you eager to learn more, my team has put together a web site at www.dynamic marketreport.com that provides further information on each.

Trading Secret Number One: How to Profit from Cyclicality

Every six months, our editors Christian DeHaemer and Ian Cooper compile a handy little planning tool they call Year of Profits, a calendar that marks the best time to buy, short, and sell cyclical investments.

For more information, see their web site at: http://yearofprofits.net.

Trading Secret Number Two: The Perfect Value Trifecta—Breakout Signal, Dividend Discount Model, and Forward Earnings Forecaster

Trading Secret Number Three: Follow the Money! (This Trading on Insider Information Is Completely Legal)

Brad Colburn's services, Value Edge and Breakaway Investor, and his volume-based trading service Volume Spike Alert share a joint daily e-letter called *Fear & Greed*, which you can follow to see both systems in action. (www .dynamicmarketreport.com/fearandgreed).

For information on his Value Edge service, go to www.value-edge.com.

For the recent scoop on his volume spike indicator, check out www .roguetraderonline.com.

Trading Secret Number Four: "Profits at the Speed of News"— Trading Extreme Volatility

Ian Cooper supplies the subscribers of his service Extreme Volatility Speculator with news-driven profit opportunities at www.vixtrader.com.

He also contributes to the RedZone Group's daily e-letter *American Capitalist*, to which you can subscribe free of charge at www.dynamic marketreport.com/americancapitalist.

Trading Secret Number Five: Stone-Cold Profit Predator—The Doji Master

For recent applications of the Doji Master system, check www.doji master.com.

Trading Secret Number Six: ActionPoint Trading—Investing in IPOs

Trading Secret Number Seven: Profits from the Red Zones

Trading Secret Number Eight: Playing the "Flying V" Lockup Indicator

Trading Secret Number Nine: The Tri-Directional Indicator

The RedZone Group team, managed by Christian DeHaemer, Siu-Yee Ng, and Ian Cooper, publishes daily market analysis in their free daily e-letter *American Capitalist*, which you can order at www.dynamicmarket report.com/americancapitalist.

More information on the RedZone Group services can be found at www.redzoneprofits.com and at www.redzonevip.com.

Trading Secret Number Ten: Trading the Money-Flow Matrix

Brit Ryle has incorporated his Money-Flow Matrix into a high-carat trading service called the Money-Flow Matrix Trader, which you can read up on at www.moneyflowmatrix.com.

He also publishes a free daily e-letter called *Daily Digest*. Find out more at www.dynamicmarketreport.com/dailydigest.

Trading Secret Number Eleven: Profiting with the WaveStrength Options Trading System

Trading Secret Number Twelve: The Secret Strategies of CBOE Floor Traders

Trading Secret Number Thirteen: Bryan Bottarelli's Six Trading Rules

The WaveStrength team, headed by Adam Lass and Bryan Bottarelli, publishes a daily e-letter called *Market Report*, which you can find at www.dynamic marketreport.com/ws-marketreport.

For more current information on the system, check out www.dynamic marketreport.com/wavestrength.

INDEX

ABOUT THE AUTHOR

As executive publisher of the Taipan Group LLC and vice president of the publishing company Agora Inc. in Baltimore, J. Christoph Amberger has assembled one of the world's most successful teams of independent financial analysts.

Born in 1963, he grew up in what used to be West Berlin, Germany, and was educated at the Freie Universität Berlin, the Georg-August-Universität Göttingen, the University of Aberdeen (Scotland), and St. John's Graduate Institute in Annapolis, Maryland. His work and travel have given him first-hand experience of Eastern and Western Europe, as well as North and Central America.

Amberger began his career as a freelance contributor to various Agora publications before emigrating to the United States in 1989, when he joined the editorial board of Taipan. In 1991, he took over as managing editor for the publication, and assumed responsibility as group publisher in 1995.

A frequent speaker at international conferences, he is the author of several books, among them the definitive treatise on historical European sword-fighting traditions, and scores of articles and special reports. His daily e-letter, the *Dynamic Market Alert*, is one of the most popular financial dailies in the world.